Clint Eastwood

Clint Eastwood
Evolution of a Filmmaker

JOHN H. FOOTE

Modern Filmmakers
Vincent LoBrutto, Series Editor

Westport, Connecticut
London

Library of Congress Cataloging-in-Publication Data

Foote, John H.
　Clint Eastwood : evolution of a filmmaker / John H. Foote.
　　p. cm. — (Modern filmmakers, ISSN 1943-183X)
　Includes bibliographical references and index.
　ISBN 978-0-313-35247-8 (alk. paper)
　1. Eastwood, Clint, 1930–　—Criticism and interpretation. I. Title.
PN1998.3.E325F66　2009
791.4302'33092—dc22　2008032610

British Library Cataloguing in Publication Data is available.

Library of Congress Catalog Card Number: 2008032610
ISBN: 978-0-313-35247-8
ISSN: 1943-183X

First published in 2009

Praeger Publishers, 88 Post Road West, Westport, CT 06881
An imprint of Greenwood Publishing Group, Inc.
www.praeger.com

Printed in the United States of America

The paper used in this book complies with the
Permanent Paper Standard issued by the National
Information Standards Organization (Z39.48-1984).

10　9　8　7　6　5　4　3　2　1

For Sherri,

Your smile warms the day, your presence keeps me safe. And your love makes me want to be a better man. You once called film my heroin, but know that you are my only true addiction. This, and everything I have done, is for you.

Clint Eastwood is now sixty-two years old; there has never been a career to compare to his. Once reviled, and justifiably, as an actor with the warmth of a girder and the depth of a raindrop, he nonetheless became for years the world's most popular performer. Having acquired power, he exploited it to create artful but essentially non-commercial movies—*Honky Tonk Man, White Hunter Black Heart, Bird. Unforgiven* is about a man who cannot escape his past. Eastwood has. Who would have thought that the cheroot-smoking, poncho-wearing star of those surreal Spaghetti Westerns would turn into one of Hollywood's most daring filmmakers?

—The late, great Jay Scott,
writing in the *Globe and Mail*, 1992

Contents

Series Foreword

The Modern Filmmakers series focuses on a diverse group of motion picture directors who collectively demonstrate how the filmmaking process has become *the* definitive art and craft of the twentieth century. As we advance into the twenty-first century we begin to examine the impact these artists have had on this influential medium.

What is a modern filmmaker? The phrase connotes a motion picture maker who is *au courant*—they make movies currently. The choices in this series are also varied to reflect the enormous potential of the cinema. Some of the directors make action movies, some entertain, some are on the cutting edge, some are political, some make us think, and some are fantasists. The motion picture directors in this collection will range from highly commercial, mega-budget blockbuster directors, to those who toil in the independent low-budget field.

Gus Van Sant, Tim Burton, Charlie Kaufman, and Terry Gilliam are here, and so are Clint Eastwood and Steven Spielberg—all for many and various reasons, but primarily because their directing skills have transitioned from the twentieth century to the first decade of the twenty-first century. Eastwood and Spielberg worked during the sixties and seventies and have grown and matured as the medium transitioned from mechanical to digital. The younger directors here may not have experienced all of those cinematic epochs themselves, but nonetheless they have remained concerned with the limits of filmmaking. Charlie Kaufman disintegrates personal and narrative boundaries in the course of his scripts, for example, while Tim Burton probes the limits of technology to find the most successful way of bringing his intensely visual fantasies and nightmares to life.

The Modern Filmmaker Series will celebrate modernity and postmodernism through each creator's vision, style of storytelling, and character presentation. The directors' personal beliefs and worldviews will be revealed through in-depth examinations of the art they have created, but brief biographies will also be provided where they appear especially relevant. These books are intended to open up new ways of thinking about some of our favorite and most important artists and entertainers.

Vincent LoBrutto
Series Editor
Modern Filmmakers

Acknowledgments

It had never occurred to me that a book was such a group effort. This one began a long time ago on a couch in a village called Seagrave, where a father gathered his three sons to watch old monster movies.

Thank you first to Daniel Harmon of Greenwood, who championed this project and believed in the idea from the very beginning.

To Susan Yates, for being a most kind, fair, and patient project manager, consistently concerned with improving the work, and always willing to work with me.

To Clint Eastwood, for an exceptional body of work, for being a consummate artist and decent human being—hearty thanks.

For my friends at the Toronto Film School—Rick Bennett, Sam Weller, Susann Imshaug, Mark Ingram, Paul French, Aric Whittom, Steve Bartolini, and Marcello Scarlato—thank you for being part of my life and for sharing in this love of film.

Thanks to Ellie for being seventy-five, funky, energetic, purple and full of life, and a huge inspiration.

Peter Hvidsten, for allowing me a forum way back when in which to write about film, and smiling upon hearing of any subsequent success—I thank you.

To George Hood, Christopher Heard, Paul Arculus, Brenda Mori, Liz Williamson, Gemma Files, Diane Lackie, David Toye, John Crocker, and Gerry Pearson—thank you for the mentoring and friendship over the years.

Thanks to the Academy of Motion Picture Arts and Sciences and Christopher Lewchuk at Warner Brothers for their assistance, and to Eve Goldin and her staff at the Toronto International Film Festival Group's Reference Library.

Thanks also to:

My parents, Skip and Dianne, for indulging their oldest son's obsession with all things cinema.

My sister Jo for being Jo.

My brothers Steve and Jeff for sharing early film memories with me—those delicious warm memories on the couch watching monster movies.

To my girls Aurora and Ariana, the two lights of my life, my reasons for getting up in the morning. I appreciate your patience with Daddy's obsession.

And to Sherri, the love of my life, my best friend . . . my everything.

Introduction

Ever the realist, had anyone told me in the late seventies that 30 years later Clint Eastwood would be among the finest directors working in modern cinema, I would have laughed at them as though they were utterly mad.

Though a top box office star in the seventies, Eastwood was an actor of limited ability; and realizing this, he chose his roles accordingly. Lacking the natural talents of Marlon Brando or Jack Nicholson, Eastwood needed to be cautious about which characters he portrayed on the screen. He was very much, on the surface at least, a movie star, and more than capable of portraying the steely eyed Harry Callahan of the *Dirty Harry* (1971) franchise and very able to send up his tough guy image opposite an ape in *Every Which Way But Loose* (1977), but for anyone to suggest Eastwood as any character in *The Godfather* (1972) would have been simply insane. Yet quietly behind the scenes, almost invisible to most moviegoers, Eastwood was forging a career as a director, making his directorial debut with the fine thriller *Play Misty for Me* (1971). The only way he could get the studio to back the film was by playing the male lead, but he generously allowed his costar to steal the film. This was a time when actors rarely stepped behind the camera, unlike today when actors are often directing. Eastwood is the only one to have emerged a great filmmaker, making many forget that he was ever an actor, even though his acting became much stronger in his later years.

Like fine California wine, Clint Eastwood has become a greater artist with age—stronger, much more complex, and fearless to attempt anything on screen that other actors and directors would balk at. In 2008, there are three major American directors looked to for masterpieces. They are Martin Scorsese, Steven Spielberg, and Clint Eastwood, who, since 1992, has put forth a body of work envied by every working director and virtually every actor who ever attempted to direct a film.

He had been directing for 17 years when he directed the biographical work *Bird* (1988), a study of jazz great Charlie Parker, in which Eastwood gave remarkable insight into a world inhabited largely by blacks. Oddly enough, this box office failure would attract a great deal of attention for Eastwood, earning rave reviews in Europe and winning awards at Cannes. Though the critical reception was lukewarm in the United States, Eastwood had broken through into the ranks of top filmmakers . . . audiences, critics, and most importantly, other directors had noticed. Upon announcing the nominees for the Directors Guild of America Award for best director, Steven Spielberg observed sadly, "I was really hoping that Clint Eastwood would be nominated this year for *Bird*," echoing the sentiments of many other directors and critics in North America. He would win the Golden Globe Award for best director, which is given out by the Hollywood Foreign Press Association, but was denied an Academy Award nomination. Having earned the right to make a film that he did not have to appear in to secure financing, Eastwood boldly told the story of Parker, who was brilliantly portrayed by Forest Whitaker. Whitaker would win the Academy Award for best actor for his riveting performance as Ugandan dictator Idi Amin in *The Last King of Scotland* (2006). There seemed to be genuine shock in the industry when *Bird* (1988) failed to find an audience, as early screenings had indicated this was Eastwood's ticket to the Academy Awards.

Four years later he not only was nominated for the Directors Guild of America Award, he won it for his dark Western masterpiece *Unforgiven* (1992). Released in the late summer of '92, by year's end the film began winning awards from various critics' groups, including the Los Angeles Film Critics who stunned the film community by honoring *Unforgiven* with best film, best director, best actor (Eastwood), and best supporting actor (Gene Hackman). A few weeks later the National Society of Film Critics followed suit, giving the film everything the L.A. scribes had except best actor. Come Oscar time, the film was nominated for nine Academy Awards, including best picture, best director, and Eastwood's first nomination for best actor. There was no stopping either Eastwood or *Unforgiven*. On Oscar night as the film coasted to four awards, including best film, best supporting actor, and for Eastwood, his first Academy Award for best director, it seemed to solidify the fact he was a filmmaker first and foremost.

In the years since that first Academy Award, he has never been one to sit on his laurels contently, but rather chose as a director to grow and expand, challenging himself with films that sometimes worked and sometimes did not. The drama *A Perfect World* (1993) never quite caught on with audiences despite rave reviews for actor Kevin Costner who gives what many, including Eastwood, believe is the finest performance of his career as psychotic killer Butch. Eastwood's direction of the adult love story *The Bridges of Madison County* (1995) earned high praise from critics and no less than for his costar Meryl Streep, but what astonished many was Eastwood's own sensitive, fine performance in which he managed to capture something on screen he had never before shown: vulnerability.

The years spanning 1996–2002 seemed to be a time of personal growth for Eastwood as a director when he attempted many different stories, some successfully, such as the over-the-hill drama *Space Cowboys* (2000), and some not, such as the adaptation of the best seller *Midnight in the Garden of Good and Evil* (1997).

In 2003 he returned with a vengeance with the film adaptation of Dennis Lehane's massive crime novel *Mystic River* (2003) in which he guided Sean Penn and Tim Robbins to Academy Award–winning performances. Beyond that he made a searing film about the choices we make in life, and how we are never completely free of those choices. Penn gave the finest performance of his career as a father tormented by the murder of his daughter, capturing raw, primal grief with such stunning power that audiences were speechless and numb after seeing the film. Nominated for six Academy Awards, Eastwood again found himself in the running for best director, only to lose to the Peter Jackson juggernaut that was the final *The Lord of the Rings* (2003) film.

One year later he would not be denied.

Released late in the year *Million Dollar Baby* (2004) was the Cinderella film that stunned critics and audiences with its startling twist that sent the film off in a direction totally unseen and unexpected, becoming in the process a radically different film than we initially anticipate. It is a sports film, but also a deep love story, and finally a film about the ultimate sacrifice for the one you love. Hilary Swank and Morgan Freeman won Oscars for their performances, and Eastwood received his second Academy Award nomination for best actor for his work, which Swank declared "the finest performance of his career." He won his second Academy Award for best director, besting no less than the great Martin Scorsese for his Howard Hughes drama *The Aviator* (2004).

He then entered into the busiest two years of his life, directing two films about the battle on Iwo Jima during the Second World War. The first, *Flags of Our Fathers* (2006), was the biggest film of his career—a 90 million dollar epic about the impact of the war on three of the young men who raised the flag on Iwo Jima and then were shipped home to help raise money for the war bond drive, their hearts and minds still on the battlefield. Though beautifully filmed and powerful in every way, and despite strong reviews, the film struggled out of the gate and never caught on with audiences, thus dashing its Oscar chances. In hopes that a second film created on the heels of the first would bring more interest to the first, *Letters from Iwo Jima* (2006), a much smaller and more personal film, went into theaters in late December, a full three months ahead of schedule, and found itself basking in some of the best reviews of Eastwood's career.

Becoming increasingly bothered that he was not telling the whole story, Eastwood decided to tell the Japanese side of the story while making the first film. Commissioning a screenplay and filming on a shoestring budget entirely in Japanese, the film was created quietly and became one of the best films of the year. The Los Angeles Film Critics voted it film of the year, and

Letters from Iwo Jima was nominated for four Academy Awards, including best director and best picture.

Eastwood now sits as one of the three finest directors working in modern American film, with Steven Spielberg and Martin Scorsese alongside him. While they may represent the old guard and the remnants of the great cinema of the seventies, there can be no question that their films are indeed among the elite of the last 30 years, surpassing the work of any single new generation director. This book is a study of how Eastwood managed to quietly get to this level, and in explaining such, I hope this book also is a celebration of his gifts as an artist.

Everybody changes all the time. I certainly hope I have. If I made Play Misty for Me *now I'd probably ruin it because that was a different mind, with less experience, that made it back then. I've always been intrigued that people like Wilder and Capra stopped directing as early as they did. I think these can be your best years . . . as long as you keep changing. The world keeps changing, so you've got to change with it.*

—Clint Eastwood, speaking with *Sight and Sound* magazine, 2008

THE SEVENTIES

Play Misty for Me (1971)

To have an actor directing a film was certainly not new to the film business in 1971.

Charlie Chaplin directed all of his major work after 1917, creating some of the greatest comedy classics of all time in *City Lights* (1931) and *Modern Times* (1936). More so than any other could have, Chaplin understood his strengths and weaknesses, and directed his films to exploit his great strength as a physical actor. American boy wonder Orson Welles would direct himself as Charles Foster Kane in the stunning *Citizen Kane* (1941), forging a career through the years as both actor and director. British actor Laurence Olivier almost single handedly saved the British film industry with his Shakespearean films *Henry V* (1945) and *Hamlet* (1948), which would become the first non-American film to win the Academy Award for best film. Though nominated for best director, Olivier lost but made a stunning impact on the business. Charles Laughton would helm the thriller *The Night of the Hunter* (1955), which was probably the greatest film ever made by a man who directed a single film and easily the best film of 1955. John Wayne, however, directed *The Alamo* (1960) with little success. Not having learned his lesson, Wayne would tackle *The Green Berets* (1968), the first American film to deal with the conflict in Vietnam and still among the worst.

When Paul Newman stepped behind the camera to direct his wife Joanne Woodward in *Rachel, Rachel* (1968), there seemed to be a watch on whether he did a good job, as though this was the turning point for actors seeking to direct. Newman did better than a good job; he did a brilliant job, earning the New York Film Critics Award for best director and a nomination from the Directors Guild of America for best director. The film was nominated for an Oscar for best picture, but in one of those bizarre nomination incidents, Newman was ignored for best director by the Academy.

It really didn't matter because the die had been cast; actors could indeed direct and direct well. Woody Allen would forge a long career of directing himself in a series of wonderful comedies in the early seventies before becoming one of the most important and vital American directors with *Annie Hall* (1977) and *Manhattan* (1979), splitting his career between meaningful comedy and still, Bergman-esque drama.

There seems to be a general, though perplexing, rule within the Academy of Arts and Sciences that if an actor directs a film, and it is remotely good, he or she deserves an Oscar for best director. Eastwood is among the few exceptions for actually deserving the Oscar he won, along with perhaps Warren Beatty for *Reds* (1981).

Robert Redford won an Oscar for directing *Ordinary People* (1980) over Martin Scorsese and his masterpiece *Raging Bull* (1980), a move obviously based on the popularity of Redford's film rather than sheer artistry. The very next year British character actor Richard Attenborough won the Oscar for his direction of *Gandhi* (1982), a paint-by-number, conservative biography of the Indian leader—the sort of film the Academy loves—defeating none other than Steven Spielberg for his brilliant *E.T.: The Extraterrestrial* (1982), which within a year was being condemned for its idiocy. Beatty took home the best director award in 1981 for his massive Bolshevik epic *Reds* (1981), one of the most deserving awards given in the last 35 years. Scorsese fell victim to an actor directing again when Kevin Costner won the Oscar for *Dances with Wolves* (1990) over Scorsese and *Goodfellas* (1990). And just five years later Mel Gibson won the award for *Braveheart* (1995), a film that had not even earned its director a nomination from the prestigious Directors Guild of America. Did Gibson and several of these other men win because they pulled it off? Because they managed to create an average film rather than a disaster? Gibson directed a better film a few years later with *The Passion of the Christ* (2004), but there was no chance the Academy was going to nominate him for that. Too dark, too bloody, and too controversial despite the fact that it was brilliant and a greater achievement than *Braveheart*. Even his Mayan epic *Apocalypto* (2006) surpasses what he accomplished with *Braveheart* and also went virtually unnoticed.

Of all the actors who have tried their hand at directing, Clint Eastwood and Warren Beatty appear to be the finest, each taking substantial risks in their work that many established directors will not take. The major difference between them is that Eastwood likes to work and does so consistently, whereas Beatty often takes years between films—nine between *Reds* and *Dick Tracy* (1990) and another eight between the comic book crime film and *Bulworth* (1998), his vicious black comedy about L.A. politics.

Scorsese has lost an Oscar to Eastwood as well, in 2004, watching his Howard Hughes epic *The Aviator* (2004) cruise to five early awards before the juggernaut that was Eastwood's *Million Dollar Baby* (2004) took over and won the top awards. Though he had previously lost to two actors, Scorsese certainly would not complain about losing to Eastwood, who by that time was thought of as one of America's finest filmmakers. The road to that status began with a little thriller titled *Play Misty for Me* (1971), a Hitchcockian work that would establish Eastwood as an artist to be taken seriously, both as an actor and a director.

The work first came to him as a treatment, a 60-page story written by a former secretary he had known named Jo Heims who had dreams of being a screenwriter. Eastwood liked the idea very much and optioned it from her, later receiving a frantic phone call from her that Universal was interested in moving on the film. He let the film go, but later it would find its way back to him as part of a three-picture deal he had with Universal in the days before he became a mainstay on the Warner Brothers lot.

Studio chief Lew Wasserman agreed to allow Eastwood to direct and star in the film on one condition: That they did not tell him, but rather his agent, that they would not pay him for his directing. Eastwood agreed to that, believing that they should not have to pay because he nor they had any idea if he could make this work. His agent would work out a deal that gave Eastwood his fee for the three-picture deal as an actor, and for his directing services he would receive a percentage of the gross. The ever-frugal Wasserman believed he had gotten quite a steal because Eastwood, he felt, would work for him again in an action film and make them a bundle.

"I like the Alfred Hitchcock kind of thriller aspect but the main thing I liked about it was that the story was very real," Eastwood states on the special feature documentary on the DVD for *Play Misty for Me*. "The story was believable because these kind of commitments or misinterpretations thereof go on all the time."

"Jo Heims had a female friend that was very much a stalker type. She didn't commit homicide or anything like that, but she went around and harassed this person," Eastwood states.

The film was made at a time when strong female characters were quite rare in films. Within a year of the release of *Play Misty for Me*, Jane Fonda had not so much as kicked in the door for women in film as smashed it open with her fierce and real performance as a stalked hooker in *Klute* (1971), a film bearing some comparison to *Play Misty for Me* in that the lead character is being stalked. Fonda's performance made clear to the industry that women could be as realistic in a role as a man; they could be as authentic, down and dirty, and completely human as men could be. Furthermore, Fonda's performance started a revolution that saw women such as Ellen Burstyn, Faye Dunaway, Marsha Mason, Jodie Foster, and later Meryl Streep achieve great success with their performances.

Eastwood needed a strong female lead. Furthermore, he understood that the key to the success of the film was the performance of the woman portraying Evelyn. He had seen a New York stage actress, Jessica Walter, in Sidney Lumet's *The Group* (1966) and was struck by the ferocious look on her face when something in the film happened to her character. Without feeling the need to audition anyone else, he called her in for a chat and they discussed the script and story. Walter, initially shy, found the confidence to be very open with him about the character. They roamed around the lot, discussing the character, the arc of the performance, and the motivation of the characters. Eastwood, believing in her as an actress, gave her the role. She then began her research into the character, with Eastwood taking her name back to his writers.

The shoot took a mere four and a half weeks. This was the beginning of the Eastwood style of incredible organization—one or two takes, and sometimes shooting the rehearsal shot, though rarely because he so disdains rehearsing, preferring the spontaneity of the first read. The film was shot on location in the Carmel area—not a single studio shot—with the rugged mountain area and smashing waves of the ocean captured in their stunning glory, giving the film an often spectacular beauty.

"Directing and acting, it wasn't as difficult as I thought it would be on *Misty*," explained Eastwood. "I'd seen it done before many times; there's many precedents for it. Everybody from Orson Welles to Laurence Olivier and all the people that had tried it, some quite successful.

"After a while you got so you could throw a switch. Don Siegel kept at me all the time, telling me not to slough yourself," discusses Eastwood about his mentor's advice on set. "He said the big temptation is gonna be to spend all the time with the other actors, then slough your own performance. I had to be careful that I always remembered those words. To this day, more than 30 years later, I still once in a while remind myself to take my time."

In later years Eastwood's actors would come to love the manner in which he worked, the freedom he allowed them, and the gentle manner of coaching he brought to the set. As an actor himself he no doubt understood that actors are very creative people who dislike being told how to play a part as they bring to the film their own ideas. Though Eastwood's skills as an actor were not yet fully appreciated, he certainly seemed to know what an actor required and gave it to them here and has been doing so ever since.

Donna Mills, cast as his estranged girlfriend, had a background in television and soap operas, and would return to that with great success in the eighties and nineties. "I was a little nervous, intimidated, of him as a director because this was the first time he was going to direct and actors directing isn't always the best idea. They generally have not a great reputation as far as doing movies," says Mills in the special features of the DVD.

"He was intimidating but I knew from the first day of shooting that he was a director who knew what he wanted and how to get what he wanted. He had everything totally planned and made me feel very comfortable. No matter what we were doing he'd look at me and say, 'Did you like that? Is that OK?'" remembers Mills.

Like the great directors before him, Eastwood had chosen to be what actors call an actor's director, meaning he was actively involved in the creative process. For far too long directors had been gods on their set, commanding the actors as to what they were to do and how to do it, never allowing them to bring in their own creativity. Elia Kana, John Huston, and Billy Wilder began incorporating the actors' ideas in their films through the forties and fifties, and by the time the method-acting explosion hit, actors had a huge involvement by some directors in their performance and the film. Of course, the bigger name the actor, the greater the power on the set. Through his years as a director, there have been very few power struggles on Eastwood's sets. If there were any, they were settled very quickly with someone leaving and it was never Eastwood, and it was never embarrassing to either party.

Portraying a deeply disturbed woman, Jessica Walter needed her director to trust her work and believe in what she was doing at all times. She found in Eastwood a kindred spirit and celebrates the memory of having worked with him.

"Actually it was a nice meeting of minds because he doesn't like to do very many takes and neither do I. So usually we would do two, three at most, and sometimes he got what he wanted on the first take. We just had the same feeling about not over-rehearsing the film, keeping things fresh. We were a great match I think," she smiled.

The story will seem familiar to today's generation because Adrian Lyne made a film called *Fatal Attraction* (1987) that is in many ways a remake or rethinking of *Play Misty for Me* but without having ever been called such.

Dave Garver (Eastwood) is a popular DJ on a jazz station in Carmel. He is a small celebrity in a small market though the larger markets are paying attention to him. While taking phone requests, there is a female voice that constantly requests of him to "play Misty for me." The voice is sexy and sultry and more than a little intriguing to Dave. With his girlfriend Tobie (Mills) having broken up with him and moved away, Dave mentions on the show that he frequents a bar called the Sardine Factory. The woman requesting "Misty" tracks him to the bar and they meet one another, finding an instant attraction. Lonely and offered a night of sex with no strings attached, Dave agrees and sleeps with Evelyn (Walter), not realizing what he has started and the nightmare it will bring to his life. Soon Evelyn is popping in on Dave whenever she feels like it, growing more and more possessive of him, and slashing her wrists when he tries to break all connection with her. She ruins any chance he has in his career of going national by insulting a woman who has contacted Dave about his program, and when Dave manages to get her into a cab after a terrible physical altercation, she screams at him as the taxi pulls away, "I love you." The harassment does not stop but becomes increasingly worse, and finally vicious and dangerous when Evelyn slashes Dave's maid when she walks in on the woman trashing Dave's home as she is slashing his clothes and art to pieces. Knowing that Evelyn is dangerously unbalanced, Dave confesses everything to Tobie in hopes she will begin to trust him again.

Evelyn calls the station again with a request for "Misty," explaining she has been cured and is headed to Hawaii to start her life over again. That night Dave awakens to find her standing over him with a butcher knife in her hand, which she plunges into the pillow beside him. To Dave's horror he finds out that Tobie's new roommate is none other than Evelyn, who he knows has murder on her mind. Sure enough, as he rushes to Tobie's home, Evelyn has bound and gagged Tobie and has begun to slash the portrait of Dave. Bursting into the home, Dave is attacked by a knife-wielding Evelyn, but finally manages to strike her hard enough to send her through a window and plunging over a cliff to the Pacific below.

The story was told with taut and tight direction; Eastwood tightened his grip on the audience when it was needed and forced them to the edge of their seats once the film got going. He lulled them into a false sense of security and then displayed Evelyn's madness with sharp, sudden cuts that startled and shocked the viewer. The use of the fast cuts, and those stunning helicopter shots, give the audience a sense of the beauty of the area and the evil and madness that lurks within such picturesque beauty.

Critics were somewhat shocked at what Eastwood had accomplished, not ready to accept him as a director when they had not accepted him as an actor at this time in his career. Nonetheless the major critics were at the very least more than fair with him.

"*Play Misty for Me* suggests strongly that Clint Eastwood is more than a multitalented actor, producer, and gunman. He is also a director who, at least in this picture, shows a good sense of what it takes to make an audience get goose pimples," wrote Archer Weinstein for the *New York Post.*

"*Play Misty for Me* marks a surprisingly auspicious directorial debut for Eastwood," said the *Village Voice.*

Ann Guarino, writing for *New York Daily News,* greatly admired the film, writing, "Eastwood makes his directorial debut in *Play Misty for Me.* After a slow start, he proves he can handle both sides of the camera ably. The contemporary thriller holds the interest of the audience for the most part. Jessica Walter is so good as the possessive and obsessive woman that the audience will want to strangle her. In fact when the much put upon Eastwood finally punches her in the jaw as she tries to stab him, this viewer wanted to cheer. . . . Eastwood is at his best when he picks up the threads of the story and carries it to its violent climax. The thriller stands out as a study of psychotic obsession."

Roger Ebert, long one of Eastwood's greatest supporters as a director, wrote, "*Play Misty for Me* is not the artistic equal of *Psycho* (1960), but in the business of collecting an audience into the palm of its hand and then squeezing it hard, it is supreme. It doesn't depend on a lot of surprises to maintain the suspense. There are some surprises, sure, but mostly the film's terror comes from the fact that the strange woman is capable of anything. The movie was Clint Eastwood's debut as a director, and it was a good beginning. He must have learned a lot during the 17 years of working with other directors. In particular he must have learned a lot from Don Siegel, who directed his previous movies and has a bit part (the bartender) in this one. There is no wasted energy in *Play Misty for Me*. Everything contributes to the accumulation of terror until even the ordinary daytime scenes seem to have unspeakable things lurking beneath them."

Not all the critics were so appreciative of Eastwood's work, though in fairness to them, no one was downright nasty.

"*Psycho* in mothballs," carped Rex Reed in the *New York Daily News*. "As for Eastwood's directorial debut, he should be credited for making up in helicopter shots what the movie lacks in plot, motivation, and script. Then to guarantee commercial success, he even throws in a nude scene, a visit to the Monterey Jazz Festival, and his best friend is black. You can't have everything, but you can sure try."

Overall the film was a success despite the fumbling of Universal in marketing the picture and getting it into theaters. Though it would make 5 million dollars, which was very good for the budget, time, and the lack of support from the studio, there must have been a sense of disappointment surrounding the picture for Eastwood. Despite some impressive reviews, Jessica Walter was not nominated for an Academy Award in what was a relatively weak year. Eastwood expected no such accolades for himself—all too aware of what the Hollywood community thought of him as an actor—but he had hoped they might recognize his leading lady.

As an actor he gave a fine performance, moving away from the Westerns he had been so popular in for so long, and coupled with his powerful work in the haunting, nightmarish *The Beguiled* (1971), in which he was both monster and victim, certainly he was breaking ground with his reputation as an actor. The answer to the comments about who would want to see Eastwood portray a DJ was loud and clear: if the film was good and the performance was strong, as it was, anyone would.

The best thing that came out of the film was the fact Eastwood made it clear he could indeed direct, on a budget and on time. He created a strong narrative film to which audiences responded strongly.

Reflecting back on the film in 2003, Eastwood stated, "I don't know if I'd do it the same now, or if I would do things differently. I suppose I wouldn't do it as well."

Did anyone in 1971 really understand that the career of one of modern American cinema's most significant directors had begun?

2

High Plains Drifter (1972)

High Noon (1952) was one of the great films of the fifties, a classic Western directed by Fred Zinnemann that was a critically acclaimed box office hit when released, and was hailed for its acting, directing, and editing.

Told in real time, beginning at ten thirty in the morning, the long-time town marshal Will Kane (Cooper) has married his lady love, Quaker pacifist Amy (Grace Kelly). Kane has sworn to his new wife that he will turn in his badge, give up his life as a lawman, and move to another town to open a store. However, word arrives that Frank Miller, a criminal that Kane helped put away, has escaped his scheduled hanging on a technicality, and, having sworn revenge, is on his way to the town with three of his gunmen to exact their revenge on Kane. The townspeople immediately begin encouraging Kane to leave, believing he is no match for the killers. He and his wife do leave town, but his conscience forces him back, despite knowing he may lose the woman he has just married. He puts the badge back on and decides to go about the town asking for help, believing the people will gladly defend the town with him, as he once did for them. His deputy resigns, and one after another the people of the town refuse to help him in any way. Beaten down but not defeated, Kane meets the four outlaws alone and guns down two of them. Amy, who had been boarding the train when she heard the gunfire, comes back and kills one of the outlaws, choosing to save her husband rather than allow him to die. But Miller takes her hostage and offers Kane a trade, his life for hers. Kane agrees, but Amy claws at Miller's face, at which point Kane fires and kills him, leaving the two newlyweds alone with one another. The townsfolk emerge from their hiding places ready to proclaim Kane a hero, but he hatefully throws his badge in the dust at their feet and with his wife leaves the town forever.

One of the great crimes of Academy Awards history is that *High Noon* and *The Quiet Man* (1952) lost the Oscar for best picture to Cecil B. DeMille's circus soap opera *The Greatest Show on Earth* (1952), easily the worst film to win the award for best film of the year. In addition to the attention from the

Academy, the film had been named best film of the year by the New York Film Critics Circle, who also named its director best of the year. Much was made of Zinnemann's choice in *High Noon* to allow the story to unfold in real time, building an almost unbearable tension throughout with the careful placement of time pieces in the picture. Grandfather clocks, bar clocks, and pocket watches counted down the minutes to high noon with a vicious precision.

Though well loved, *High Noon* was not without its critics. Among these critics was none other than John Wayne, the great star of American Westerns, who was outraged at what he perceived to be the lead character's cowardice. In retaliation to the film, he and director Howard Hawks created *Rio Bravo* (1959), a similar tale, but with a decidedly different story arc and outcome. Wayne felt that Cooper's marshal was a coward for asking for help and should have stood against the bad guys on his own, as he was prepared to do in *Rio Bravo*.

Although many considered him too old for the role, Cooper won the Academy Award for his riveting performance as Will Kane, the finest work of his long career. The film also took the Oscar for film editing and best song, but the loss of the best film and director honors was stunning not only to the makers of the film but also to the industry itself. Generations later, *High Noon* stands as one of the great American Westerns.

It is more than a little ironic that John Wayne despised both *High Noon* and *High Plains Drifter* (1972), though in fairness his reasons for hating the two films were different. He despised *High Noon*'s supposed cowardice, and he was offended by *High Plains Drifter*'s pioneer spirit and the realistic portrayal of the Old West. Perhaps the unfavorable comparisons between Eastwood and Wayne stopped here, as Eastwood had always maintained that he had no desire to be the next John Wayne. He knew he could not be John Wayne, and he wanted to be his own man.

Eastwood first received the idea for *High Plains Drifter* as a draft not more than 10 pages long. He brought in writer Ernest Tidyman, famous for the *Shaft* (1971) novels and films and for recently having won the Academy Award for his screenplay for *The French Connection* (1971). Together they asked the question, "What would have happened if Will Kane, the marshal in *High Noon* had been killed?"

"I decided to do it on the basis of a treatment of only nine pages. It's the only time that's happened to me. The starting point was, 'What would have happened if the sheriff of *High Noon* had been killed? What would have happened afterwards?' In the treatment by Ernest Tidyman the sheriff's brother came back to avenge the sheriff, and the villagers were as contemptible and selfish as in *High Noon*. But I opted for an appreciably different approach; you would never know whether the brother in question is a diabolic being or a kind of archangel. It's up to the audience to draw their conclusion," he would tell the press in the early 1970s, "You like characters who form part of the system or at least appear to form part of it, but don't play the rules of the game it has established and end up revealing its corruption. . . . I'm aware that type of character attracts me. Why? Maybe because I've hated corruption within the system, no matter what it is. In this respect *High Plains Drifter* goes further than *High Noon*. When the hero helped them get organized the townspeople believe they can control him, manipulate him. As soon as he leaves they fall back into the error of their ways and their failure is obvious, their disgrace is unpardonable."

This became the basic premise for the film *High Plains Drifter* (1972), the second feature Eastwood would direct. Directing a Western seemed a natural progression for him, having become a major international star in the Spaghetti Westerns of Sergio Leone, and there was little doubt that the influence of the Italian master would be apparent on the screen.

Although the studio wanted Eastwood to use their back lot, he had no such inclination and was soon on the road scouting locations. The spot he found was Mono Lake, which is situated near a desert in California. The lake has stalagmites rising out of the water and giving the place a hellish look. Very quickly upon visiting the area he found all the locations he would need for the film, with the exception of the desolate desert from which his character emerges, which ended up being shot outside of Reno, Nevada.

Henry Bumstead, the gifted designer still working with Eastwood more than 30 years later, was hired to create the Western town, and brought to the screen a unique and highly original look. Building the village in a scant 28 days, he gave the picture a raw and rough look with his unpainted lumber and lived-in look. Unlike the Western towns we had seen in previous films, this one looked terribly foreboding, as though the townspeople knew not to plan for growth or even consider a future. The town became almost a secondary character, devoid of any real hope.

The story opens over the credits as a stranger moves through the wilderness, riding past the graveyard in a strange sense of foreshadowing and into the desolate and seemingly tragic little town. The stranger will not go unnoticed for long, as he is harassed by a local prostitute, whom he takes into an alley and rapes. Menaced in a barbershop, he makes quick work of the bullies and earns the respect of the townsfolk. The townsfolk seemed to be afraid of something, and it turns out they have every reason to be very frightened. They had stood by and watched their former sheriff be whipped to death by a group of cowboys, who are now threatening to turn them all in and make the law aware of their being complicit in the crime.

Rumors circulate about the stranger: Who is he? Is he the sheriff's brother? Is he another lawman who has come for revenge? Or is he an avenging angel or ghost that has come for revenge? The townspeople offer him whatever he wants, and he takes full advantage of this by befriending the midget Mordecai and pinning the star on him.

"What people fear is what's inside them," he tells Sarah (Verna Bloom), the wife of the hotel owner and the only person who actually tried to come to the dead marshal's aid. She and the stranger strike a bond and enjoy a night together, each knowing that it will not last.

Working with the people in the town, he convinces them that they can defeat the criminals with an ambush, but they will need to follow his every word to make this work. He talks the people into painting the town hell red, and then all but abandons them, leading to the failure of the ambush. The convicts tear the town apart, setting fire to this town called hell, only to be killed at the last minute when the stranger reappears to kill them. As he leaves, he is again asked his name, and he replies almost sadly, "You know who I am." Then he rides away and seems to vanish into thin air, leaving the audience and townsfolk believing he may indeed be the ghost of their dead sheriff.

Eastwood shot the film in sequence, a tactic he has employed when able, allowing the actors to grow into character, but likely done this time out of necessity, in order to burn the town down.

Actress Verna Bloom was among those with praise for his directing style. "He doesn't give you a specific direction about how to do this or how to do that, but he has a very clear idea about what the scene is about and how he wants the scene," she stated. Eastwood was developing already as a fine director of actors, allowing them the freedom to do the job he had hired them to do without infringing on their artistic space.

The film drew praise for its realistic depiction of the Old West, something Western icon John Wayne did not appreciate when he saw the film. A few years after the release of the film, Wayne wrote Eastwood a letter in which he made clear his displeasure with the film and the depiction of the pioneers of the Old West. Wayne believed that Eastwood's pioneers were killers, and the older actor felt that the filmmakers needed to stick together. I believe the major difference was that for Wayne the American West was so much a part of his legacy and his career that it had become something of an obsession, but for Eastwood the American West was just a location in which his film was set. Wayne, though a champion for realism on film, also did not want audiences ever to be offended by what they were seeing, and in Eastwood's films he saw the potential for that to happen simply with the portrayal of the realism of the violence. Although he became famous making Westerns, first on television and then in Italy, it is telling that Eastwood himself has only directed four of them.

Critics were split on *High Plains Drifter*, some finding the film very good, with exciting set pieces, and others snickering openly at Eastwood's continued work as a director.

Vincent Canby, writing in the *New York Times*, stated, "With its fragmented flashbacks and bizarre, austere locations, *High Plains Drifter*'s stylistic eccentricity lends an air of unsettling eeriness to its revenge story, adding an uncanny slant to Eastwood's antiheroic westerns . . . part ghost story, part revenge western, more than a little silly, and quite often entertaining."

"Shows Clint Eastwood to be a genuinely talented filmmaker; not at all a likable film, but an impressive one," was the review in the *London Observer*.

"Even Clint Eastwood makes fun of Clint Eastwood's pitifully narrow range as an actor. *High Plains Drifter* should put an end to those jokes, because Eastwood the director gives notice of a solid and exciting talent. There are already traces of a distinctive Eastwood style. His performance is redeemed by his work on the other side of the camera; it's a future to build on," wrote Jerry Oster for *New York Daily News*.

Perhaps most savage was Rex Reed, also of *New York Daily News*, who spit venomously, "One of the year's most hysterical comedies. The acting is a riot; the direction is as interesting as the rear end of Eastwood's horse. I've seen better westerns at the Pepsi Cola Saloon at Disneyland."

With two films under his belt as a director, each radically diverse, there was little doubt that Eastwood's work as a director was allowing for artistic growth. No one would be prepared for his next project, the heartwarming love story *Breezy* (1973), which perhaps more than any of his early work made clear his intention to grow with each film and move from genre to genre.

3

Breezy (1973)

I'd forgotten what it was like to make pictures this agreeably, I'll work with Clint any time he asks.

—William Holden on Eastwood

With two films under his belt as a director, both strong hits at the box office and drawing the attention of film critics, Eastwood sought to stretch his creative muscles with a film that would confound the industry and the critics. The romantic comedy genre seemed the last place Eastwood would be at home, but the screenplay for *Breezy* (1973) offered him the chance to explore a genre that he had not previously worked in and the chance to work with a genuine movie legend, Oscar winner William Holden, an actor Eastwood had grown up watching.

Written by Jo Heims, the May–December romance did indeed seem like an impossibly odd choice for Eastwood, now the top box office star in the world. Yet he liked the subject matter and was attracted to the storyline of a young girl teaching an older man a thing or two about the world. Eastwood also believed the film would allow him to show a side of himself not previously seen by critics. Although Eastwood and producer Bob Daley knew the film would not make major money, neither of them seemed concerned because the film would not cost much to make either, and frankly they were both more interested in making the movie. Hooked by what he called "the rejuvenation of the cynic through this naïve creature," Eastwood believed there was a fine story waiting to burst forth from behind the rather lightweight screenplay. Universal was against making the film from the beginning, believing it to be everything Eastwood was not, perhaps initially unaware that the actor had no intention of being in the film. Still, a debt of sorts was owed to Eastwood, and the decision to allow the film to go forth was made at a budget of $750,000, which would make it easier for the film to turn a profit.

After rejecting Heim's suggestion that he should play the role of the depressed real estate agent Frank Harmon, an older man who falls in love with the much younger girl, Eastwood seemed to have decided that only one actor could play the part: William Holden. As far as anyone knows, Holden was the only actor personally approached by Eastwood to be in the film.

Long a fan of the Academy Award winner, Eastwood realized that for the first time he would be directing a major movie star. This would be perhaps a true test of his abilities as a filmmaker, because here was an actor who had worked with no less than directing titans David Lean and Billy Wilder. If ever there was to be a test of his gifts as a director of actors, this was it for a variety of reasons. Specifically, it would be a challenge because it was a known fact that Holden made himself part of the creative team and liked to be involved in decision making. More challenging for Eastwood than any other single factor in the film, however, would be the fact that the picture was outside his comfort zone as a director. If Universal was worried about the box office without Eastwood in the film, they said little and let their star make his movie unbothered.

William Holden belonged to another age of cinema, the golden age. The actor had exploded into the business with a superb performance in *Golden Boy* (1939), leading him to roles throughout the forties, and to greater and more interesting roles such as his doomed writer in Billy Wilder's caustic *Sunset Boulevard* (1950) opposite the great Gloria Swanson, in what would be the performance of her lifetime. Solidifying his reputation as a leading man, he became a favorite of many directors throughout the fifties. He specialized in the cynical antihero, beaten down by the world and life yet hopefully looking around the corner for something better, always knowing it does not exist. Performances in *Born Yesterday* (1950), *Stalag 17* (1953)— for which he won the Academy Award for best actor—*The Country Girl* (1954), *Picnic* (1955), and *The Bridge on the River Kwai* (1957) had allowed Holden to become one of the most exciting and sought-after actors in the business. The loneliness he brought to his roles was very real, and over the years he became a bitter, rather cynical man, disgusted with the movie business, much preferring his time in Kenya. He drank heavily, and by the time he came to Eastwood he had a reputation as an alcoholic. Eastwood was well aware of the actor's drinking as well as the ravages of the disease on the actor's good looks, but he placed his trust in Holden. Many in the industry believed Holden's best work was long behind him, but ironically it was yet to come, in the form of a sterling performance in Sidney Lumet's scathing satire about the corruption within television, *Network* (1976), for which Holden was nominated for an Academy Award. Holden was quite extraordinary in the film, playing the only sane man within a television network allowing an obvious madman on the air to preach what he believed God was saying to him. Entering into a torrid affair with the woman who steals his news division, his character, Max, learns a harsh life lesson too late, realizing that the younger executives around him are television incarnate and unable to connect with anything real. Holden brings to the film a sense of decency, a lone voice of reason in a world gone utterly mad.

The older actor, thrilled to be cast in *Breezy*, placed himself at Eastwood's disposal for readings with countless young women seeking to play the young girl in the film. Major stars do not do this sort of thing, and the fact that Holden made himself that available was not lost on Eastwood, who knew that the chemistry between Holden and the young girl was all-important to the picture.

Casting Breezy, the young hippie girl that Holden falls for, proved more challenging for Eastwood than he thought it would be. Every young actress in the movie industry auditioned for the role, including his future love and costar Sondra Locke, before he decided on relatively unknown Kay Lenz, perhaps best known for her marriage to pop star David Cassidy.

Sometimes on a film set—and on *Breezy*—something magical occurs between actors and director, a merging of minds, a recognition that they are doing something special; and even though the film is not likely to be widely seen, there is a feeling that they have the chance to do something unique. That feeling abounded on the *Breezy* shoot, with Holden on his best behavior, consistently on time and ready to work at all times, always kind and sensitive to the younger Lenz, who admitted at the time and later on that she really knew nothing. During the difficult nude scenes, the actress stated that Holden never took his eyes off of hers, allowing her to be comfortable at all times. The moment they had the shot, he would carefully take his shirt off and drape it around her shoulders, thereby covering her. Lenz adored Holden, realizing that the older man was taking care of her on the shoot in much the same way his character cared for hers on film. Perhaps what she did not realize at the time was that the older actor was building trust, which is an all-important factor for characters in such a highly emotional film. Holden actually seemed to elevate the work of Lenz through his careful work with the younger actress throughout the shoot.

The film explores the relationship between Frank and Breezy, a young hippie girl he encounters wandering around the grounds of his home. Offering her a ride appears to be the only way to get rid of her, so he does just that, although she ends up back at his home that night to retrieve a guitar she left behind. A fast talker, the young woman manages to chat her way into the house and get a bath before he tosses her out. The very next night she is brought back to his home by two police officers, who ask him if he is indeed her uncle. Knowing that she is going to go to jail if he does not go along, he assents, and against all better judgment he asks her to stay with him for a while. Although their age gap is huge and their opinions of everything differ, Breezy takes a bizarre hold on Frank, and he finds himself becoming more and more involved with her, eventually succumbing to desire and making love to her.

Their affair takes flight, and Frank finds himself coming out of the shell he had long been hiding in, allowing life to slip by while he made money but no friends or serious relationships. Breezy falls in love with him as well, but Frank becomes embarrassed by her when meeting friends, in particular his ex-wife. Despite knowing he will break her heart (and his own), he tells her they can no longer see one another. A short time later a close friend of Frank's is killed in a car accident, and upon experiencing heartache and loneliness in the grieving process, he comes to understand that life is too short to let true love pass by. He finds Breezy and professes his love to her, but tells her he gives them just a year. With a look of wonder, a winning smile, and a glance of pure love she tells him, "Imagine that . . . a whole year!"

Critics were reasonably kind to the film, seeming to understand that Eastwood had stepped beyond what he was used to creating as a director with this odd little comedy. They certainly recognized that his skill with actors was apparent, as he drew very strong performances from both Holden and Lenz. Although the film did not earn rave reviews, the critics were most respectful of what they saw Eastwood attempting to do with his career.

"Clint Eastwood continues to rise as a director with *Breezy*. He proved what he could do with *Play Misty for Me*, conquered the western form of film with *High Plains Drifter*, and now hits the bull's-eye with a sentimental April–December romance that could have been awful, but isn't," stated Arthur Winstein for the *New York Post* in one of the film's strongest reviews.

Molly Haskell of the *Village Voice* gushed, "Clint Eastwood's most accomplished directorial job so far . . . a love story in which almost everything works." "Fine work from William Holden and low-keyed direction from Clint Eastwood sustain the narrative flow and mood in this film," wrote Howard Thompson of the *New York Times*.

At the other end of the critical spectrum, there were some expected out-and-out assaults on the film. Judith Christ savaged the picture with her comments in *New York Magazine*, "So perfectly awful that it's almost good for laughs."

Both Holden and Lenz gave fine performances, bringing to their roles an honesty in their characters that was both refreshing and becoming essential in modern cinema. Audiences were no longer willing to accept the standard conventions of Hollywood romance; they needed characters they believed in with a story line that made sense. Unlike the black comedy *Harold and Maude* (1971), in which the elderly Maude (Ruth Gordon) brings joy into the life of the morose and often suicidal Harold (Bud Cort), *Breezy* breathes life into its "Harold," allowing him to find his inner youth and enjoy life once again. Into his dark world Breezy came bursting forth like a bright ray of sunshine, which he basked in. Holden enjoyed working with Eastwood very much.

"He's also even-tempered, a personality trait not much in evidence among directors. The crew is totally behind him, and that really helps things go smoothly. There's been no temperament, nothing. We do our own work and we like it," he stated after completing the film.

Holden gave himself over to the role and gave a terrific performance, inhabiting the character throughout the film, and delivering one of his best though least seen performances. The film would allow him to continue in other pictures such as the high-profile disaster picture *The Towering Inferno* (1974), the aforementioned *Network*, and his last great work in Blake Edwards's savage black comedy *S.O.B.* (1981).

Eastwood's instincts as an actor served him well on this film in directing the role of Frank, who, though outside his comfort zone in terms of age, was the very sort of isolated outsider that Eastwood found himself attracted to in future roles. It is quite remarkable that the best reviews of the film praise Eastwood's substantial growth as a director even at this early stage of his directing career.

Eastwood, however, was deeply disappointed and rather bitter about the film's failure at the box office, and again he blamed Universal for what he felt was a shoddy job of marketing the picture. Here was a sweet-natured, offbeat love story that failed at a time when romantic pictures were doing very well at the box office. Granted, *The Way We Were* (1973) had the box office appeal of Robert Redford and Barbra Streisand and was a sweepingly beautiful love story, but other such films were doing strong business because their studios were behind them. *Cinderella Liberty* (1974), a down-and-dirty love story, featured James Caan as a sailor who falls hard for a hooker portrayed by Marsha Mason, while *A Touch of Class* (1973) won Glenda Jackson her second Academy Award for best actress. Why then was Eastwood's film missed? Did the studio have so little confidence in the film that they dumped it into theatres and then walked away—a common fate for pictures they have no clue how to release? It was simply another slight in the growing animosity between Eastwood and Universal, and it would eventually lead to a parting of ways.

A recent viewing of *Breezy* shows the film to be still a lovely little love story with an offbeat romance that holds up. Holden's cynical real estate man finds love in the least likely of places, in the arms of a goofy, naïve hippie who barely notices his age and does not see him as an older man, but as the man she loves. He finds in her something he thought was forever gone from his life—wonder. Eastwood beautifully captured the sense of hope that comes with every new relationship, that wonderful freshness, in which people hope to find the best parts of themselves for the other. In this film, no one is more surprised than Holden's character when he discovers that this young girl makes him want to be a better man, and she, through her sheer love of life and innocence, allows him to discover the man he once was. Her youth, her exuberance, is infectious, and he, partnered with her, finds his younger soul to link with hers.

4

The Eiger Sanction (1975)

The year 1975 was one of the major turning points in the history of American cinema. The impact of Francis Ford Coppola's *The Godfather* (1972) and *The Godfather Part II* (1974) had firmly put a stamp on the New American Cinema, his films hailed as two of the finest films of all time. In the summer of 1975, Universal released Steven Spielberg's thriller *Jaws* (1975), which within a few months had surpassed *The Godfather* as the highest grossing film of all time, but more importantly, made clear to the industry that blockbuster releasing was the future of the cinema. So great was the box office impact of *Jaws* that it is often forgotten what a superb piece of film-making it truly was. That same year Milos Forman's *One Flew over the Cuckoo's Nest* (1975) would sweep the Academy Awards, finally earning Jack Nicholson his Oscar for best actor for his breathtaking performance, while Sidney Lumet would give audiences his finest film, *Dog Day Afternoon* (1975), containing an electrifying piece of acting from Al Pacino. Gene Hackman would stun audiences in *French Connection II* (1975) as a cop taken hostage and addicted to heroin, left to withdraw on his own, while Walter Matthau and George Burns would delight in *The Sunshine Boys* (1975) as a pair of old vaudevillians at one another's throats.

Stanley Kubrick's *Barry Lyndon* (1975) was adored by critics but dumb-founded audiences, while Robert Altman's *Nashville* (1975) would become one of the first major films almost entirely improvised. Filmmakers found new freedom in American cinema, and they were now able to make films about subjects previously considered taboo with studios and the public. Suddenly movies were incredibly authentic and realistic about their subject matter. However, there were still some purely entertainment films, such as the genre films *The Poseidon Adventure* (1972) and *The Towering Inferno* (1975). As the top-ranked box office star in North America, Eastwood by now was deeply disappointed with the manner in which Universal had handled his directing projects *Play Misty for Me* (1971) and *Breezy* (1973) and was seriously considering moving to Warner Brothers, who were holding their door wide open for the artist. Knowing he owed Universal a film, he had an interest in yet another Paul Newman reject, *The Eiger Sanction* (1975). In this film he would portray Jonathan Hemlock, a government assassin and spy who climbs mountains in his spare time. Hemlock strikes a deal to assassinate two Communist killers in return for the Internal Revenue Service (IRS) turning a blind eye to his lucrative art collection, which is, frankly, stolen. Though Eastwood never had been particularly interested in subject matter such as this, the film offered him two things that appealed to him: first, a way out of the contract with Universal, and second, the chance to work on location, in isolation in Switzerland. He was most aware that some of the film's crucial scenes took place high atop the Eiger in Switzerland, and he agreed that a small crew would go with him for the shoot, all of them performing double duty, himself included, hauling cables and equipment.

Eastwood had never been terribly impressed with the screenplay, which was based on a series of novels with Hemlock as the lead character, but he did believe that if he could shoot on location and capture the climbing sequences he hoped to shoot, audiences would forget the plot and be in awe of the film's visuals.

"I took a book Universal owned—a best seller—and I couldn't figure out what to do. The book has no ties. In other words, the character that is killed at the beginning has no relationship to anybody else. I just took it and tried to make the guy relate to the hero so the hero had some other motivations. The way the book was written, he had no motivations for anything. He just went up there strictly for monetary gain, no other motivations, period," Eastwood explained. "At the end he's not with any of the people he started with—including the girl. It just rambled on that way.

"The challenge of it for me was to actually shoot a mountain-type film on a mountain, not on sets. The only ones done in the past were all done on sets; the mountains were all papier-mache mountains," he continued to Patrick McGilligan in *Focus on Film*.

Warned that the Eiger, which means "ogre" in German, was grouped with Everest and K2 as being among the world's most difficult climbs, Eastwood clearly understood the risks he was about to undertake. Had he known the eventual outcome, one wonders if he would have pushed ahead. In 1974 the Eiger had claimed the lives of 41 climbers, so in order to ensure maximum safety, Eastwood hired Mike Hoover as climbing advisor to the film. The greatest concern to the climbers involved in the film seemed not to be that the Eiger was that difficult to ascend, but rather that it was described by Jim Fargo, the film's assistant director, as "a pile of rotting limestone." This kind of surface meant that it could be difficult to find something solid to grab onto, and the possibility that if grabbing something then gives way, it would make rock slides much more of a threat.

Knowing all of the dangers and knowing that the film required his character to be an expert climber, Eastwood pressed on, training with Hoover in Yosemite. Though in excellent physical condition, Eastwood found that climbing was brutally difficult, and although he accomplished what Hoover asked of him, it was not without difficulty. Furthermore, beyond the obvious physical rigors of the filmmaking itself, there was the plot that Eastwood was not entirely happy about, because he saw many complications with the story.

"There were in fact three stories in one, and it was a very difficult picture to make. A good thing our gadgets were limited in number; we were running the risk of heading in the direction of the James Bond movies," he explained to McGilligan. "And especially the mountaineering sequences posed enormous problems. We had to shoot with two crews, one crew of technicians and one crew of mountain climbers. Every morning we had to decide, according to the weather report, which to send up the mountain. The three actors and myself had to undergo intensive training."

In one of the final days of training in the United States before leaving for Switzerland, Eastwood, Mike Hoover, Oscar winner George Kennedy, and a skeleton crew shot a short sequence for the film in Monument Valley, home to countless John Ford Westerns. One of Eastwood's happiest memories is sitting high and alone atop the Totem Pole gazing out at Monument Valley, the ghost of John Ford perhaps dancing around him as the sun fell in the sky.

The Eiger proved as difficult as he had been warned, and the decision was made to do the toughest shots first. To Eastwood's satisfaction and the surprise of Hoover, the first couple of days went very well. However, on August 13, disaster struck when Hoover and 26-year-old David Knowles were descending the mountain after accomplishing a couple of very difficult shots. Hoover heard the sound of a huge rock on the move and instantly moved into a crouch to avoid being hit. The rock hit him full in the back, and the pain he endured from the pelvic fracture was incredible, but he was alive. Knowles was not as lucky. He was killed as the rock struck him on the head, killing him instantly. Eastwood was devastated, having never dealt with death on one of his sets before. He felt responsible and considered calling off the shoot, but he was urged to continue by the climbers who made it clear that each of them understood the risks of what they were doing. After many heart-to-heart discussions with his climbers and crew, Eastwood finally came around to the thinking that to cancel the project and shut down production was to state that Knowles's death meant nothing. The shoot continued, though a pall had fallen over the project with the death of the climber. Forging on with the film, Eastwood would take part in a dangerous stunt that would see him doing a free fall, or appearing to do a free fall, of some 4,000 feet. Harnessed and safe, Eastwood still found himself nervous about the stunt, yet he pulled it off without a hitch.

The plot of the film resembled a thriller in the style of the great Alfred Hitchcock, which Eastwood no doubt recognized when he first read the screenplay. In fact, it is hard not to see the similarities between *The Eiger Sanction* and *North by Northwest* (1959), which features that classic chase across the faces of Mount Rushmore.

Summoned by a secret U.S. intelligence agency to perform a sanction—a killing—Hemlock agrees to do the job only because it will keep the IRS off his back over his highly valuable art collection. After executing the person he was hired to kill, it seems he is not going to be able to return home because the agency is now blackmailing him to perform an even more dangerous sanction that will have him scale the dangerous Eiger Mountain, find his target among a climbing party, and kill him without being detected. Aided by Ben Bowman (George Kennedy), an old friend, Hemlock begins the climb and begins to deduce who the target is. He is stunned to learn that it is none other than his friend Bowman. When Bowman learns that he is to be killed, he attempts to climb down the mountain. Circumstances see Hemlock make a drastic climbing mistake that leaves him hanging thousands of feet in the air facing certain death. When Bowman appears to save him, Hemlock is confused and stunned by his friend's loyalty. Bowman explains the reasons for his actions to Hemlock and convinces Hemlock that he was in the right, and has been right all along about what has been happening. Hemlock listens and allows his friend to leave by refusing to carry out the sanction. He then deludes his employers at the agency by telling them that Bowman has indeed been killed, gaining a small degree of justice, betraying them for the greater good, as they had tried to betray him by asking him to work against his moral code.

In 1975, the film opened in the spring, which is now considered one of the worst times to release a film, as audiences are still viewing the films nominated for the Academy Awards. It is a season usually set aside for the pictures the studios do not know how to release. There were no strong films released at that time, yet *The Eiger Sanction* was still a failure, both with audiences and critics, who saw little in the film to praise other than the outstanding climbing sequences that Eastwood had fought so hard to make realistic. Actor Jack Cassidy, best known as the husband of Shirley Jones and the father of pop sensation David Cassidy of *The Partridge Family*, earned some good reviews for his wildly over-the-top performance as a gay spy; though in other quarters his work was attacked as being offensive and stereotypical.

"Eastwood, who also directs and according to the studio did his own mountain climbing without doubles, manages fine suspense both in the Swiss and Monument Valley climbs, as well as strong delineation of character. His direction displays a knowledge that permits rugged action," praised *Variety*.

"It has a plot so unlikely and confused we can't believe it for much more than fifteen seconds," wrote Roger Ebert in the *Chicago Sun-Times*, "but its action sequences are so absorbing and its mountaintop photography so compelling that we don't care . . . and so we get wrapped up in the situations and we're seduced by the photography, and we enjoy the several pretty girls who happen along the hero's path, and if the plot doesn't make any sense, well, no movie's perfect."

Ebert seemed to sum up the consensus on the film in that it was not very good or believable. However, the sequences atop the mountain were truly breathtaking, which in the end was all that Eastwood was really after. He had always been aware of the issues with the script, and considering his great concern for a strong story, one wonders if *The Eiger Sanction* was made to get him out of his contract with Universal and allow him to establish a new connection at Warner Brothers, which would end up lasting more than 30 years.

5

The Outlaw Josey Wales (1976)

The American bicentennial marked the last great year of the American Western—the only entirely American genre, and certainly among the most beloved in cinema history. When John Ford's *Stagecoach* (1939) first thundered across screens 37 years earlier, the Western became engrained in the culture of film and was linked with myth and history. Though widely loved by audiences, the Western had not always enjoyed the admiration of critics and historians, who often dismissed the films as fluff and formulaic. Yet by the seventies, with a new breed of filmmaker emerging—artists who grew up on the Westerns of Ford and Howard Hawks and spent time in colleges and universities studying film—there was a renaissance in the American Western. John Ford's *She Wore a Yellow Ribbon* (1949) and his masterpiece *The Searchers* (1956) finally became appreciated for the works of art they were, admired by no less than Martin Scorsese, George Lucas, Steven Spielberg, and John Milius. As the New American cinema emerged, critics looked into the past at great Westerns such as *High Noon* (1952), *The Gunfighter* (1950), *Shane* (1953), and *Rio Bravo* (1959), finding in them the art that had always been there but perhaps had not been noticed until now. There was a renewed respect for the performances of American icon John Wayne, who, like Eastwood, was badly underestimated as an actor for much of his career. How sad that within four years the American Western would suffer a terrible death at the hands of Michael Cimino's overblown epic *Heaven's Gate* (1980), which at 44 million dollars would bankrupt United Artists, one of the oldest existing studios in Hollywood.

In 1976, four Westerns were released, two of them destined to become classics of the genre, and the other two interesting, if not noble, failures.

Robert Altman would bring his unique brand of realism to the legend of Buffalo Bill in *Buffalo Bill and the Indians* (1976), with Paul Newman as the Western hero in a rambling film about the famous Wild West Show that made Buffalo Bill famous around the globe. Audiences ignored the film, critics were lukewarm in their response, and it became little more than a curio.

On a higher profile, a film that was expected to be a masterpiece was *The Missouri Breaks* (1976), bringing together two acting icons, Jack Nicholson and Marlon Brando, in a film directed by Arthur Penn. Though fireworks were expected from the two stars, the film suffered immeasurably from Brando's bizarre behavior on the set, and his very odd performance in the film, which seemed to change from frame to frame. Audiences were put off by the film; they did not know what to think and certainly were not willing to take this quirky journey.

Ironically, the year Eastwood broke through as a great American director, his friend and mentor Don Seigel directed the finest film of his career, *The Shootist* (1976), which offered John Wayne the last role of his career as a gunfighter dying of cancer. Sadly, in a tragic stroke of irony, Wayne himself was again suffering from cancer during the film's making, and though he would give one of his finest performances, he was in very bad shape for the shoot. When the film was released to rave reviews, there was every belief that Wayne would earn an Academy Award nomination for best actor; but sadly Paramount mishandled the film's release, and no such nomination came. That said, *The Shootist* is widely considered one of the finest Westerns ever made, and a heartbreaking study of a "dying man, afraid of the dark." Years later it seems a fitting epitaph to the career of a giant of the cinema.

Eastwood's film, *The Outlaw Josey Wales* (1976), like *The Shootist*, instantly would be recognized as a great American Western, and critics began to take notice of Eastwood's substantial gifts as a director. Yet the road to *The Outlaw Josey Wales* was not an easy journey, and by the time the film was released, the Directors Guild of America had created a new rule, called "the Eastwood rule," in response to events that transpired during the film's troubled shoot.

Eastwood did not begin the film as director, choosing to allow Phillip Kaufman, a newcomer, to handle the directing duties. Having been impressed with Kaufman's work on the Jesse James Western *The Great Northfield Minnesota Raid* (1972), Eastwood felt the younger man was a solid choice to bring the screenplay to the screen.

The story first came to Eastwood through producer Bob Daley, who had been given a story written by Forest Carter, a middle-aged half-Cherokee Indian, who had written the little-known book *The Rebel Outlaw Josey Wales*. Both Eastwood and Daley responded strongly to the story and, as Carter had hoped, the actor committed to portraying the lead role in the film. Eastwood brought in Kaufman initially to polish the screenplay that became *The Outlaw Josey Wales*, and then made the decision that he also would direct the film. Eastwood felt that Kaufman had found in the story the strength of the narrative and, based on that understanding of the story, trusted the director with the film.

However, the troubles started almost at once on location. Kaufman, a strong visual director, lacked Eastwood's take-charge approach, and was content to arrive on set not quite knowing what he wanted or what he was going to do that day. Eastwood does not work that way at all, having thought through the entire process. And though able to handle improvisational moments on set, Eastwood certainly did not care for Kaufman's seeming lack of organization. Operating on the "what if" theory, Kaufman very quickly alienated his star and producer. Eventually things came to a nasty peak during a series of shots on which Kaufman could not decide. Whether Eastwood acted properly in the situation is not for us to say, as we were not in the awkward position in which he had placed himself. Fiscally responsible to the studio (as always), he asked Kaufman to hop in a truck and go scout some locations for upcoming shots. While the director was off scouting, Eastwood told the Director of Photography (DOP) where to put the camera. Although obviously bothered by this turn of events, James Fargo, the DOP, did as he was told, and Eastwood directed the sequence. Kaufman then returned to realize what had happened, and recognized at once that his authority on the set had been seriously impaired. Eastwood, whether or not it was his intention, had made it clear who was in charge. Wanting to confront Eastwood but asked not to do so, Kaufman could see the writing on the wall. Anguished about what he had done and the decision he needed to make, Eastwood fired Kaufman from the film and decided to take over the directing reins himself. In fairness to Kaufman, he went on to an impressive career, directing the masterpiece about the American space program *The Right Stuff* (1983) and the superb sexual dramas *The Unbearable Lightness of Being* (1988) and *Henry and June* (1990), more than proving himself as an artist. He simply was not Eastwood's type of artist or director.

Perhaps more than the rift that had developed between them was Eastwood's growing confidence in his own abilities as a director. He knew he could do the job. From the moment he took over as director, the film became a labor of love.

The film opens on a farm, the homestead of Josey Wales and his family, where Josey is content to work the land and stay away from the Civil War that is ravaging the country. Raided by renegade Union soldiers, Josey's wife and son are butchered while he is left for dead. Enraged and seeking revenge, Josey joins the Confederate army, but eventually he escapes with his life when their leader betrays them. Josey heads into Indian country hoping to escape the eyes of Terrill (Bill McKinney), the man responsible for the killing of his family. While there he encounters Lone Wolf (Chief Dan George), an old Cherokee who also has been victimized by many hardships in his life. Taking a liking to the old man, Josey invites him to come along with him to Mexico, and while on the road they allow a young Indian woman portrayed by Catherine Keams to come with them, somehow forging a surrogate family. Once they arrive in Texas, Josey decides that he is tired of running from Terrill, and they settle on a farm, hoping for a better life. Terrill, however, will not leave them alone and arrives to kill them, but in turn is slaughtered by Josey, who finds some element of peace in his revenge that had long since escaped him since the death of his family.

Eastwood gave one of his most effective performances as Josey, and surrounded himself with a series of strong supporting performances to enhance the story and complement his screen presence. Best among them was the wily old Native Canadian Chief Dan George, who had earned an Academy Award nomination for his performance in *Little Big Man* (1970), Arthur Penn's sprawling story of Little Big Horn as an allegory for Vietnam. The old chief was 76 when he made the film with Eastwood, and the director was sensitive to the fact that a man of George's age was not likely to remember his lines as well as the seasoned pros on the film. Eastwood simply asked that the Chief act naturally, and that was precisely what happened, allowing George to give an excellent performance. The old actor brings dignity and a gentle wise humor to the role, which is very similar to what he brought to the part of Old Lodgeskins in *Little Big Man*.

Bill McKinney and John Vernon were superb as the villains in the film, but this is Eastwood's film. He gives a towering performance as a man who has everything he holds dear ripped from him, but then slowly exacts a terrible revenge. Many critics and audience members felt that Eastwood's performance was not great because he portrayed a variation of the strong, silent character he had portrayed on a number of occasions before. Yet look closer, study the slow building rage and the obsessive need for revenge that overtakes not only his life but also his very being. In many ways the performance is like that of John Wayne in *The Searchers* (1956), a man motivated by revenge and obsessed with setting right the score as he sees it in his mind. When Wayne's seething performance was first seen by audiences, no one quite knew what to make of it because suddenly John Wayne was so unlike the characters he had portrayed before. The same applies to Eastwood in *Josey Wales*. Suddenly he was portraying a different kind of character very well. Although dismissed at the time as just another Eastwood film by the majority of critics, those sharp-eyed film reviewers saw the merit in the film and celebrated what Eastwood had accomplished, pushing the envelope of his own gifts as both actor and director. Like *The Searchers*, it would be several years before *The Outlaw Josey Wales* was fully appreciated for the revisionist Western that it was, though ironically Orson Welles, himself once a great director, made it clear he believed the picture to be a wonderful film, and spoke highly of Eastwood as a director on the Merv Griffin Show.

Writing in the *Los Angeles Times*, Kevin Thomas called the film "imaginatively and eloquently devised," adding, "a timeless parable on human nature."

Hailed as one of the year's 10 best by *Time* magazine, *The Outlaw Josey Wales* was not without its admirers. Roger Ebert liked the film very much, saying, "Clint Eastwood's *The Outlaw Josey Wales* is a strange and daring Western that brings together two of the genre's usually incompatible story lines. On one hand it's about a loner, a man of action and few words, who turns his back on civilization and lights out for the Indian nations. On the other hand it's about a group of people heading West who meet along the trail and cast their destinies together."

"Eastwood is such a taciturn and action-oriented performer that it's easy to overlook the fact he directs many of his movies—and many of the best, most intelligent ones," finished Ebert in high praise of Eastwood's film.

Nominated for an Academy Award for best score, it represented the first film Eastwood had directed that had drawn the attention of the Oscars, though it would by no means be the last.

6

The Gauntlet (1977)

A gauntlet is defined in the dictionary as to defy or to take up a challenge, or as an assault from both sides, all of which I suppose define and explain the basic premise of Eastwood's film *The Gauntlet* (1977), one of the worst films of his career, both as an actor and a director. Released in December as Warner Brothers' major Christmas blockbuster, the film died a quick death at the box office as better work, such as Steven Spielberg's *Close Encounters of the Third Kind* (1977), *The Goodbye Girl* (1977), and *Julia* (1977), drew moviegoers with their excellence. It is rather shocking that in the year after *The Outlaw Josey Wales* (1976), which made clear Eastwood's obvious talents as a director, he would make such a huge mistake with this picture. What is more disturbing is that at one point Eastwood actually believed the film was on the level of such classics as *The African Queen* (1951).

It originally came to him as a vehicle for himself and Barbra Streisand, whom he had dated for a short time. Streisand had been cast opposite Steve McQueen in *The Gauntlet,* but fighting between the two forced the actor, who was known to be surly, to quit the film, causing it to be shut down. The writers, Michael Butler and Dennis Shryack, with Streisand still attached, sought out Eastwood, believing he might want to do a film with Streisand. She had exploded into American film with an Oscar-winning performance as the legendary Fanny Brice in *Funny Girl* (1968) and then starred with Robert Redford in *The Way We Were* (1973), one of the seventies' most popular, iconic love stories, for which she was nominated for another Academy Award. However, her star was tainted somewhat by her behavior and controlling ways on the set of *A Star is Born* (1976), a remake of the 1954 classic transplanted to the world of rock and roll, with Kris Kristofferson as her alcoholic rock star husband. As producer of the film, along with her ex-hairdresser boyfriend Jon Peters, Streisand frequently was accused of bullying the film's director, Frank Pierson, which did not endear her to anyone in the business. When the film was released, the reviews were merciless in attacking her, but the film made a fortune, and Kristofferson won a Golden Globe for his moving performance. Streisand won another Oscar, for the song *Evergreen* she wrote for the film, which also became a gold record and Grammy Award winner.

When she hesitated about being the costar in a major Clint Eastwood vehicle, knowing she would be very much the second banana, Eastwood became impatient and forged ahead, casting to no one's surprise Sondra Locke. Eastwood saw the film as a comedic romance rather than an action adventure as it read, comparing the film to *It Happened One Night* (1934) and believing that Locke would have the acting skills to pull off the demanding role. One can only think he was blinded by his infatuation for the actress, who proved through the years to be most limited.

Working with the highest budget of his career, 5 million dollars, he agreed with Warner Brothers to act and direct the film, with Warner Brothers fully expecting a film that would make them a great deal of money.

"What attracted me to the story was that it was a good relationship story," Eastwood explained to *Film Comment* in 1977. "It's an action picture with a ton of action, but at the same time, great relationships. The girl's part is a terrific role, not just token window dressing like in so many action films. Her part is equal to the male part, if not even more so. It's in *The African Queen* tradition: a love-hate thing that turns out to be a love story. It's a bawdy adventure, too."

In comparing the character he would play in *The Gauntlet*, Ben Shockley, with Harry Callahan, Eastwood stated, "Ben Shockley in *The Gauntlet* is a guy who's never had the big cases Callahan's had. The big case is happening to him right during the movie: that's where they're different characters. Shockley fumbles through a few new situations that Callahan would have handled much slicker."

"There are little moments, gestures between them as they grow together, that become symbols—but they're not overt gestures. He never goes to bed with her even though she's a hooker and that would have been the obvious thing to do," explained Eastwood about the connection between the characters. "It's a relationship built on another plane. A cop who's had a lot of disappointments, never had a personal life that reached any great heights—it becomes a very pure love affair, with great friendship, great regard for one another."

His character in the film, Ben Shockley, was light-years away from Harry Callahan, as Eastwood decided this time to portray a dumb cop who drinks far too much. His character is even chosen for this glorified babysitting mission because he is expected to fail, being a lousy cop. Surprisingly, Eastwood's performance earned him some of the best reviews of his career, as critics saw in the actor a willingness to stretch himself beyond what the expectations of the audience might have been. For perhaps the first time in his career Eastwood was willing to make a fool of himself on screen, which translated into the audience believing him to be spoofing his own screen persona.

Gus (Sondra Locke) is a hooker who has witnessed a killing that the government considers high-profile enough that someone is now trying to kill her to prevent her from testifying at the trial. The moment she is in Shockley's custody, she warns him that her evidence is going to incriminate many police officials and that, by protecting her, he is putting his life in danger. Of course, Shockley does not believe her. When one attempt after another is made on their lives, Shockley becomes convinced that Gus is telling the truth, and knows now that his boss, Blakelock, is behind the attempted murders. Vowing revenge and livid with the betrayal of a fellow police officer, Shockley concocts a wild escape plan that involves a hijacked bus. Riding the bus into the gauntlet of gunfire set up by Blakelock, the bus is riddled with bullets, its metal torn to shreds, but Shockley manages to deliver the destroyed vehicle into the building that houses Blakelock's office. As they emerge from the bus, no one, including Blakelock, can quite believe they have somehow survived yet another massive attack. Wildly hysterical and out of control, Blakelock orders the men to shoot, but they refuse, seeing their commanding officer slipping over the edge into utter madness. Enraged, Blakelock shoots Shockley, wounding him, before Gus gets her hands on a weapon and fires at Blakelock, killing him. Having survived betrayal from within the ranks of those they should have been able to trust, Gus and Ben are free to find a new life together.

Watching *The Gauntlet* when it was first released, one was aware immediately that it was a very poor film, the worst Eastwood had directed up to that time. Why he thought there was any connection between this picture and the classic *The African Queen*, I do not know, but the comparison stops at the characters finding love together in harsh surroundings. Eastwood and Locke have very little chemistry between them, which is of course what every good love story is made upon: if we do not feel the heat they have for one another, there is no love story. Furthermore, Locke was not believable as a tough hooker because she appears too gentle and fragile. She is game, and gives it everything she has, but there is not a single frame of film in which her performance seems the least bit natural. Her portrayal looking forced, she commits the worst crime an actor can commit: "acting" and being caught doing so.

It must be stated here that Locke is an actress of limited talent and owes her meager film career to Eastwood, who repeatedly cast her through the late seventies and early eighties, despite some dreadful reviews of her work. Obviously, a fierce loyalty clouded his judgment concerning Locke, as there were certainly stronger actresses capable of bringing greater depth to the parts Locke portrayed.

Now it is also unfair to lay the failure of this film entirely on Locke's shoulders, as one has to wonder how Eastwood saw this film as a screwball comedy in the vein of Howard Hawks's best works, such as *Bringing Up Baby* (1940). Wisely, he gave the film a comic book feel, starting with the poster, which features an over-muscled Eastwood brandishing a massive weapon, looking nothing like he did in the picture. Further, the ridiculous amount of violence in the film became cartoonlike over the course of the narrative. It is impossible to believe that trained sharpshooters would not have the common sense to aim for the wheels of the bus and shoot them out, or that with thousands of bullets being fired, no one would be hit with even a ricochet. Imagine that! Tens of thousands of rounds of ammunition rain down on the bus carrying Eastwood and Locke, but not a single cop is hit or injured.

Directors are permitted weak films, and the studios rarely mind so long as the film makes money. What was shocking about *The Gauntlet* was that Eastwood had begun a promising directing career, impressing audiences and critics alike with *The Outlaw Josey Wales*, only to take a huge step backward by making the weakest and most unnecessary film of his career. Granted, he must have seen something in the screenplay, but after more than 30 years I am still baffled as to what.

When the work of Eastwood is discussed or debated, as it will be more and more in the years to come, *The Gauntlet* will be a curious smudge on that filmography. No doubt time will be even less kind to the film than the critics of 1977 were, and it will be described as two hours of nothing, which in itself is being generous.

The National Lampoon declared the film the worst of the year, as did the *Toronto Star* and several other publications, and even those who found something to admire admitted it was a struggle to do so.

THE EIGHTIES

7

Bronco Billy (1980)

The genre of comedy has many subgenres, among them the screwball comedy, which was one of the more popular subgenres during the thirties and forties. The main characteristics of screwball comedy are class issues, in which the upper class tends to be shown as pampered and spoiled, struggling to get around in any world but their own, whereas the lower class is able to appear as upper class with relative ease. Screwball comedy often uses a combination of fast-paced dialogue, slapstick humor, mistaken identity, and wildly over-the-top characters that are impossible to believe as real. Film scholar Andrew Sarris has been quoted as calling the screwball comedy "a sex comedy without the sex."

The genre reached its zenith in the mid-thirties, perhaps beginning with *It Happened One Night* (1934) and hitting its peak with *Bringing Up Baby* (1940). In the years after 1940, the genre became increasingly rare because modern directors were almost fearful of the genre's demands. This led to only a very few being released in recent years, among them *What's Up Doc?* (1972), *A Fish Called Wanda* (1987), and *Intolerable Cruelty* (2003).

Of the many genres Eastwood would explore through his directing career, none seemed as odd or as uncharacteristic as the screwball comedy; yet it would lead to one of his sunniest, most gentle films, and a film that he believes to be one of his finest, *Bronco Billy* (1980).

The screenplay came to Eastwood through a young woman who worked for one of the writers. Spotting Eastwood having dinner, she wandered over and asked if he would be interested in reading the work. Thinking it might be about silent screen star Bronco Billy Anderson, Eastwood was immediately interested. The screenplay was dropped off the next day, and Eastwood glanced through the work but found he could not put it down. Once he finished reading the story, he knew at once this would be the next picture he would direct.

Like reviewers, Eastwood recognized in the film the qualities of early Frank Capra films, in which the underlying message was "love thy neighbor" or "basic human decency." There was a soft quality to it that his other films had never shown, and a chance for him to stretch as both actor and director. Although Eastwood had scored at the box office with the goofy comedy *Every Which Way but Loose* (1978), in which his costar was an ape, this offered him the chance to work in a genre he had never been subject to before. Although he was very eager to make the film, because he knew that it would strengthen his art as a director, he was initially hesitant, because it was indeed so far from anything he had previously made. Urged on by Sondra Locke, who adored the work, he decided to make it. Of the many films Eastwood has directed over the years, none has the sunny disposition or utter charm of *Bronco Billy*, which clearly is a film that might have been directed by Frank Capra or Preston Sturges had the property been there in the thirties and forties.

The story is, like many Eastwood films, deceptively simplistic. Bronco Billy (Eastwood) was once a shoe salesman in New Jersey who, after training himself to shoot, immerses himself in the world of the Wild West (in modern-day America). One day he packs up and hits the road, creating his own version of Buffalo Bill's Wild West show. The group of misfits he surrounds himself with are an odd group to say the least: Chief Big Eagle (Dan Vadis), who handles nonpoisonous rattlesnakes (unbeknownst to the audience); his wife, Running Water (Sierra Pecheur); the wily old ringmaster Doc (Scatman Crothers); draft dodger Lasso Leonard James (Sam Bottoms); and Lefty Lebow (Bill McKinney). Each offers some sort of unique skill to the show, and together they make up a most dysfunctional family with one common trait: they believe in and love Billy to the point of working when they have not been paid for months.

There is one other character in the show, though the person in this role is constantly changing—the woman tied to the spinning wheel while Billy throws knives at her. Though Billy is very good, incredibly good considering his background, there are times when he misses, which causes him to lose girls, who leave the show terrified about what has happened and happy to be alive.

Into their lives walks Antoinette Lily (Sondra Locke), an heiress on the run. We have learned that she must marry to claim her inheritance and she foolishly chooses the nasty schemer John Arlington (Geoffrey Lewis), who sees money, money, money. When it becomes clear to him that the woman he married is a walking nightmare and impossible to deal with, he leaves her in the middle of nowhere without a penny to her name.

Billy and Lily first meet one another at a gas station miles away from civilization and instantly take a disliking to each other. Needing a girl for the show, Billy offers her the job; and needing a ride back to somewhere other than where she is, Lily takes the job and immediately causes havoc among the others in the show. She refuses to do anything Billy's way; her selfishness and self-centered attitude always blind her to what he truly believes in. She then learns that her husband has declared her dead and is trying to get his hands on her money, which eventually leads her to leave the show.

However, while she is still with them she comes to understand what makes Billy tick. There are certain things Billy lives by with an almost religious fervor: a devotion to children, a firm belief that one must take care of his friends, and a deep, almost ferocious love for America. He treats everyone he meets with great respect, is almost gravely well mannered when around women, and only raises his voice when something threatens to shut down his beloved Wild West Show. Many of the shows they do are for free, because Billy will not turn away a chance to see a child smile at their antics in the ring. Although initially Lily cannot believe that Billy is the real thing, she learns that he is precisely that and falls in love with him.

When he speaks to little children, he does so with the knowledge of what they see when they look at him, perhaps fueled by what he saw when he looked at a cowboy as a child. He teaches them right from wrong, calling them "little partners," and offers such homespun advice as "I don't take kindly to kids playing hooky from school" or "I want you to finish your oatmeal at breakfast and do as your ma and pa tell you because they know best." He understands what he is to them, which is a hero, and as the camera pans the faces of the adoring children, we understand just how well Billy knows both his audience and his impact on them. There is goodness about Billy, an innocence, but also sometimes a naïve sense of what the world is—or perhaps an absolute awareness of what it is with a decision to look the other way and find some goodness.

What is suggested by Billy's adoration for children is the fact that he obviously adored cowboys and heroes when he was a boy, and knows what he represents to these little ones. He believes he can make a difference in their lives, and does his best to bring to them honesty and integrity, which of course are the rules he lives by as best he can.

Many critics complimented Eastwood on his performance, which was by far the finest of his career up to this time, surpassing his superb work for Don Siegel in *Escape from Alcatraz* (1979) the previous year, and certainly moving in a different direction from anything he had previously done. Many spoke of the scene in which the bullying sheriff humiliates Billy, who does not fight back or exact any sort of revenge later in the film. He does what he has to do to keep the show rolling, which in this case means being harassed by a bully.

What meant more to Eastwood was the fact that critics were continuing to notice his skill as a director, recognizing that the artistic growth between *The Outlaw Josey Wales* (1976) and this new film had been substantial.

Writing in the *New York Times*, Janet Maslin raved, "Mr. Eastwood turns Billy . . . into one of the warmest and most memorable characters. . . . Mr. Eastwood, who can be as formidable behind the camera as he is in front of it, is an entertainer too."

Maslin cited the film as being "the best and funniest Clint Eastwood movie in quite a while," and was struck by both Eastwood's boyish performance and the Capra-esque Americana within the film.

"His achievement in *Bronco Billy*, as star and director is to chisel some emotion and innocence and a passel of likability into those features. It is as if one of the faces on Mount Rushmore suddenly cracked a crooked smile. Watching *Bronco Billy*, millions of moviegoers are likely to smile back," wrote Richard Corliss in *Time Magazine*.

If the film had a major weakness, it was the shrill and often wildly erratic performance of Sondra Locke as Lily, who was doing the sort of character made famous by the thirties comedian Carole Lombard. Lombard played these comedic characters with a devilish glint in her eye to let us know she was in on the joke. Locke is no Carole Lombard. In fact, her skill as an actress is suspect, and is growing more so with every passing film, leaving critics to ponder why Eastwood cast her in film after film when he could have had his pick of actresses in Hollywood. This is the sort of role that an actress like Diane Keaton would have turned into an Oscar-nominated performance. Oddly enough, despite the lack of praise for her performance, no one doubted the love the two had for each other on screen, which of course was also happening off screen.

The film caught critics off guard with its charm, and specifically the manner in which Eastwood deftly dealt with the genre, which is without question screwball comedy. Known for its use of improbable characters, this genre is among the most popular of the forties' films. But Eastwood? Doing screwball comedy? That he even had the sheer audacity to direct such a film seemed to both anger and stun critics, but the fact that he pulled it off and made an excellent film was even more stunning. The only thing left to say was the obvious fact that Eastwood was quietly becoming one of the finest directors in cinema. It was the great Orson Welles who noticed what Eastwood was accomplishing and stated on television, "I suppose Clint Eastwood is just about the most underappreciated director working in movies today." Welles was referring to Eastwood's directing in *Bronco Billy* and the soon-to-be released *Honky Tonk Man* (1982), in which Eastwood did things that Welles had done so well in the forties—taking risks.

8

Firefox (1982)

All great artists have that one project where their involvement is unexplainable, and that stands out like a sore thumb when compared to the rest of their work. For the great John Huston, it was *The Bible . . . In the Beginning* (1966), and for Francis Ford Coppola it was the quagmire that was *One from the Heart* (1982) and again years later the wretched *Jack* (1996). Even the seemingly untouchable Steven Spielberg failed miserably with *1941* (1979), his out-of-control comedy that was not very funny. In many cases it is simply that artists wish to stretch their artistic muscles and see if they can pull off something radically different from what they are used to creating, but stepping outside of that box can be very difficult. Martin Scorsese found that out with *New York, New York* (1977), his ill-fated and misunderstood musical that merged classical musical format with stylized seventies expressionism.

For Eastwood, a director becoming known for his lean storytelling and focus on people, that project was *Firefox* (1982), a misguided science fiction thriller made at the height of the science fiction/visual effects explosion that came at the end of the seventies and beginning of the eighties. Fueled by *Star Wars* (1977), *Close Encounters of the Third Kind* (1977), *Superman* (1978), *Star Trek: The Movie* (1979), and *The Empire Strikes Back* (1980), business was booming for these types of films, which featured excitement throughout by virtue of nonstop action, reasonably strong stories, and most of all, stunning visual effects. Not since Charlton Heston as Moses parting the Red Sea in *The Ten Commandments* (1956) had there been so much excitement over special effects, with that leap to light speed in *Star Wars* (1977), one of the singular great visual effects ever put on film, defining a generation. Audiences were willing to go cinematically to places they had never gone before, therefore they were more accepting of a story happening "a long time ago in a galaxy far, far away . . ."

In a year bloated with films driven by high-tech special effects, Eastwood's *Firefox*, based on the novel by Craig Thomas, was something of a lame duck from the moment it was released. The film could not compete against obvious audience favorites, such as *E.T.: The Extraterrestrial* (1982), *Star Trek II: The Wrath of Khan* (1982), *Poltergeist* (1982), *Tron* (1982), and Ridley Scott's masterpiece *Blade Runner* (1982), which at the time was a box office dud that would be rediscovered on home video years later. Spielberg's *E.T.: The Extraterrestrial* (1982) was driven by visual effects to the extent that the leading character *was* a visual effect. The tiny alien, who is stranded here on earth and befriended by a little boy who helps summon his own kind to come back for his friend, was a large chunk of carved latex with soulful eyes modeled on those of Albert Einstein and was operated by a dozen technicians. Audiences fell in love with the amazingly lifelike E.T. and made the film the highest moneymaker of all time within months of its release. The effects in this film were astounding because they were very realistic, as this alien seemed to be as real as the actors on the screen.

Did Eastwood have his eye on the box office and, knowing that science fiction was hitting with audiences, intentionally set out to make such a film? Or was he simply responding to what he always did, his instincts as a director seeking a strong story? The story had come recommended to him by a helicopter pilot he used for the aerial sequences in *The Eiger Sanction* (1975).

"I liked the story and the script," Eastwood would tell Michael Henry in 1984. "It started out a classic spy film, but then there were pertinent reflections on the arms race and the imbalance of strengths caused by a new technological advance. What worried me a little was the special effects. Luckily they only came at the last part of the film. The problem in particular was that these special effects played out against a background of the atmosphere of our planet and not some far away galaxy off in the future somewhere. I must confess, I'm not crazy about special effects. I'd prefer a thousand times over to have to deal with human beings and their problems."

In response to Eastwood's concerns about the film's visual effects, the studio hired for him John Dykstra, the Academy Award–winning special effects artist who brought those far away galaxies to life in *Star Wars* (1977). Although Eastwood was worried about the special effects, he was also profoundly attracted to the leading character in the film, which was again a damaged man with a haunted past, something he was beginning to specialize in portraying.

Mitchell Gant, the main character in the film, was an American hero emotionally scarred by his time in Vietnam, where he was a POW and responsible for the deaths of innocents. Gant was prone to freezing up at key moments while in the line of duty, which led him to retirement. Those flaws, of course, were the very qualities that attracted Eastwood to the role.

"He's a professional, and he doesn't have any idea before he goes over there of what his mission implies for the dissidents. He doesn't know anything about the behind-the-scenes political machinations and over there, he doesn't have a single moment when he's at ease. Except when he takes command of the prototype, because there at last, he's in his element," Eastwood continued.

A retired pilot, Gant is recruited back into duty by the government to go to Russia (he convieniently speaks the language) to steal a new weapon they have developed, code-named Firefox, and return it to the United States. Firefox is a unique plane that is controlled by telepathy and can reach extraordinary speeds in the sky. To the United States, it represents a most formidable foe.

Once in the Soviet Union, Gant begins the complicated task of stealing the plane, which is fiercely protected by the Russians. In addition to overcoming the tight security of the KGB and Russian army, Gant is forced to overcome his old psychological demons to keep control of his mind. Once the plane is in his possession, he is pursued by another Firefox jet piloted by a Russian who understands exactly how to control the plane, which forces Gant to call upon his wealth of knowledge from past dogfights and shoot the Russian out of the sky. Narrowly escaping death, Gant returns the plane to the United States and NATO, receiving a hero's welcome for his efforts.

If the picture has a primary weakness, it begins with a screenplay that is overly technical in its discussion of the plane's mechanics. Over and over we hear advanced technical jargon about the plane and the mechanics of it, which is far too much for the average audience to grasp. There is no sense of action, pacing, or swiftness to the plot, which is instead bogged down by entirely unnecessary narrative.

Working for the first time with a large budget, 20 million dollars, Eastwood was nonetheless just as careful as he always had been throughout his career with someone else's money. He brought to the production a profound sense of responsibility, again working quickly with the actors, and only slowing with the complicated visual effects. He was right in that the effects needed to look realistic, as the film was not quite fantasy in the vein of *Star Wars* (1977) or other such films. His patience was tried time and time again with the seemingly endless waits for the effects to pan out.

Upon release of the film, critics were quick to point out the film's weaknesses, realizing at once that this film was so out of the realm of Eastwood's filmography and leaving many wondering why he made the picture in the first place. Obviously Warner Brothers was hoping for a massive science fiction hit as the other studios had experienced with their films, but it was not to be. Audiences stayed away from the film, and the critics pounced on it.

Vincent Canby, writing in the *New York Times,* thought the film to be "a James Bond without the girls, a Superman movie without the sense of humor."

"A sagging, overlong disappointment, talky and slow to ignite," wrote Sheila Benson in the *Los Angeles Times.* "It is the first time that Eastwood the director has served Eastwood the actor-icon so badly, and it is unnerving."

"It's a good thing for the West that Clint Eastwood is available for the job. There's a bit of suspense as he slips past the entire Soviet security system, and a bit more when he skedaddles with the coveted craft. But most of the way, this is a very talky film, stretching a slim plot into more than two hours of familiar Hollywood maneuvers," complained David Sterrit of the *Christian Science Monitor*.

Yet out of this mess came one of the first real indications that Eastwood was rising in appreciation as a director. Appearing on the *Merv Griffin Show*, iconic director Orson Welles made some disparaging remarks about *Firefox*, but quickly made clear his admiration for Eastwood's other work. He admitted to admiring *The Outlaw Josey Wales* and *Bronco Billy*.

"They [audiences, critics, Hollywood] don't take him seriously," spoke Welles. "They can't believe they can act if they are beautiful—they must be a little ugly to be taken seriously by men. And an actor like Eastwood is such a pure type of mythic hero-star in the Wayne tradition that no one is going to take him seriously as a director. But someone ought to say it. And when I saw that picture for the fourth time, I realized it belongs with the great Westerns. You know the great Westerns of Ford and Hawks and people like that. And I take my hat off to him. I'm glad to have a chance to say that," finished the one-time Hollywood wunderkind.

Thus, although *Firefox* was not well received by the critics, it might have been the beginning of some recognition for Eastwood in the business. Welles's words carried weight, and almost immediately there was a new appreciation for Eastwood the director that had not been there previously. In the end *Firefox* was reasonably profitable but certainly not the blockbuster Warner Brothers hoped for.

9

Honky Tonk Man (1982)

The critical success of *The Outlaw Josey Wales* (1976) had given Eastwood the confidence to make *Bronco Billy* (1980), still his sunniest and most optimistic film, and though audiences did not flock to see the picture, it did respectable business and earned some solid reviews. Buoyed by that success, and perhaps the recognition from critics that he was growing as a director, Eastwood next tackled his most intimate and personal character study yet, *Honky Tonk Man* (1982).

Based on the book by Clancy Carlile, which had been given to Eastwood by his agent, Lenny Hirshan, the film provided him with his greatest challenge as an actor—portraying a dying country and western singer on his way to an audition at the Grand Old Opry. The role required him to sing on screen—something he had not done since *Paint Your Wagon* (1969)—and though music was a huge part of his life, there was definitely some fear in that prospect.

In addition to the challenge as an actor, the work behind the camera would tax Eastwood as never before; his performance was the anchor for the film, and though that was not necessarily new to him, he was acutely aware of just how strong a performance he needed to give to make the film work. There was no doubt of his growth as a director or of his strong confidence as a filmmaker, but *Honky Tonk Man* was light-years away from what he was used to making and certainly from what audiences were used to seeing.

What audiences and fans of Eastwood tend to forget is that he was an actor first, and actors thrive on challenge. Even John Wayne, to his fans forever a Western character, wanted change and challenge, agreeing to portray Genghis Khan in *The Conqueror* (1955), one of the most woeful films ever made. Wayne, like Eastwood, had no intention of failing; he just desperately wanted to be challenged as an actor. And Eastwood saw in *Honky Tonk Man's* character Red Stovall the chance for this.

Red is accompanied to his Nashville audition by his 14-year-old nephew, who also will do much of the driving, given Red's poor driving skills and tendency to drink on the road. Eastwood, who believed his son Kyle would do a fine job in the role of the nephew, had reached a certain standing in the industry where his casting choices were not questioned. If he wanted his son, he got his son. Certainly excited about the prospect of directing his boy, Eastwood went to work on preproduction, scouting locations in and around the back roads of Sacramento, which would stand in for Oklahoma in the film.

The five-week shoot, like all Eastwood shoots, was uneventful, and the film was released in the summer of 1982. The gentle story seemed a natural for audiences, offering them a different look at Eastwood.

Red Stovall returns to his sister's farm in Oklahoma during the Depression as a dust storm wipes out the property, leaving her penniless and facing the prospect of heading to California with the thousands of "Okies" who have already left. Having spent a lifetime working in whorehouses and bad bars passing the hat for change, Red has become a heavy drinker and developed tuberculosis, which is ravaging his body. The one thing not dimmed is his hope for some sort of singing career. When the Grand Old Opry in Nashville offers him an audition, his greatest obstacle is getting there. Even though he has a car, he lacks the skill to drive it, and driving drunk will get him killed. His sister convinces her son, 14-year-old Whit (Kyle Eastwood), to go on the journey with her brother and take care of him.

During the long trip the two males bond, forging a friendship that will stay with the boy long after the trip and certainly after the death of Red. Upon arriving in Nashville, Red attends a recording session, but the coughing (a symptom of tuberculosis) has gotten worse to the point where he can no longer finish a song. Against the advice of his doctors who fear for his life, he goes ahead and records the songs, though the pain is excruciating to him, before succumbing to the disease. As Whit prepares to move his family to California, Red's song starts playing on the radio with the announcement that the song comes from a true Honky Tonk Man. In death Red has become what he always believed he was.

Eastwood's performance surprised the critics because he dug deep and inhabited the character beautifully, leaving us little or no trace of Eastwood the movie star, something of a major challenge for him as he was such a visible star. Being considered a star as opposed to an actor may have made it a greater challenge for Eastwood to be accepted by audiences in this sort of role, but he quietly slipped into character and became Red. Through the course of the film Red evolves and seems to physically deteriorate before our eyes. Although we understand the hard drinking, which is the result of broken dreams, it takes some time for us to comprehend his obsession with music. Only when he is broken, racked with pain and coughing blood, yet insisting on carrying on, do we understand why he is indeed, first and foremost, before even being a human being, a honky tonk man. The difficulty in seeing a movie star give such a performance is the fact that the audience can never quite let go of the movie star persona. Many viewers could not let go of the fact that the man on the screen was Dirty Harry to them—a macho tough guy more likely to blow someone away than pull out a guitar and sing a song.

Somewhat ironically, one year after this film was released, actor Robert Duvall played a similar character in *Tender Mercies* (1983). He portrayed a washed-up country and western star who finds happiness with a pretty widow. This film earned him rave reviews, and he won not only the Academy Award for best actor but also awards from the Los Angeles and New York Film Critics Associations. The major difference between these two actors is that Duvall is an actor through and through, and Eastwood will always have the stigma of movie star attached to him. There is something rather dubious in critical circles when someone is the top box office draw, the thinking being that if they make money, they cannot be making money in good films. Steven Spielberg represents an example of this. For so long it was thought that if his films were moneymakers, how could they possibly be considered art? Yet *Jaws* (1975) is a brilliantly artistic piece of filmmaking that deserves to be recognized as such. There are times when critical snobbery (and there is no other word for it) can truly hurt a film's chances of success. This was certainly true with *Honky Tonk Man,* for what the critics missed in their focus on Eastwood the celebrity was a sensitive and strong performance from a movie star growing into an actor before their eyes—and in a self-directed performance, which often is even more difficult. In hindsight, the performances, both very good, are not so very different.

"This is a sweet, whimsical low key movie; a movie that makes you feel good without pressing you too hard. It provides Eastwood with a screen character who is the complete opposite of the patented Eastwood tough guys, and provides a role of nearly equal importance for his son Kyle as a serious independent and utterly engaging young nephew named Whit," wrote Roger Ebert for the *Chicago Sun-Times,* continuing, "This is a special movie. In making it Eastwood was obviously moving away from his Dirty Harry image, but that's nothing new; his spectacular success in violent movies tends to distract us from his intriguing and challenging career as a director and/or star of such offbeat projects as *Bronco Billy* (1980) and *Play Misty for Me* (1971)."

Long a supporter of Eastwood's evolution as actor and director, Roger Ebert might have been the single American film critic who understood where Eastwood was going with *Honky Tonk Man*. He saw the stretch, the growth, and eventually the budding of a new and very fine American director.

Later his biographer, *Time* magazine critic Richard Schickel, would write of *Honky Tonk Man,* "Eastwood has fashioned a marvelously unfashionable movie as quietly insinuating as one of Red's honky tonk melodies. As both actor and director, Eastwood has never been more laconic than he is in this film. It reminds one . . . of *Bronco Billy*, although it disdains the farce and romance of that underappreciated movie.

"If there are any people left who doubt Eastwood's accomplishment as a screen actor, they had better come around for this lesson in underplaying a long, strong scene," Schickel finished.

Writing for the *New York Post*, critic Archer Winstein struggled with the film, finding both strengths and weaknesses: "The pace is slow, very country, but it rises to touching moments. Eastwood never outdoes his acting—maybe he can't—always playing it very close to the vest. It works for the larger portion of the picture, falling somewhere between the Eastwood sincerity and changes of mood that put the picture in a special class—not at all perfect by any means, but ultimately a story of occasional awkward truths."

"*Honky Tonk Man* is one of those well-intentioned efforts that doesn't quite work. It seems that Clint Eastwood took great pains in telling his story of an aging, struggling country and western singer but he is done in by the predictability of the script and his own limitations as a warbler," carped *Variety*.

Sadly, most of the reviews echoed what Joseph Glemis would write in *Newsday*: "Clint looks the classic country western singer in dark suit, string tie, boots, and ten gallon hat. It would be a great pleasure to report that his courage pays off. But the scenario's ultimate ambition is kitschy bathos, to make you weep in your popcorn . . . the mild humor of *Honky Tonk Man* devolves into the gross sentimentality of a Clint Eastwood *Camille*," stated Glemis with caustic charm.

The film admittedly was a tough sell, and whether it was because audiences would not accept Eastwood in the role of a dying country and western singer has become moot. His skills as an actor through the nineties and beyond display an actor willing to challenge himself, growing as an artist and making a very personal work that mattered to him. Most directors are celebrated for that sort of courage. Eastwood had not yet reached that plateau in his career.

If Eastwood was the least bit stung by the critical attacks on his attempt to grow as an artist, the fact that critics in France compared the film to *The Grapes of Wrath* (1940) must have eased that sting.

The words of the great Norman Mailer would have eased Eastwood's pain: "The steely compassion that is back of all the best country singing . . . and the harsh, yearning underbelly of America . . . making out with next to nothing but hard concerns and the spark of a dream that will never give up."

"A subtle man," Mailer wrote of Red Stovall, "brought to life with minimal strokes, a complex protagonist full of memories of old cunning deeds and weary sham. It was one of the saddest movies seen in a long time, yet on reflection, terrific. One felt a tenderness for America while looking at it."

Mailer, more than any film critic of the time, understood exactly what Eastwood was trying to do and say with *Honky Tonk Man*, something he celebrated in his own art form.

10

Sudden Impact (1983)

Ah . . . I know what you're thinking . . . did he fire six shots or five? . . . Well to tell you the truth in all this excitement I've kinda lost track myself. But being this is a .44 Magnum, the most powerful handgun in the world, and will blow your head clean off, you gotta ask yourself . . . Do I feel lucky? Well, do you . . . punk?
—Detective Harry Callahan (Eastwood) in *Dirty Harry*

Go ahead . . . make my day . . .
—Detective Harry Callahan (Eastwood) in *Sudden Impact*

With that first speech, as the cliché states, a star was born, who then became an icon. The second piece of dialogue became a part of pop culture and was repeated by President Ronald Reagan, though certainly not within the same context. Eastwood claims that the moment he read the line, he knew it would become synonymous with the film.

His first monologue is said over a man wounded in Harry's attempt to break up a bank robbery. Eastwood and the character he was portraying became an instant part of American pop culture; and the actor found a role that suited him as perfectly as a form-fitting shirt. Becoming one of the major stars working in Hollywood was a transforming moment for Eastwood. He gained more power than he ever thought imaginable, and he knew even then that he would use this power to further his career as a director.

As John Wayne *is* Ethan Edwards in *The Searchers* (1956), and Harrison Ford *is* Indiana Jones in *Raiders of the Lost Ark* (1981), Clint Eastwood *is* forever Dirty Harry Callahan.

The role of Harry Callahan—now identified with Eastwood and only Eastwood—was not initially even offered to him until Paul Newman turned the part down because of his political convictions. Stating that he had none, Eastwood read the script and saw immediately what Newman was concerned about, and he demanded rewrites of the work. The original screenplay seemed to challenge, if not take away, the constitutional rights of criminals, something Newman had found repulsive. Eastwood was not quite as appalled, and suggested with some effort they could flesh out a fine story within the work. However, movies being what they are—green lights being difficult to obtain, and projects coming and going—Eastwood became busy with other work, and the project fell away from him, eventually going to Frank Sinatra, who was formally signed as Harry. An injury prevented Sinatra from shooting the role, and Eastwood, now with a window of time, stepped in. The screenplay, having been finally overhauled, loosely based the killer, Scorpio, on the Zodiac killer, who had terrorized the San Francisco area since the late sixties.

The now famous story sees Harry on the hunt for a dangerous, psychotic killer who kills at will, demands money for him to stop killing, kidnaps a child, and admits sexually assaulting her. Scorpio (Andy Robinson) was the sort of Hollywood bad guy the audience wanted to see killed in the worst possible way. Yet the twist here was that the character was very smart and always seemed to be one step ahead of Eastwood's character. However, Harry finally catches him and kills him to the cheers of audience members, repeating the speech he had made over the bank robber at the beginning of the film, though this time with barely concealed rage.

At a time when the New American Cinema was emerging with profoundly strong works of art, such as *A Clockwork Orange* (1971), *The Last Picture Show* (1971), *Klute* (1971), *McCabe and Mrs. Miller* (1971), and the Academy Award–winning cop thriller *The French Connection* (1971), *Dirty Harry* (1971) seemed an odd choice as the year's top moneymaking film; yet it was just that. It struck a chord with audiences and brought them a character they felt an instant rapport with, someone they could identify with and someone who offered them a sense of justice as they sat there in the dark. Ironically, what *Dirty Harry* shared with *The French Connection* was the lead character being a rogue cop who played by his own rules, almost a vigilante in many ways, and who was consistently at odds with his supervisors but committed to upholding the law, even if it meant breaking the law. Made with an almost documentary-style realism, *The French Connection* was new cinema, something previously unseen in its honest and startlingly authentic portrayal of police work, namely narcotics investigation. Gene Hackman's gritty, Academy Award–winning performance as Popeye Doyle was light-years removed from Eastwood's Harry Callahan, yet oddly enough they shared the same code. *Dirty Harry* was not realism, and everyone involved with the film knew that; the film was first and foremost an entertainment piece. At the outset how could anyone have known what the impact of this tough character would be?

Eastwood became the most popular actor on the planet, surpassing John Wayne who was now in the twilight of his career as world-box-office king. This popularity led to some snipes from various critics, such as Pauline Kael, who had always held Eastwood's acting ability in contempt.

The box office success of *Dirty Harry* could not be denied, and in the seventies with box office success came the inevitable sequel. *Magnum Force*

(1974) was written by no less than future Oscar winner Michael Cimino, who would also direct Eastwood in *Thunderbolt and Lightfoot* (1974) before finding success with *The Deer Hunter* (1978) and before bankrupting United Artists with his blatant self-indulgence with *Heaven's Gate* (1980). Two years after *Magnum Force,* the second *Dirty Harry* sequel followed, *The Enforcer* (1976), which was met with tepid reviews but strong box office draw. Audiences loved this character despite the inferiority of the films, each progressively weaker than the one before it—with the exception of *Sudden Impact* (1983).

By 1983 Eastwood had grown substantially as a filmmaker, with *The Out-law Josey Wales* (1976), *Bronco Billy* (1980), and *Honky Tonk Man* (1982), establishing him as a director and actor willing to take risks. One wonders why he would decide to do another *Dirty Harry* film, other than the obvi-ous fact that he was given the opportunity to star as well as direct. Although Eastwood believed he had nothing more to say about Harry Callahan as an actor, he believed that if he directed the film, he might be able to bring a new spin to the character and to the story.

Upon reading the screenplay for *Sudden Impact* for the first time, he came across a line he knew at once would become the film's signature tag: "Go ahead . . . make my day," which Harry says to a criminal holding a terrified civilian hostage—the threat being of course that the moment the person is killed, Harry will fire and end the life of the criminal. One wonders if Eastwood had any idea how powerful that line would be not only on his own career but on North American pop culture.

Eastwood cast his current lady, Sondra Locke, in the crucial role of the young woman hell-bent on avenging herself and her sister, who had been brutally beaten, raped, and left for dead 10 years earlier by a gang of vicious cutthroats. Locke, a one-time Academy Award nominee, had struggled to find roles before meeting Eastwood. After meeting Eastwood her luck changed dramatically, and she was cast in many of his films, often not neces-sarily for the better. Eastwood cast Locke in the same manner that Woody Allen cast Mia Farrow in one film after another, and one wonders what Allen and Eastwood saw in the ladies they chose to lead their films.

There is a decided lack of mystery and tension in *Sudden Impact* because of the choice to show the audience who the killer is from the very begin-ning. Furthermore, this is, after all, a *Dirty Harry* film, and there is no doubt he is not going to die and is more than likely going to do some killing before the film is through. Jennifer (Sondra Locke) is a painter in the style of Edvard Munch (pain, rage) and was brutally beaten and raped 10 years earlier by a marauding gang of thugs, who also attacked her sister into a state of catatonia. After tracking down the men who did this to her, she sys-temically begins to exact her revenge on each one by firing a gunshot into his genitals, leaving him in excruciating pain for a few moments, and then into the head, giving him a quick and all too merciful death. Harry is assigned to the case and slowly figures out who the killer is, while falling in love with her at the same time. He allows her to finish the killings, and thereby (we assume) exorcise her demons. Around the same time this film was released, there was a deplorable film titled *I Spit on Your Grave* (1983), which became something of a cult classic, with its softcore porn images merged with a series of revenge killings. A young woman is repeatedly beaten and raped by a gang of rednecks only to come back and achieve her own brand of revenge that leaves them either dead or incomplete. The only major difference between the films is that Eastwood brought good taste to his project. Although Eastwood's film was at times violent and brutal, it was not as exploitive as this other work of trash. Eastwood deserved a great deal of credit for bringing the darkest of the *Dirty Harry* films to the screen and in the process challenging audiences to think about the true meaning of justice. We watch a woman who was brutalized—and whose sister was left in a catatonic state—exact her revenge on the monsters that raped her, and we are then asked, what is justice? That her rapists walk free, or that she get the chance to serve them her own brand of American justice? It was a daring film that at the time critics found more exploitive than anything else, which is rather unfortunate.

Much credit must be given to the writers and creators of the films for finding strong roles for women in the pictures—beginning with Tyne Daly as Harry's doomed partner in *The Enforcer* and ending with Locke as the avenging angel in this film. In most action films women are merely eye candy, but in the *Dirty Harry* series they are front and center with powerfully written roles.

"Directing the material himself, Clint Eastwood has attempted to retell the *Dirty Harry* myth in the style of a forties film noir. Much of *Sudden Impact*, including all the scenes of violence, was actually shot at night. In a stiff, sensational, pulp-filmmaking way, the mayhem is impressive: As the camera glides through the dark, sinister thugs emerge from the shadows, or Sondra Locke, blonde hair curtaining her face in the style of Veronica Lake, moves into the frame, and violence flashes out, lightning in the air," praised David Denby of *New York Magazine*.

Pauline Kael continued her merciless attacks on Eastwood that started when she first saw *Dirty Harry*. She seemed enraged that the actor would dare to step behind the camera. Kael, one of the foremost American critics, was a brilliant writer—her reviews actually superb essays on cinema—yet she was often sadly mistaken. Her negative reviews became personal assaults on individuals she deemed not suitable for the film industry. Eastwood was an easy target for her, as his acting skills in the sixties and seventies were limited or at least not apparent at that time. Kael, however, failed to notice him growing into a better actor with each film he did. By 1980 Eastwood was earning recognition from the industry as a first-rate director. She seemed offended that he would even think of directing a film when she had decided and written that he was nothing close to an artist. Her review of *Sudden Impact* was no surprise.

"*Sudden Impact* . . . might be mistaken for parody if the sledgehammer-slow pacing didn't tell you that the director (Eastwood) wasn't in on the joke. . . . America has gone to hell, Harry can't cross the street without interrupting some heinous crime," she ranted, continuing with an attack on Eastwood's acting ability: "What expressions would be appropriate to this movie? By out-deadpanning Clint Eastwood, she (Locke) comes across as the one and only right woman for him. . . . Eastwood's moviemaking might be euphemistically described as . . . basic."

Despite Kael's venomous review, the film was a major success at the box office, which is all Warner's was asking of Eastwood.

I began this chapter by stating that Eastwood was forever identified with the role of Harry Callahan and that often when we think of Eastwood it is with a .44 Magnum handgun at his side. As the years slipped by and he evolved into a first-rate director, the image of Eastwood in the iconic role of Harry faded from public view. And although Warner Brothers released a handsome *Dirty Harry Ultimate Collection* in June of 2008, it seems nothing now prevents audiences from thinking of Eastwood first and foremost as a filmmaker.

11

Pale Rider (1985)

Shane . . . come back . . .

—Joey Starrett in *Shane* (1953)

Michael Cimino was the toast of Hollywood with the release of his powerful film *The Deer Hunter* (1978), a searing study of the impact of the war in Vietnam on Americans and small-town America. Having worked with Eastwood before, directing him in *Thunderbolt and Lightfoot* (1974), Eastwood had been both a friend and mentor to the director. When Cimino signed with United Artists to direct his follow-up film to *The Deer Hunter*, the film had not yet won its five Academy Awards, including those for best film and director. Being newly crowned by Hollywood seemed to have had an effect on the hot director that fueled an already substantial ego, and the production of *Heaven's Gate* (1980) spiraled radically out of control. The shoot went much longer than anticipated, and the budget soared from $9 million to $44 million, both driven by Cimino's unreasonable self-indulgences. The four-hour film was pulled from release the day after its disastrous premieres in Los Angeles, New York, and Toronto. Cimino's blatant disrespect for his studio bosses, massive overages, and seemingly arrogant attitude were to blame for this disaster. The film bankrupted United Artists and, even worse, killed the American Western.

In hindsight, *Heaven's Gate* was nowhere near the dreadful film it was attacked for being back in the fall of 1980. On the contrary, though long and sometimes tedious, and without question self-indulgent, it was and is a visually stunning picture that captures the look and mood of the Old West and "the poetry of America." The roller skating sequence remains one of the most breathtaking scenes I have ever witnessed in an American film. Now 28 years later, the film is widely considered the greatest flop in movie history; but for those who actually have seen it, the experience was not at all terrible. In fact, though aspects of the film are rather boring, and there is a decided lack of action, there are moments when the film soars with utter brilliance, which was clearly unappreciated at the time of release of the film. The war between Cimino and United Artists was well documented in producer Steven Bach's seminal book *Final Cut*, perhaps the finest book made about the making of a major Hollywood film. While he details how the film went wildly out of control, how the studio went bankrupt, and how Cimino's career was ruined, what he failed to understand fully was that the American Western, once the most popular genre, making up one-fifth of all films released, was dead. The Western had become box office poison.

One of the earliest films in America was a Western—*The Great Train Robbery* (1902). "If you consider film as an art form as some people do, then the Western would be a truly American art form, as much as jazz," explained Eastwood when challenged as to why he would want to make a Western.

"In the sixties American Westerns were stale, probably because the great directors—Anthony Mann, Raoul Walsh, John Ford—were no longer working a lot. Then the Italian Westerns came along, and we did very well with those. They died of natural causes," explained the director.

"I don't know if the genre (Westerns) has really disappeared. There's a whole generation, the younger generation that only knows Westerns from seeing them on television. And I notice that audience ratings for *High Plains Drifter* and *The Outlaw Josey Wales* continue to be excellent. When someone asks me, 'Why a Western today?' I'm tempted to answer, why not? My last Western went over very well. It's not possible that *The Outlaw Josey Wales* could be the last Western to have been a commercial success. Anyway, aren't the *Star Wars* movies Westerns transposed into space?" smiled Eastwood.

While Michael Butler and Dennis Shryack were working with Eastwood on *The Gauntlet* (1977), they had mentioned that they would be interested in making a Western sometime. Eastwood invited them to bring back any idea they might have to him, and that is precisely what they did. The three of them brainstormed and came up with the idea for *Pale Rider* (1985), which would be the only film Eastwood would commit to doing without a written screenplay.

The film owes more than a small debt to George Stevens's Western classic *Shane* (1953), one of the greatest of the genre and easily the best film of its year despite the Academy Awards going to *From Here to Eternity* (1953). Seen through the eyes of a child (superbly realized by Brandon De Wilde), *Shane* tells the mythical story of a gunfighter, Shane (Alan Ladd). He flees his old life hoping for something new and stumbles into a valley where a war is being waged between the homesteaders and cattle barons for the land. The nasty old baron has called in a gunfighter named Wilson (Jack Palance) to deal with the farmers. Wilson is a man Shane is quite familiar with. In a stunning sequence that makes clear Wilson's lack of regard for human life, he guns down one of the farmers in the mud, goading the little man into a fight he cannot possibly win before shooting him in cold blood. Knowing that a showdown is inevitable, Shane dons the buckskins he had given up for a set of farmer's clothes, and straps on his guns to go to town and face Wilson.

The film opens with Shane descending from the mountains (the heavens), and at the end of the film he ascends back into the mountains (toward death), mortally wounded. Stevens allows Shane to be a hero not only to the boy but also to everyone around him. The film is quite simply one of the finest Westerns ever made, with a mythic quality due to Shane's near-angelic nature.

Pale Rider has many similarities, though there is a supernatural tone to the film that is clearly not in *Shane*, and the young boy is replaced by a 14-year-old girl who has sexual feelings for the character Eastwood portrays, who is known only as Preacher and who may or may not be a ghost. There is a moment in the film when Preacher stands to reveal that his back is decorated with the scars left by bullets that had gone through him, which is something no man could possibly have lived through at this time in history.

In 1850s California, a small group of miners have formed a community mining for gold while being terrorized by LaHood (Richard Dysart), who heads a strip mining corporation and has no use for the settlers, and his men. The wealthy LaHood is raping the land with his hydraulic water system, which blasts water with enormous force into the earth, tearing it apart, in his search for gold. The miners, however, work with their hands. They toil by day, working in the mud and rock, hoping for that find of gold that could change their life. Angered that the miners will not give up, LaHood sends in his men to tear apart their makeshift village. They kill Megan's dog in their campaign of violence. As the child buries her pet, she prays for a miracle; and as she says the word "Amen," the film cuts to a lonely figure moving toward the town on horseback. This is the Preacher. The leader of the miners, Hull (Michael Moriarty), happens to be in town for supplies when the stranger arrives, and when Hull is attacked by LaHood's men, the stranger comes to his rescue, beating the hoods to a pulp. Earning Hull's gratitude, the stranger is invited for dinner, where Hull's woman Sarah (Carrie Snodgrass) berates him for bringing home a killer, only to find that the stranger is a preacher, a man of God.

The first time Megan (Sydney Penny), Sarah's 14-year-old daughter, and the population of the miners' village lay eyes on the Preacher, he is astride the pale horse, and we will later learn that he has a past marked by killing and mayhem. "And I looked and beheld a pale horse; and his name that sat on him was Death, and hell followed with him," says the Book of Revelation. This is the first suggestion in the film that the Preacher may be of supernatural background, perhaps a ghost or an avenging angel of some sort.

Megan and Sarah also see the scars on his back left by the bullet holes, which makes it clear that the man is no stranger to trouble. Megan falls hard for him and offers herself to the man, who politely turns her down.

However, he does not respond in the same way to her mother, Sarah, whose advances he embraces, despite his friendship with her lover.

The Preacher unites the miners by making them understand that together they are stronger than one person and that they have every right to the land and what is in it. If they remain a community, they stand a chance at beating LaHood. But the businessman brings in hired guns to fight the miners, leaving the Preacher no choice but to fight them his way. Although the townspeople ask the Preacher to not go to town and fight because they are afraid that he might die, the Preacher does indeed go to war against LaHood's hired guns. At least one of them is stunned and more than a little frightened at seeing the Preacher, whispering "Not you . . ." when he gets a look at him for the first time. And of course, the Preacher guns them down, leaving the mining community free of tyranny and free to mine their land and hope for a better way of life. Yet unlike the ending of *Shane* (1953), when the Preacher leaves, no one cries for him to return.

Critics saw at once the obvious parallels between *Pale Rider* and *Shane*, some even stating the film was no more than a remake of that classic film. Several lowbrow critics called the film a "ripoff of *Shane*," failing to see that the film, like many before it, was paying homage to that great Western, and under no circumstances was ripping it off. The wiser film writers admired what Eastwood had accomplished with the film, recognizing that rather than ripping off the previous classic, he was paying homage and putting his own spin on the story by adding to it a touch of mysticism.

"*Pale Rider* is the title of Clint Eastwood's entertaining, mystical new Western, and the name of him who sits on the pale horse is simply the stranger, also called Preacher, when he comes to wear a turned collar. However, no matter what his costume, he's still Death," wrote Vincent Canby for the *New York Times*.

"The veteran movie icon handles both jobs (actor and director) with such intelligence and facility that I'm just now beginning to realize that though Mr. Eastwood may have been improving over the years, it's also taken all these years for most of us to recognize his very consistent grace and wit as a filmmaker," finished Canby.

"Clint Eastwood has by now become an actor whose moods and silences are so well known that the slightest suggestion will do to convey an emotion. No actor is more aware of his own instruments, and Eastwood demonstrates that in *Pale Rider*, a film that he dominates so completely that only later do we realize how little we saw of him," raved Roger Ebert in the *Chicago Sun-Times*.

Yet Ebert followed that opening praise with some concerns.

There are moments when the movie's myth making becomes self-conscious. In one scene, for example, the marshal's gunmen enter a restaurant and empty their guns into a chair where Eastwood had been sitting moments before. He is no longer there; can't they see that? In the final shootout, the preacher has a magical ability to dematerialize, confounding the bad guys, and one shot (of a hand emerging from a water trough) should have been eliminated—it spoils the logic of the scene. But *Pale Rider* is a considerable achievement, a classic Western of style and excitement. Many of the greatest Westerns grew out of a director's profound understanding of the screen presence of his actors; consider for example John Ford's films with John Wayne and Henry Fonda. In *Pale Rider*, Clint Eastwood is the director, and having directed himself in nine previous films, he understands so well how he works on screen that the movie has a resonance that probably was not even there in the screenplay.

There are many major differences between the two films that I believe many critics never gave proper credence to. First and foremost, the 10-year-old boy has been changed to a 14-year-old girl who professes her love to the Preacher just as the boy did with Shane; however, there is now a sexually charged element that did not appear in *Shane*. She boldly approaches the Preacher about making love, and he politely declines. However, he does no such thing with her mother, something that also did not happen in *Shane*, although there was little secret about the way Joey's mother felt about the gunfighter. Shane was fleeing his life as a gunfighter because he saw the end of an era; the Preacher is searching for someone, someone that hurt him, someone that did him harm, and he intends to exact revenge. There is darkness within *Pale Rider*, a growing sense of dread that is not apparent in *Shane*. Eastwood's Preacher is clearly a dark force, whereas Alan Ladd's Shane gives off an almost heavenly glow; their greatest similarity is that they have come to save the weaker group from the larger forces of evil and commerce. Of course, Shane is beloved within the community, whereas the Preacher is feared and respected, and while the little boy chased Shane begging him to come back, no one goes after the Preacher.

The film proved popular at the box office, dismissing the myth that Westerns could not make money and grossing more than 50 million dollars in its initial release. There had been initial hope that this film would bring back the American Western, which of course it did not do. Neither audiences nor critics seemed quite ready for a supernatural Western, believing that the genre should be realistic. Eastwood's next Western, eight years later, would be exactly that, and one of the very best of the genre ever made.

12

Heartbreak Ridge (1986)

You're an anachronism. You ought to be in a glass case with a sign saying, Open only in case of war.
—Remark about character Tom Highway in *Heartbreak Ridge*

Of the many characters Eastwood has portrayed over the years, none gave him so much obvious pure acting fun as Tom Highway, the tough-as-nails, napalm-spitting Marine in *Heartbreak Ridge* (1986), one of the year's biggest hits. In the manner of Colonel Kilgore (Robert Duvall) in *Apocalypse Now* (1979), the surfing nut who loves the smell of napalm in the morning, Tom Highway is at home only in war and uneasy and frustrated when without it. Although it may make him a great warrior, it does little to help him function in society.

At a time when military films had become comic book fantasies, such as *Rambo: First Blood Part II* (1985) and *Top Gun* (1986), Eastwood made a film that explored machismo to an extreme. Like those films, it was very much a fantasy and a comedy merged with adventure. There was never any doubt that *Heartbreak Ridge* was a fairy-tale movie, pure entertainment, and wildly fun to watch, but not realistic in any way. Though he had been taxed as an actor before in *The Beguiled* (1971) and under his own direction in *Honky Tonk Man* (1982), here was a film that allowed him to go over the top and give audiences exactly what they expected of Eastwood when heavily caffeinated: a brawling, cursing son of a bitch sent in to whip a group of Marines into a fighting machine.

"*Heartbreak Ridge* is my ultimate statement about macho," he would explain to biographer, Richard Schickel. "He's super-macho—and he's full of shit. He's ignorant." Eastwood decided to do the film based on reading a dozen or so pages written by James Carabatso, though he concedes that the final version should have been credited to Joe Stinson. Certainly the part offered Eastwood the broadest, loudest, most profane, and most repressed rage–filled character he had ever portrayed. He was a warrior without a war to fight. Highway was a Marine lifer who had dedicated himself to the Corps on every level, sacrificing everything outside of the Marines for his life there, including his marriage to Aggie (Marsha Mason), with whom he is still deeply in love. The United States Marine Corps initially agreed to take part in the shoot, which was something they had refused to do on other films, such as *Apocalypse Now* and later *Platoon* (1986). But during the shoot, they expressed concern with the objectionable language in the film and the homophobic nature of the script. Consequently, they withdrew their support. Eastwood's other issues during the shoot were minor—specifically Marsha Mason, who questioned Eastwood's style of shooting and printing the first take. An actress from the theatre, Mason had come to prominence in the seventies with an Oscar-nominated performance in *Cinderella Liberty* (1973). Married to playwright Neil Simon, she would end up the leading lady in many films based on his work, including *The Goodbye Girl* (1977) and *Only When I Laugh* (1980), both of which earned her Oscar nominations for best actress. She was clear in telling Eastwood she needed rehearsal before the scene was shot, and recognizing that all actors had different needs, he made clear to her that he would never roll film until she was ready. Once again, a true actor had found that Eastwood was among the more sensitive directors toward actors at work, and the result was an excellent performance from Mason.

We hear Tom Highway before we see him. That gravelly voice is bragging about his exploits in a prison cell when a very large man takes exception to something he says. Without hesitating, Highway hands his cigar to another man in the cell, deals with the much larger man in seconds, and takes back his cigar to continue his tale. It is perhaps the most memorable introduction to any character Eastwood has ever portrayed, and it sets the tone for the entire film. This was to be a study of a man tough as nails who late in his life realizes his antics and devotion to the Marine Corps have cost him the woman he loves. During his last assignment, training a group of young men for combat, he begins reading women's magazines in hopes of wooing Aggie back. She works close to the base at a bar, and though she claims to be with the owner of the bar, Highway has no doubt there is still heat between the two of them.

Upon arriving at the base, he finds that his new commanding officer is a much younger man who has never known combat and who sees Highway, the much older warrior, as something out of ancient history. Highway takes charge of the recruits and quickly begins putting them through their paces. Repeatedly clashing with his commanding officer and at war with his men, he finds that they begin respecting him when they learn that he received the Congressional Medal of Honor in Korea. The men also are aware of Highway's personal troubles with Aggie, and they watch as he manages to convince her to briefly reconcile before he and the men are shipped off to Grenada. Dropped into a war zone to rescue medical students, Highway and the men are forced to improvise when nothing seems to go right in Grenada, but their training, however unorthodox, comes in handy time and time again. Disobeying direct orders, they manage to take a fort, and though initially threatened with court martial, Highway is elevated to the status of hero for his initiative. He returns to the United States and to Aggie, hoping for the second phase of his life to be less chaotic than the first.

Eastwood loved playing this character, and during the making of *Unforgiven* (1992) he was told by no less than Gene Hackman that it was his finest performance. Tom Highway was, without question, the most boldly theatrical portrayal of Eastwood's career, one of the rare times the actor went over the top without resorting to caricature. Walking that fine line can be dangerous for actors who are not acutely aware of what they do well and how their audience perceives them. Very few actors know their strengths and weaknesses better than Eastwood does. Like Robert Duvall's war-loving Kilgore in *Apocalypse Now* (1979), Tom Highway is first and foremost a warrior who is at home in the thick of battle, smart enough to never let fear enter his mind, and compassionate enough to know that the young men around him are quite terrified of combat and of him. Compared with any other character Eastwood had ever portrayed, Highway is by far the broadest, and frankly, one of the most entertaining.

"As the gritty, raspy-voiced sergeant, Clint Eastwood's performance is one of the richest he's ever given. It's funny, laid back, seemingly effortless, the sort that separates actors who are run of the mill from those who have earned the right to be identified as stars," wrote Vincent Canby in *The New York Times*.

Not all critics felt the same as Canby, and although the film was a strong box office hit, critical acclaim was difficult to come by.

"Why do we go to Clint Eastwood movies?" asked Paul Attanasio of the *Washington Post*. "To watch Clint whisper killer lines, stand tall for American virility against his milquetoast bosses and, with fist and gun, knock the stuffing out of his foes. Those with an endless appetite for this sort of tough-man-tender-chicken melodrama will enjoy watching Clint go up against these young punks and outrun, outshoot, outdrink, and outpunch them, in the process lending an idea of what it means to be a . . . Marine."

Roger Ebert seemed to understand that Eastwood had taken a screenplay laden with cliché and made it his own, and that this was not art but, without question, entertainment. "Clint Eastwood's *Heartbreak Ridge* uses an absolutely standard plot and makes it special with its energy, its colorful characters, and its almost poetic vulgarity. We have seen this story in a hundred other movies, where the combat-hardened veteran, facing retirement, gets one last assignment to train a platoon of green kids and lead them into battle. But Eastwood, as producer, director, and star, caresses the material as if he didn't know B movies had gone out of style," wrote Ebert.

"*Heartbreak Ridge* is Eastwood's 13th picture as a director, and by now he is a seasoned veteran behind the camera. He has starred in all but one of his films, and who knows Eastwood better? This time he makes himself look old, ragged, and scarred, with a lot of miles behind him," Ebert finished in gentle praise for the film, which he compared to a low-budget Sam Fuller war picture.

"*Heartbreak Ridge* is not great Eastwood," wrote his biographer, Richard Schickel, for *Time* magazine, "but it will tide us over until the next *Bronco Billy* or *Tightrope* swaggers into view."

Ironically the same year this film was released, a former Vietnam veteran and Academy Award–winning screenwriter—for his adaptation of *Midnight Express* (1978)—would bring his experiences in Vietnam to the screen in *Platoon* (1986). Oliver Stone's low-budget masterpiece would obliterate the comic book mentality of Vietnam that existed at that time in Hollywood and end the reign of movies such as *Rambo: First Blood Part II* and *Missing in Action*—and, I suppose, to a lesser extent, *Heartbreak Ridge*, which was nowhere near as exploitive as the aforementioned pair. The impact of *Platoon* was astonishing; the little film grossed in excess of 180 million dollars and won four Academy Awards, including best picture and best director.

War films were never again the same, with Stanley Kubrick weighing in with *Full Metal Jacket* (1987), and later Steven Spielberg with *Saving Private Ryan* (1998). The next movies Eastwood made about combat would be realistic and powerful back-to-back studies of the conflict on Iwo Jima as seen through the eyes of the Americans and then the Japanese, each in its own way a superb work of art.

13

Bird (1988)

Upon announcing the annual nominations for the Directors Guild of America's highest honor, Steven Spielberg said with some genuine regret, "I had really hoped that Clint Eastwood's name was among the nominees . . . ," echoing the sentiments of many in the film community who felt Eastwood deserved to be recognized for his film *Bird* (1988).

Eastwood's love of jazz has been well documented in various books and publications. He has served as executive producer on documentaries, and in his later career, composed the scores to both his own films and those of others, including his daughter Alison's picture *Rails and Ties* (2008).

Through the seventies there had been attempts to make a biography of jazz great Charlie Parker, which Eastwood had followed with great interest. In the mid-eighties he became aware of the screenplay written by Joel Oliansky belonging to Ray Stark at Columbia Pictures. Hearing that Stark coveted a property titled *Revenge* (1990), Eastwood arranged a deal with Warner Brothers and Columbia that would see a trade of screenplays. *Bird* would come to Warner, and *Revenge* would go to Columbia—and eventually become a box office dud with Kevin Costner and Anthony Quinn. Eastwood now had a script for his dream project on Parker, and nothing was going to stop him from making the film.

"Parker was an exceptional human being, his story had never been told and I'd been interested in jazz since I was a boy," the director explained to writer Milan Pavolic of *steadycam* in 1988. "My mother had a collection of Fats Waller records. When I was growing up there was a Dixieland revival in the San Francisco area, and that was when I saw Bird for the first time."

That event had a profound impact on Eastwood's life, as he never forgot the magic he saw Parker wield with his saxophone on the stage, redefining and recreating a new musical form. It was 1946 in Oakland at an event called Jazz at the Philharmonic. Eastwood sat and watched his idol Lester Young, but while there he was given the golden opportunity to see the legendary Parker, an experience that would galvanize him.

"I'll never forget how Parker moved, how he walked, and how he stooped, and of course the sound," said Eastwood in 1988. "This stirring, joyous music, which didn't hint at the player's tragic fate. It's a tragedy. Everyone who plays the alto saxophone today has been influenced by him, and he left his mark on audiences; he introduced people like me to a completely new music."

Charlie Parker, known as Bird, was a musical genius who broke down the conventional boundaries of jazz music and, in doing so, evolved the art form and created a new one in the process. He fell in love with jazz as a boy, growing up in poverty with a deep love of music. Attempting to see his heroes at every opportunity, he learned to play the alto sax and, by the early forties, was a leading figure in the fast-emerging bebop scene. Parker had hit upon a method of musical improvisation for developing his solos that enabled him to play what he had been hearing in his head for some time. He built his solos on the chords at extended intervals, such as the ninth, eleventh, and thirteenth. Although many of the masters disdained this new form of jazz in its early stages of development, the great Benny Goodman was confident of its emergence and potential.

And of course, it did indeed emerge, making Parker the leading jazz figure of his generation through the late forties and into the fifties. Yet with all of his fame and success, he was a tragic figure, battling an addiction to drugs that he had been fighting since his teenage years, succumbing first to morphine and later to heroin. When drugs were not available, he drank heavily to take the edge off the withdrawal that came upon him fast and with brutal consequences. His addiction had an enormous impact on his life, as it got him fired from various gigs, caused him to miss shows, led him into a dark depression, and eventually was responsible for his death at age 34. The doctor, upon studying Parker's body, believed he was looking at a man in his mid-sixties, not a 34-year-old, because the drugs and alcohol had so ravaged Parker.

The screenplay for *Bird* had been in existence for several years in various forms and with several different actors attached to the project. At one point production was set to move forward with comedian Richard Pryor in the lead role, but various events transpired to prevent this from happening. Eastwood made no secret to Warner Brothers that he wanted to cast an unknown in the lead role, believing a name actor would forever be seen as just that—a name actor playing Parker, which was not what he wanted. The thought of Richard Pryor in the role was to Eastwood, with all due respect to the comic actor's memory, grotesque.

"I told them that we weren't going to use a name actor, and they went along with me. Columbia had the script first, and they were talking about Richard Pryor, which I think would have been wrong. He's done some wonderful things, but you'd see Richard Pryor, not Bird. People would be expecting gags. I wanted very good actors people could see as the characters," he explained to Nat Henhoff before the film's release.

Eastwood, like many of the older actors, had long followed the career of Forest Whitaker, a large actor who had come to attention for the first time as a football star in *Fast Times at Ridgemont High* (1982) before stealing *The Color of Money* (1986) from under the nose of Paul Newman as a potentially brain-damaged pool hustler. It was in this Scorcese film that Eastwood first took great notice of the actor.

"I'd liked him for a long time," he explained. "I'd enjoyed him in supporting roles, particularly *The Color of Money* (1986). He had always conveyed a truthfulness. I looked at a few other actors but decided in favor of him very early."

Whitaker spent a great deal of time researching the role. He interviewed Chan Parker, wife of the jazz great; listened to old recordings of his music; and learned to play the sax in order to match the finger movements of the music on the track. A method actor, it was important to Whitaker that he inhabit the character, going beyond a mere performance and immersing himself so deeply in the character that Parker came to life again on screen through Whitaker.

For the coveted role of Chan Parker, Eastwood chose Diane Venora, a recognized stage actress with few film credits, but again he had the trust of the studio behind him in the choice.

Eastwood believed that Oliansky's screenplay needed no work and moved quickly into production on the film. With the memories of Parker firmly in his mind, Eastwood spent a great deal of time with Chan Parker as well as Dizzy Gillespie and Red Rodney, both portrayed in the film and both able to provide insight into Parker's world. Of chief importance to Eastwood was the truth and honoring the spirit of Parker's work. He knew his film was dark because it dealt with an artist heavily addicted to drugs to the point that his addiction ended his life. This would not spell box office hit, but he wanted the truth in the work, and all involved knew from working with him before that nothing less would do.

An added bonus for Eastwood was sound wizard Lennie Niehaus discovering a manner in which to isolate the saxophone played by Parker on some of the old recordings by fading out the piano and string bass and cleaning up the background, allowing for a pristine sound to Parker's sax, something not heard in years. Many of the recordings were loaned to Eastwood and Niehaus from Chan Parker's private collection, and the work Niehaus did on them was simply revolutionary.

In making the film like a jazz piece, Eastwood captured the improvisational style in which Parker both played his music and seemed to live his life. By all accounts, although Parker was a deeply troubled man, he also was a gentle soul who was full of love for those around him. However, he was forever obsessed with his music, which dominated his life and thoughts. Eastwood's final cut of the film was nonlinear—moving back and forth in time—which forced audiences to pay attention to the happenings and events in Parker's life, but also provided insight into the workings of his mind. We think nonlinearly, as past events of our lives always come to the forefront of our mind when we are doing something of importance to us. Eastwood discussed the look of the film with his director of photography Jack Green, wanting to capture the look of the glossy black-and-white photographs of the jazz scene that appeared in the trade magazine *Downbeat* at the time. Working closely with his director of photography, who seemed to understand where he was going, they created the dark look of the film, capturing with extraordinary realism the worlds in which Parker moved, from the smoky clubs to the dark apartments to which he came home in the early hours of the morning.

With the relatively small budget (for a period film) of 10 million dollars, Eastwood shot the film in his usual manner, bringing the picture in on time and under budget and impressing both Whitaker and Venora with his attention to detail.

"I feel he trusts his people, from the top to the bottom. He knows who he hires, he likes what they are, and he trusts that they will work according to what he liked in them. He wants an uninhibited response, so his feeling of not rehearsing is to create that off-balance for an actor," raved Venora.

Whitaker added to her praise, "He's very cool, calm, and very relaxed."

For the first time in his career, Eastwood broke from linear storytelling, bending time and taking the film into an almost expressionistic form in execution. Utilizing a moment from Parker's past in which an angry band member tossed a cymbal at him in a rage, Eastwood employed a cymbal in mid-flight throughout the film, perhaps as a reminder that Parker was constantly trying to evolve and become greater than he was. The lesson Parker took from that tossed cymbal was to never stop trying to improve and to get better at what he was doing. Thus the cymbal signifies rebirth and renaissance throughout the film. During the later years in Parker's life, in which he is ferociously supported and defended by Chan, the drugs have taken their toll on him, and he is spiraling downward about to hit bottom. In flashback sequences we see how his life has unfolded, both the good and the bad. Eastwood has made the finest type of biography in showing the character, warts and all. Often Hollywood biographies are little more than a series of "greatest hits" moments in the character's life. Richard Attenborough's overrated *Gandhi* (1982) was such a film, as it failed to show any negative aspects of the Mahatma's life, the very aspects that humanize the character. Eastwood's Parker was all too real. He was a man battling the landscape of his subconscious while creating a new musical form on the stage each night. Unafraid to place on the screen a man at war with his demons, Eastwood's film was what he had wanted it to be: real. He knew his severest critic would be Chan Parker, who upon seeing the film announced she loved it.

Perhaps what Chan Parker admired most about the film was that Eastwood made no moral judgment about the character, choosing to allow the audience to make their own decisions about how Parker had lived and died. Whitaker's mesmerizing performance was everything both Eastwood and Chan had hoped it would be, capturing the essence of a man who would redefine a musical form, yet struggle forever with his addictions, and finally allow them to take control of his life as he hurtled toward the end of it. Eastwood's belief in Whitaker had been well founded, and throughout the next 20 years he would become one of the most reliable and eventually important actors in modern film. Performances in *The Crying Game* (1992), *Phenomenon* (1996), *Ghost Dog* (1999), *Phone Booth* (2002), and *Panic Room* (2003) all served to make him a much sought-after actor. As former Ugandan dictator Idi Amin in *The Last King of Scotland* (2006), Whitaker became the fourth African American actor to win the Academy Award for best actor, winning in fact every major acting award available to him for that astonishing performance. Obviously what Eastwood saw in the actor was on the money.

Bird would have its world premiere at the Cannes Film Festival in May of 1988. The audience inside the massive Palais Theatre honored the film with a long ovation upon its ending, and strong word of mouth swept through the festival, tipping the film as a potential prizewinner. Two-time Academy Award–winning screenwriter William Goldman was on the Cannes jury that year and made clear his unabashed love for the film.

"It was by far the outstanding directorial work of that fortnight [festival]. The only stigma being Eastwood and all those action movies," explained the acid-tongued writer. "How dare he attempt to make a serious movie? And bring it off? I believe if Francis Coppola had directed it, frame for frame, the critics would have put him back on top with Woody Allen. And if Allen had directed it, they would have elevated him alongside Orson Welles."

Goldman believed Eastwood had a shot at the directing prize, and did his best with the jury, to no avail. As the prizes were awarded, Eastwood was overjoyed that his actor Whitaker won the best actor award, but that would be the only honor for the film at Cannes. Although Eastwood was disappointed, he kept the sting of rejection to himself. Eastwood returned from Cannes hoping the film would find acceptance among the American film critics when released in the fall. He found his nemesis Pauline Kael, who had hated all of his work, attacking the picture after seeing a screening, calling it a "rat's nest" and calling Eastwood an "atrocious director." Because she had never admired anything Eastwood had either acted in or directed, Kael's comments could not have stung the director as much as one would think, particularly since it seemed she was in the minority of the critical community.

"Clint Eastwood's vision of the jazz scene of the 1950s is touched appropriately by the austere romanticism of fifties' existentialism," wrote Roger Ebert in the *Chicago Sun-Times*.

"Exhilarating!" began Gene Shalit on NBC-TV. "Clint Eastwood's consummate directing and flawless cast send *Bird* soaring. A prodigious movie."

Writing in the *New York Times*, critic Janet Maslin stated with reverential adoration, "*Bird* is a moving tribute and a labor of love. The portrait it offers is one Charlie Parker's admirers will recognize. The soundtrack is superb."

"Eastwood's *Bird* is a hypnotic, darkly photographed, loosely constructed marvel that avoids every possible cliché of the self-destructive celebrity biography, a particularly remarkable achievement in that Parker played out every cliché of the self-destructive celebrity life," wrote Jay Scott in Toronto's *Globe and Mail*. "Forest Whitaker holds the camera with a towering performance . . . Venora is as supple and sultry as a Parker solo."

"Clint Eastwood's *Bird* is a film from the heart. He has done a daring thing; Charlie Parker's music and Bird lives," wrote Jami Bernard in the *New York Post*.

"Clint Eastwood's ambitious 1988 feature about the great Charlie Parker is the most serious, conscientious, and accomplished jazz biopic ever made and almost certainly Clint Eastwood's best film to date," raved Jonathan Rosenbaum at the *Chicago Reader*.

Finally Jack Kroll, writing in *Newsweek*, exclaimed, "*Bird* is an extraordinary work made with honesty, insight, and unmistakable love . . . a film of remarkable sensitivity."

Despite Kael's somewhat vicious attack, the film earned strong reviews overall, though it was admittedly a tough sell at the box office because the subject matter was so downbeat. As expected, it did not do well, but the studio was hoping for Academy Award consideration.

The year-end critics' awards had one bright spot: a supporting actress win for Diane Venora from the New York Film Critics Circle, one of the most prestigious of the pre-Oscar honors. When the Hollywood Foreign Press announced their nominations for the Golden Globes, Eastwood was among the nominees for best director, his first such nomination, with a best actor nomination for Whitaker, and Venora in the running for supporting actress. Suddenly the chance for Oscar consideration became brighter.

Eastwood would win the Golden Globe for best director, but with the announcement of the Academy Award nominations, *Bird* was nominated for a single award, best sound. Obviously Lennie Niehaus's miracle-working with the old recordings had been noticed by the soundmen in the business.

Bird remains one of Eastwood's best films, though admittedly it is a demanding work that requires some dedication from its audience. To quote Arthur Miller, "Attention . . . attention must be paid," for with all the time shifting and broken linearity, it is easy to get lost in the narrative. More than any other film that Eastwood had directed, *Bird* demonstrated his audacity as a director and his willingness to risk and move outside his comfort zone. On display in this film are his artistry, his sublime skill as a director, and his immense courage in choosing to make a film about such a downbeat subject, finding in it a glimmer of humanity. Critics were beginning to take note of the body of work Eastwood had amassed as a director. They were noticing his growth as a director, and most important, they were paying attention to the fact that Steven Spielberg and the rest of the directing community seemed to know something they did not about Eastwood's consummate skill as a director. It was time they caught up with what everyone in the film business seemed to know: as a director, he had arrived. By this point in his career no one considered him just an actor anymore. He was a filmmaker to be reckoned with and appreciated.

THE NINETIES

14

The Rookie (1990)

I had nothing to do, so I made this . . .

—Eastwood

Very likely the worst reason to make a film is because one has nothing to do or because the studio sees in the idea another franchise.

Every director has one film they wish they had not made. For Francis Ford Coppola I suspect it is *Jack* (1994); for Steven Spielberg it is no doubt *Hook* (1991); and for Martin Scorsese it is *Bringing Out the Dead* (1999). While I am not sure if that is the case with Eastwood and *The Rookie* (1990), which is without question the weakest film of Eastwood's career, I suspect in hindsight he might have some regrets.

Just three years earlier, Warner Brothers had an enormous hit with *Lethal Weapon* (1987), a cop-buddy film directed by Richard Donner that featured a wild, star-making performance from Mel Gibson as a suicidal cop and former Vietnam veteran who has lost his beloved wife and is struggling with the grief of that loss. In one of the film's opening scenes, he loads a gun and puts it to his head before realizing that he does not want to kill himself, though he may, in fact, want to die. Certainly his self-destructive behavior and the wild risks he takes lead his superiors to believe that he is dangerously suicidal, whereas others see it simply as crazy courage. Partnering him with a steadfast family man played by Danny Glover, who is just a short time away from retirement, the two form an unlikely team—a team that does indeed get the bad guys, but more importantly, gets the audience. It became one of the year's biggest hits, receiving great reviews in the process. Gibson, already a star, shot into superstardom with this performance, which led Italian director Franco Zefferelli to cast him in *Hamlet* (1990). He, like Eastwood, would parlay his stardom into work as a director, winning the Academy Award in 1995 for his Scottish epic *Braveheart*, though his masterpiece would be *The Passion of the Christ* (2004), which he personally financed and then watched make 700 million dollars worldwide.

Lethal Weapon would, of course, become a franchise for Warner Brothers, with sequel after sequel. Joe Pesci was added into the mix as comic relief that quickly became annoying, and the films slipped in quality as sequels often do.

There was a sense in the industry that Eastwood was slipping at the box office, with the failure of *Pink Cadillac* (1989) fresh in the minds of the studio. Looking at the success of *Lethal Weapon*, Warner Brothers believed that such a film might do Eastwood some good at the box office, and perhaps launch a second franchise for them. Though they were not saying so, Warner Brothers had been deeply concerned about the reaction to *Bird* (1988) and even more so about the reaction to *Pink Cadillac*, both of which were box office failures. However, they did acknowledge that *Bird* was never intended to be a massive hit. They believed Eastwood needed a solid hit, but they also were aware the actor would not do another *Dirty Harry* film, having gone as far with the character as he could. As the studio shopped for a franchise film for him, he was looking for a challenge.

The Rookie (1990), oddly enough, would not offer him that at all. The film's screenplay featured a career cop (Eastwood) paired with a spoiled rich kid portrayed by Charlie Sheen, who at that time was one of the hottest young actors in movies, largely due to his work with Oliver Stone in the Academy Award–winning *Platoon* (1986) and *Wall Street* (1987). The pair would portray cops trying to break a ring of auto thefts run by German criminals, who, ironically, were portrayed by Spanish actors Raul Julia and Sonia Braga.

Eastwood's choice to direct the film seemed to have been borne out of boredom and the fact that the actor believed he had little to do at this time in his life, despite the fact that he was very busy preparing the press launch of *White Hunter Black Heart* (1990), a film much closer to his heart. He would, in fact, often seem distracted while working on *The Rookie*, as he dealt with the press and the film he held so dear to his heart. The shoot of *The Rookie* was interrupted by Clint's attendance at Cannes, where *White Hunter Black Heart* was screening, and though they wrapped principal photography in June, the post-production schedule was fraught with festival interruptions in Telluride and Toronto, where the film *White Hunter Black Heart* also was screening. The issue seemed to be that Eastwood had two projects of radically different importance to himself on the go: first and foremost *White Hunter Black Heart*, which taxed him both as an actor and as a director, and *The Rookie*, which was made for the studio and no other reason. Eastwood had no emotional investment in *The Rookie*; it was not a film close to him or a film he was particularly fond of.

The story was simple enough. After the murder of his partner, Detective Nick Pulovski (Eastwood) becomes obsessed with bringing criminals to justice and breaking the ring of car thefts that led directly to the killing of his friend. Against his wishes, he is assigned a new partner, David Ackerman (Sheen), who is much younger and does little to help simmer down his rage.

They come from different worlds. Nick is a blue-collar hard-working man who earns his money, and Ackerman is a wealthy, pampered, and spoiled son of a millionaire, whose father is horrified that he is a cop. When the pair manage to do damage to the theft ring, the criminals kidnap Nick and hold him for ransom for the sum of 2 million dollars. Defying the police, Acker-man borrows the money from his father and makes arrangements to free Nick, knowing that the criminals will kill both of them the first chance they get. In the meantime, Liesl (Sonia Braga) has raped Nick, forcing herself on him while he is tied up and feeding Nick's will to free himself, which he does. They encounter the criminals at the airport, where they gun them down, Nick earning the rank of captain for his efforts. His first act is to assign a rookie to Ackerman, who has earned his respect and grudging admiration.

When *The Rookie* finally was released, critics were merciless in attacking the film, and one must admit that not since *The Gauntlet* (1977) had Eastwood made a film so weak, so lacking his artistry, and so open to attack. What had he been thinking? After the success of *The Outlaw Josey Wales* (1976), *Pale Rider* (1985), and most importantly, *Bird* (1988), audiences had come to expect something more from Eastwood, something substantial. While direc-tors need box office hits to be able to make the films they want to do, surely there were better scripts coming his way than this one. Since his debut with *Play Misty for Me* (1971), he had grown into a substantial directing artist, and perhaps the best-kept secret in cinema.

None of that artistry was evident in this film. Instead it often felt like the debut film of a newcomer not yet in command of his strengths and weak-nesses, throwing everything at the screen with no sense of discipline.

From the bizarre casting of Spanish actors Raul Julia and Sonia Braga as German criminals to the utter lack of chemistry between Eastwood and Sheen, the film was a disaster. There is no humor, no drama, no tension, and not a single moment of authenticity in the entire film. Even in the infamous reverse rape sequence, when Eastwood's character has been captured and is straddled by Braga as she sexually assaults him, the film packs no punch, leaving viewers reeling, sometimes sickened, in the aftermath of its often poor taste.

Lethal Weapon had a buzz to it, an internal energy that seemed to begin with the actors and shot off the screen into the audience, who picked up on the energy and responded. The villains in the film were vile but interesting to watch, especially Gary Busey's bleach blond hitman—the psychotic Mr. Joshua, fervently devoted to his commanding officer, now a drug run-ner. Above all there was an exciting chemistry between Gibson and costar Danny Glover. There was something interesting in their work together, the manner in which they delivered their lines, and their reactions to one another. Everything about their work together was thrilling to watch. Eastwood and Sheen had no such chemistry going on. In *The Rookie*, there are many awk-ward aspects, from the performances of the actors and their interaction with one another, to the villains as they struggle mightily with their accents (when they bother at all) and who look ill at ease doing many of the scenes. Braga looks somewhat embarrassed during the rape sequence, leaving us to wonder why Eastwood the director did not handle the sequence in a different manner. Was he hoping that the film would offer audiences something new? Perhaps he had hoped for this, but because he was now the master of his own destiny, there was no one to blame but Eastwood, who had made one of the worst films of his career. The film is, along with *The Gauntlet* (1977), the least personal of his career, made while he was distracted. Of course, the screenplay was as deep as the paper it was written on, offering the actors no chance to portray real characters of any sort. Without a strong script, no director has any chance of making a good film, which always starts with the story. Committed as he is to telling a good story, one wonders why Eastwood was interested in this tale at all. Was he truly bored and looking for something, anything, to do?

The film did not do well at the box office, and critics, expecting so much more from him, moved in for the kill and were merciless in their attacks.

"Overlong and sadistic and stale even by the conventions of the buddy pic genre, Clint Eastwood's *The Rookie* may well fill the cupboard with some early box office coin, but won't survive long in the big leagues. Toe tag this as one of the season's major holiday turkeys," fired off *Variety*.

New York Times critic Vincent Canby disliked the film intensely, but seemed more concerned that Eastwood had taken a step backward as a director, writing, "*The Rookie* is an astonishingly empty movie to come from Mr. Eastwood. He sometimes overreaches himself, but his ambitious ones are unusually noble (*White Hunter Black Heart*) . . . this one ranks alongside pigeon feeding."

"Clint Eastwood's new film *The Rookie* plays like an anthology of stuff that has worked before in action pictures. It's jammed with material, and the budget was obviously large, but somehow not much pays off. It's all there on the screen but lifeless," wrote Roger Ebert in the *Chicago Sun-Times*. "What's the deal with Raul Julia and Sonia Braga as the chop shop tycoon and what appears to be his mistress? They're given hardly any dialogue together that isn't flat and functional," he finished.

Ebert's stinging criticism was justified, and it was echoed by many other members of the North American press, who pondered why Eastwood, by all accounts a smart and savvy filmmaker, had cast Spanish-speaking actors as Germans in his film. Further, Raul Julia was a gifted actor, superb in *Kiss of the Spider Woman* (1985) but given so little to do in *The Rookie* he must have thought Eastwood was angry at him. Braga, a powerfully sexual actress, was—dare I say—exploited in the reverse rape sequence; she was used for her burning sexuality, when the sequence would have been far more effective with a less attractive actress in the part. Was it really such a devastating experience to be sexually assaulted by the likes of Braga? Many men, upon seeing the film, laughed out loud at the prospect, no doubt having fantasized about that sort of encounter in their own lives. Rape is an act of violence; yet in this film, it is not portrayed as such, which is very sad. Eastwood had proved himself a fine director of women in the past, and he would take that to greater heights in the years to come, never again exploiting an actress in the manner, however unintentional, he did Braga.

The bottom line for *The Rookie*, despite some impressive box office, is that it is a bad movie. Eastwood and Sheen so utterly lack in chemistry we barely notice when they are on screen together, each appearing bored and in a different film than the other. Neither actor has ever expressed pride in the film, nor is likely to, as both are well aware that the film was a terrible failure on every level.

15

White Hunter Black Heart (1990)

Filmmaker John Huston is regarded as one of the finest directors in film history—a sharp intellectual who also was an adventurer and as at home on a film set as he was boxing the likes of Ernest Hemingway and Errol Flynn. Outspoken and surly, Huston did not suffer fools, and was as brilliant a screenwriter as he was a director, making his mark in the writing game early with an Oscar nomination for his script for the Oscar-winning *Sergeant York* (1941). His directorial debut, *The Maltese Falcon* (1941), was sensational and all but created the film noir genre, but it was overshadowed that year by the debut of another enfant terrible, Orson Welles, and his *Citizen Kane* (1941). Huston was among those to appreciate what Welles had created with his film. After returning from duty in the Second World War as a filmmaker for the War Department, his documentaries classified, Huston set about forging his career as a brilliant director.

Among the great works in Huston's filmography are his masterpiece, *The Treasure of the Sierra Madre* (1948), *The Red Badge of Courage* (1950), *The African Queen* (1951), *Moby Dick* (1956), *Fat City* (1972), *The Man Who Would Be King* (1975), *Prizzi's Honor* (1985), and *The Dead* (1987), which he directed from a wheelchair, an oxygen tank never far from sight because his lungs were racked with emphysema. *The Treasure of the Sierra Madre* would earn him the only Academy Awards of his long career, for best director and for his screenplay adaptation. Through the years his work became an extraordinary collection of literary or theatrical adaptations with very few missteps, and late in his career he directed the superb black comedy *Prizzi's Honor*, which many critics noted seemed to be the work of a much younger man.

Huston's storytelling technique was lean and true, much like that of Eastwood, with emphasis on the story and the acting. And like Eastwood, as an actor, he was infamous for leaving his actors alone to create their characters. In fact, his only direction to Katharine Hepburn when creating her iconic character in *The African Queen* (1951) was "play her like Eleanor Roosevelt," which she did, creating one of her most famous performances.

Similar to Eastwood, when Huston failed, he did so with films outside of his comfort zone, such as the dreadful biblical epic *The Bible* (1966) and the woeful musical adaptation of *Annie* (1982).

Eastwood's film *White Hunter Black Heart* (1990) is based directly on an incident from Huston's life; in fact, the book was written by writer Peter Viertel on location with Huston in the African Congo during the shoot for *The African Queen* (1951). During this shoot Huston wanted to kill an elephant while on safari as much as he wanted to make a film. Eyewitnesses to the events state that which one was more important to Huston was often blurred. Delighted with the property, Eastwood made the radical decision of casting himself as John Wilson, who is a very thinly disguised incarnation of Huston. This decision surprised those close to him after the limited success of *Bird* (1988). Some thought he was out of his acting range and not capable of capturing the essence of Huston, though Eastwood understood better than anyone his limitations as an actor—and, frankly, always had.

As John Wilson, he plays a Hollywood director of some esteem, known as much for his outstanding films as for the havoc he wreaks on producers who do not give him everything he wants. Insisting on shooting on location despite studio objections, he has but one thing on his mind upon landing in Africa: shooting an elephant. While his actors and crew wait for him, he makes arrangements to go on a safari and kill one of God's noblest creatures for the sheer sport of it.

Along for the ride, and the conscience of the film, is Pete Verrill (Jeff Fahey), a writer struggling with his career and a good friend of Wilson's. Verrill is someone the older man can take under his wing, a younger protégé who seems to enjoy the arrogant peacock Wilson seems to be. Verrill, it appears, is around as much for Wilson's amusement as he is to work on the film itself, a means of feeding the director's ego.

Wilson is among the most dislikable characters Eastwood has ever portrayed over his long career, which is clearly a risk for the actor, who is now willing to stretch those acting muscles. Wilson was a man who gladly would go on location with someone else's money to satisfy a whim (of sorts), something Eastwood himself clearly would never do. Wilson, like Huston, speaks whatever is on his mind, no matter who he offends, and has little patience for foolish people. More than once he condemns stupidity in his presence, once to the utter amusement of all around him. Most important in revealing the character's flaws is the fact that he places his own desires above the safety of those around him, which leads to a guide being ravaged and killed by an elephant.

If the film has a major weakness, it is the one-sided approach to the story, painting Wilson/Huston as a heroic rebel with an honesty that is brutal but just. The fact was John Huston spent a great deal of the studio's money on his hunting, and there was no small amount of drinking and irresponsibility during the production in the Congo. Eastwood chose to focus his film almost entirely on Wilson's obsession with killing an elephant, leaving such colorful characters as Humphrey Bogart and Katharine Hepburn firmly in the background, virtually nondescript, when in fact their involvement in the making of *The African Queen* was substantial. Legendary tales circulate around Hollywood about the many long nights fueled with liquor in which Bogart and Huston talked well into the night, and Hepburn was very clear in her memoirs about her romantic fascination with Huston; her description of his massages is near erotic in tone. None of that is in the film, and in this writer's opinion that would have humanized Wilson, making him less of the soulless monster he becomes. He finds his elephant but does not kill it, instead watching in horror as his poor guide is attacked while he is unable to pull the trigger. In the eyes of the Africans, Wilson has become the title, "white hunter, black heart," because he is merciless in his quest for the kill, does not recognize the death he has caused, and has no regard for life.

The last word uttered in the film is "action," the very word the actors and crew have been waiting to hear from Wilson.

Beautifully filmed on location in Africa, the picture is dominated by Eastwood's performance, as he is in every frame of the picture. Obviously it helps to have some knowledge of John Huston and *The African Queen* (1951) to fully appreciate the achievement of the film, which is substantial. Though often portrayed as a monster in the film, with a single-minded obsession, Wilson is no less an artist, as was Huston, an adventurer in life, who brought such adventure to the screen.

White Hunter Black Heart was selected as a Gala Presentation for the Festival of Festivals in Toronto, which in two years would become the Toronto International Film Festival, the single most important film festival on the globe. Eastwood worked tirelessly on the film from postproduction to promotion, appearing at Cannes for the film and being interviewed by press from around the globe. At the time he was working on his action film *The Rookie* (1990), which no doubt suffered from the distraction of this film.

Critical reaction was mixed. Some critics praised Eastwood's daring performance, whereas others attacked him for attempting too much and for reaching farther than his talents allowed. Some reviewers were willing to concede that Eastwood was growing as an actor, stepping farther and farther away from the granite-jawed Harry Callahan, whereas others could not see past what the actor had previously attempted. Perhaps they failed to understand or grasp that Eastwood always had wanted to be more as an actor and always had wanted to attempt these sorts of roles, going far beyond the macho heroes the public wanted to see. Past icons such as John Wayne had dealt with these same problems, as audiences and critics loathed seeing Wayne in anything other than Westerns or war films.

Eastwood did not attempt a direct impersonation of Huston, who was familiar to audiences because of his many fine performances in films, perhaps best of all as the evil Noah Cross in *Chinatown* (1974). His deep, rich voice and that manner of drawing out the vowels in his speech was slightly suggested in Eastwood's performance, which captured the soul of the adventurer. Best of all, Eastwood did what great biographical performances should do, that is, capture the soul of the character. There was something familiar in that long-legged walk, as though he could not wait to get to wherever he was going, and that stare that leveled those opposing him. For Eastwood, loved by his audiences for his tough, macho, shoot-first cops, this was light-years away; the actor made every attempt to create the incarnation of John Huston without doing an absolute impersonation. In *There Will Be Blood* (2007), actor Daniel Day-Lewis would give one of the greatest performances ever put on film as a corrupt oilman, his speech pattern clearly paying homage to Huston, suggesting that perhaps this was his *Chinatown* (1974) character years before.

Rex Reed was among the greatest supporters of *White Hunter Black Heart*, writing for *Coming Attractions*, "Brilliant and witty, and exciting . . . Big Clint gives the finest performance of his career. . . . Eastwood impersonates every flaw with a characterization eerie enough to transcend tricks of voice and manner, offering a larger-than-life figure of Huston as an artist and bully. Clint Eastwood finally hangs up Dirty Harry's brass knuckles and like a born Olivier grafts the skin of a new talent onto himself." Reed ended by saying that he believed the film was among the finest of 1990.

"This material marks a gutsy, fascinating departure for Mr. Eastwood, and makes clear that his directorial ambitions have by now outstripped his goals as an actor," wrote Janet Maslin in the *New York Times*. "Mr. Eastwood's direction here is more fluid than it was in *Bird* (1988), the other recent testament to his far-reaching ambitions. But *White Hunter Black Heart* often suffers from a lack of irony in scenes badly in need of it," Maslin continued in her rather mixed review. More than most critics, she seemed to understand that Eastwood was growing past the image audiences had of him; and his audience was about to find out just how fine an artist he truly was.

Peter Travers at *Rolling Stone* considered, "The film is talky and often stilted. But Eastwood's compassion for the characters, warts and all, feels genuine. His performance, like the movie, is a high-wire act that remains fascinating even when it falters."

Rita Kempley, critic for the *Washington Post*, was certainly not as kind. "His performance is a bungle in the jungle, an absurdly mannered patrician pretense that leaves the rest of the cast stymied."

White Hunter Black Heart ended up as a fine character study as opposed to the grand adventure many expected it to be. When one explores the life of John Huston, who walked with kings and led the life he chose to live, one would expect an adventure as opposed to a character study. In fairness to Eastwood, the character study is a fine one, but sadly not strong enough to bring in audiences. The film barely made 2 million dollars, deeply disappointing Eastwood, who felt he had reached farther as an artist than he ever had before.

Even when released on DVD, the film was tepidly reviewed by critics, with some admiring the picture and others not. In hindsight, *White Hunter Black Heart* has a most important place in the Eastwood filmography because it was the first time audiences saw him stretch as an actor and the last time one of his major works would fail so miserably, at the box office at least. Although audiences may not have responded to his marked change of character as an actor, the film seemed to announce that Eastwood would continue going in new directions, whether he succeeded or failed.

In recent years the film has come to be much appreciated by audiences and critics, who see in hindsight the steady evolution of Eastwood the actor, expanding his depth, willing to take risks and go beyond what audiences were comfortable seeing him do. As a director he was finally ready to make the jump to great American filmmaker, and though very few people knew it at the time, Eastwood had grown supremely confident in his talents and was finally ready to bring a long-cherished project to the screen.

16

Unforgiven (1992)

The Western was for many years the most popular genre in film. It was enormously popular at the box office, and while not necessarily the sort of film that won Oscars, it had a certain standing in the industry. John Ford, the great visual poet, once made clear that he cherished his Westerns, announcing, "I'm John Ford—I make Westerns." Ford's impact on the genre is legendary, as he was the first to take his cast and crew to the remote locations in Death and Monument Valleys, allowing the staggering beauty of the landscape to be captured on film and dwarf the actors in his films. Characters in their own right, the images themselves became iconic.

The major themes of the American Western—man versus man, man versus himself, and man versus the landscape—are evident in all of Ford's Westerns, but are presented most vividly in his masterpiece *The Searchers* (1956), with his favorite actor, John Wayne, who gives what might be his greatest performance. Eastwood had commented that Wayne really took a risk with this performance by portraying a vicious racist at the time of his greatest popularity at the box office, going as dark as he had ever gone in a role before. His character, Ethan Edwards, returns home to his brother's ranch after the war hoping for a life of peace, but finds despair when Indians attack and slaughter the family after drawing him away. His brother and his sons are massacred, his brother's wife Martha is brutally raped and killed, and the two daughters, Laurie and Debbie, are taken to be raised as Indians. Ethan and his step-nephew Martin Pawley embark on a search that will take many years, following a renegade Indian tribe from place to place until they finally come face to face with the chief responsible for the attack and subsequent massacre, Scar. With Scar they find Laurie, who has been violated and butchered, and the sight seems to permanently ignite Ethan's wrath. "Long as you live, don't ever ask me again," he roars out when asked about what he had found. What is astounding is the recognition that comes partway through the film that Ethan is searching for Debbie not to bring her home but to kill her because she has been defiled by the Indians. For years he searches, finally coming face to face with a teenage Debbie, his last known kin. Ethan then finds the one thing he did not expect to find on his search, his humanity. Lifting Debbie high over his head as he did when she was a child, he sweeps her into his massive arms and whispers, "Let's go home Debbie."

With this performance, Wayne silenced many of the critics who loudly stated whenever they could that he could never play any other role than himself. He had to be careful about the roles he took, to be sure, but he often shaded his characters with small colors, allowing them to change from one film to the next. And although he never challenged Marlon Brando as the cinema's greatest actor, Wayne was a damned fine actor in the right role.

His career is not unlike Eastwood's, though Eastwood has forged a strong career as a director, something Wayne could never quite do. Each got better as an actor as he grew older, and in fact Wayne's final performance in *The Shootist* (1976) remains arguably his finest work. Ironically the last time we might see Eastwood in a film is *Million Dollar Baby* (2004), which also might be his finest work as an actor. The parallels between the two are obvious, though certainly Eastwood would have the edge as an artist.

Ford's *The Searchers* is widely considered to be the greatest American Western put on film, though when released neither audiences nor critics recognized its raw power. That came years later, when university professors teaching cinema hailed its strengths, followed by directors such as Martin Scorsese, George Lucas, and John Milius, who adored the film, often paying homage to it in their work. Westerns had been kind to Eastwood over the years, his first major work coming on television in a Western at a time when there were more than 30 prime time Westerns populating the airwaves. His performance in Sergio Leone's Spaghetti Westerns of the sixties made him an international star, and his own three Westerns, *High Plains Drifter* (1973), *The Outlaw Josey Wales* (1976), and *Pale Rider* (1985), were minor classics of the genre. But as mentioned previously, Michael Cimino's *Heaven's Gate* (1980) had obliterated the chances for more Westerns to be made, with the 44 million dollar failure bankrupting United Artists Studios and subsequently ending the directors' era of the seventies.

Eastwood found *The Cut Whore Killings* in 1983, an original work by David Peoples. Peoples had just finished seeing *Blade Runner* (1982), which he adapted to the screen, fail and then become one of the greatest cult classics of its time. The property had been owned by Francis Ford Coppola, who had let the option go, allowing Eastwood to buy it and sit on it to age into the role. The project seemed a curious one for Coppola, the genius behind *The Godfather* (1972), *The Godfather Part II* (1974), and *Apocalypse Now* (1979), who had fallen on hard times with the terrible reception of *One from the Heart* (1982). "I can't do what Francis Coppola would do," Eastwood smiled, "but I can bring something to it."

Whether it was the stunning success of Kevin Costner's Western *Dances with Wolves* (1990) or the fact that it was just the right time, Eastwood decided to make the film in 1991 for a 1992 summer release. *Dances with Wolves*, a three-hour-plus film told largely in the Lakota language, was a massive hit and went on to win seven Academy Awards, including best picture and best director. Widely praised, the film was a smash hit with audiences, elevating Costner to superstardom.

Eastwood initially had decided to do some rewrites to *The Cut Whore Killings*, but after reviewing what had been done, he changed his mind and reverted to the original script Peoples had written, with one minor change. He changed the title to *Unforgiven*.

When initially offered the role of Little Bill, Gene Hackman refused the part, saying he no longer wanted to be involved in films with excessive violence. He had recently given up the role of Hannibal Lecter in *The Silence of the Lambs* (1991), which also was to have been his directing debut. Even Hackman's children were after their famous father to ease out of the more violent roles he had been seen in on screen, though he won his Academy Award for best actor for his tough-as-nails cop in *The French Connection* (1971). More recently he had been nominated for his performance as an unorthodox and violent special agent trying to find the killers of black students in the Civil Rights drama *Mississippi Burning* (1988). Upon being turned down, Eastwood called the actor, and the two artists talked for a long time about what Eastwood wanted to say with the film—the lasting impact of violence and murder, and how one loses one's soul upon using violence and taking another's life. Understanding that Eastwood was going after something important, in many ways analogous to a modern Rodney King study, Hackman agreed to be part of the cast.

Richard Harris was vacationing in the Bahamas and watching *High Plains Drifter* (1973) on television when Eastwood got in touch with him. He could not believe the director and star of that film was on the phone offering him the plum role of English Bob in his new picture.

Morgan Freeman committed the moment he got the call for two reasons: the first obviously was "to work with Clint" and the second was to be in a Western, which long was a dream of his. An outdoorsman who loved horseback riding, Freeman cites *Unforgiven* as one his favorite shoots, because when he was not working he could enjoy the beauty and splendor of western Canada.

The location was far from Hollywood, which Eastwood liked, in Alberta, Canada, 25 miles from any real civilization and much farther from any sort of city. The town of Big Whiskey, the fictional place in the film, was constructed in the open, and the cast and crew met largely for the first time in Alberta for the shoot. Like all Eastwood shoots, this one went without incident, and the actors again loved their time with Clint and his unique style of direction. There was a vibe on the set that seemed to say what they were creating was something very special.

The story was deceptively simplistic, and Eastwood infused it with an enormous and dark depth and an undercurrent of rage. In Big Whiskey a young whore, Delilah, is mutilated by a couple of cowboys when she laughs at the size of one man's penis. The cowboy slashes her face, disfiguring her for life and limiting the amount of money she can earn for her boss, the barkeep Skinny, who laid out money to transport her to him. The sheriff, Little Bill, is called, but he does not see the situation the same way the other whores do and orders the men to pay the barkeep with ponies come spring for his loss. The women, led by Strawberry Alice (Frances Fisher), believe a terrible wrong has been committed—in their minds nothing less than murder—and they wish to see justice done. Strawberry Alice is enraged that Little Bill thinks so little of the women that he does virtually nothing for them. She convinces the other whores to pool their funds and come up with a bounty of one thousand dollars paid to the man who brings the cowboy who did the cutting to justice.

Among those who come to town is English Bob (Richard Harris), an infamous gunslinger who is best known for shooting the Chinese on the railroad, but who fancies himself a legendary gunfighter. Traveling with his biographer in tow, he arrives in Big Whiskey and ignores the signs stating he is to turn over all firearms. Upon exiting a barbershop he encounters Little Bill, who disarms him of his weapons and then beats him to a bloody pulp, kicking and stomping the man senseless in front of Mr. Beauchamp (Saul Rubinek), his biographer.

Meanwhile on a pig farm in a filthy pigsty, William Munney (Eastwood) is trying to separate hogs, keeping the sick ones from the good ones. His children are helping, but it is not going well. A young man calling himself the Schofield Kid (Jamz Woolvett) rides up and asks him if he is the same William Munney of legend. If so, he is headed to Big Whiskey to kill the man who cut up Delilah, and if Munney were to join him, he would split the bounty with him. Munney insists he is not the man the Kid is looking for, but once the younger man leaves, Munney has second thoughts. That money would help get his kids a better way of life and offer them all a second chance. He heads to his friend Ned Logan's (Freeman) house, and the pair head off in search of the Kid. Once they find him, they are forced to listen to his constant tales of adventure and killing sprees, though they come to realize that he is nearly blind and likely has never killed a man. Upon arriving in Big Whiskey, Munney, too, ignores the sign about firearms and is whipped nearly to death by Little Bill, who begins each interrogation with a smile that quickly turns into a sadistic one. He very nearly kills Will, who is taken away and cared for by the whores.

When he awakens, he finds that Ned does not have the stuff for killing anymore. Ned leaves, but he does not get far. Little Bill catches him and whips him to death, propping his body outside of the saloon in town. The Schofield Kid finally gets his chance to kill the man who cut Delilah, and he does indeed kill him while the man sits in an outhouse doing his business. The killing does not have the desired effect on the Kid's life, however, and when the whores bring the two remaining men their money as they wait just outside of town, he breaks down with the horror of what he has done in committing murder for the first time.

The young whore forever scarred in the act of violence that sets the action in motion, Delilah, makes clear to Will that Ned is dead and lying in a coffin outside the bar. Ned's death unleashes the demons within Will's soul, and he mounts his horse during a ferocious thunderstorm and rides into town. Gone is the unsteadiness that dominated Will's early days of this journey. It is replaced by a deadly sense of purpose as he boldly rides into town and sees his friend dead in front of the saloon.

Walking into the bar, he guns down Skinny for having the audacity to decorate his bar with his friend. He then turns his sights on Little Bill, but not before the other men in the bar attempt to take him down. Munney kills five men in all, never stopping to reload and just firing his guns at them, saving the last shotgun blast for the head of Little Bill, who cannot quite believe he is going to die like this. Like a man possessed, he slaughters everyone he intends to kill, seeming to summon the demons that so worked through him in the past and becoming the legend before the eyes of those in the bar. Finished with what he came to do, Munney rides out of town on a pale horse, just as death did in the Book of Revelation, and threatens anyone who comes after him with sure death. The last title card states that he moved to San Francisco and prospered in dry goods for some time.

Eastwood made a seething statement on violence and death that stunned those who saw the film with its raw, visceral power. In this film there is no glory in death, and there is nothing pretty about the violence. One pulls the trigger and someone dies, and one is left to deal with that for the rest of one's life. There is so much more to killing a man than pulling a trigger; in this West, killing eats away at a man's soul, leaving him forever haunted and unforgiven. Like John Ford did with *The Searchers*, Eastwood made a film in which the tone was exceptionally dark, and it remains so throughout the film, never redeeming any of the characters. In fact, there seems to be something awakened in Munney after he takes a savage beating at the hands of Little Bill, rising, resurrected to go at these men with guns blazing.

Eastwood's performance as Will Munney was by far the finest of his impressive career, finding the perfect tone for the character to suggest the depths of hell in his work. Munney has done terrible things willingly, will do them again willingly, and knows that he is utterly damned for what he has done but must live with it. He throws his goodness into his wife and kids, and when Little Bill unleashes the demon from hell inside of him, he takes it out on those who deserve it. Never before had Eastwood so dominated the screen; never before had he been so real and so authentic in a role, leaving behind the movie star persona.

Equally brilliant in an unsettling way was Gene Hackman as the sadistic Little Bill, a sheriff who believes that what he is doing is for the absolute good, which is truly terrifying because power in the hands of a man like that always has gone terribly wrong. The look of sick joy on his face as he whips Ned, leaning in to tell him it is going to get much worse, is disturbing. Hackman's very presence radiates menace and pure danger, a maniac hiding behind a smile. Perhaps what is most troubling about his character is that he so believes in what he is doing, and his sense of right and righteousness is frightening. Like Nurse Ratched in *One Flew Over the Cuckoo's Nest* (1975), there is nothing quite so frightening as someone utterly wrong who believes without question that they are right.

Morgan Freeman did solid work as Ned Logan, as did Richard Harris as English Bob. Young Canadian actor Jamz Woolvett had some impressive scenes as the Kid, and Frances Fisher gave her usual excellent acting job as Strawberry Alice.

When the film opened the following August, the it immediately received rave reviews, as critics fell over themselves trying to find superlatives to describe the film.

"A classic Western for the ages," wrote Todd McCarthy in *Variety*, the industry trade bible. "Clint Eastwood has crafted a tense, hard-edged, superbly dramatic yarn that is also an exceedingly intelligent meditation on the West, its myths, its heroes. Playing a stubbly, worn-out, has-been outlaw who can barely mount his horse at first, Eastwood, unafraid to show his age, is outstanding in his best clipped, understated manner." McCarthy seemed to understand what Eastwood was trying to say and where he was going with the film, something that would quickly become apparent to most North American film critics.

Rex Reed of the *New York Observer* raved, "One of the best films of the year. A profound work of art."

"They [the years] have given him [Eastwood] the presence of some fierce force of nature, which may be why the landscapes of mythic, late 19th century West become him never more so than in his new film, *Unforgiven*," raved Vincent Canby of the *New York Times*. "The center of attention from the moment he rises out of a hog pen until the darkest fade out in Western movie history is Mr. Eastwood," Canby finished, making clear his belief the film was a masterpiece.

"*Unforgiven* is the most provocative film of Eastwood's career," wrote Peter Travers in *Rolling Stone*, continuing with "the graying gunfighters of David Webb People's acutely observant script recall such classic films as John Ford's *The Searchers*, Howard Hawks's *El Dorado*, and Sam Peckinpah's *Ride the Wild Country*. Eastwood gives the film a singularly rugged and sorrowful beauty."

Kathleen Carroll at *New York Daily News* raved, "A gripping and haunting work of art that should finally establish Eastwood as one of America's finest directors." How prophetic were those words.

Christopher Frayerling, critic for *Sight and Sound*, perhaps the most intellectual of all film journals, wrote, "Eastwood's best Western—the most distinguished film he has appeared in and directed since *The Outlaw Josey Wales.*"

And Joel Siegel wrote what was on everyone's mind at the time, "A great Western. One of the year's best films. Eastwood deserves an Oscar nomination for directing."

It was the critics in North America who embraced *Unforgiven* the tightest, as the Los Angeles Film Critics kicked off award season by stunning the industry and giving the Western no less than five awards, including best film, best actor (Eastwood), best director (Eastwood), best supporting actor (Hackman), and best screenplay. A few weeks later the National Society of Film Critics honored the film with best film, best director, and best supporting actor, while the New York Film Critics gave Gene Hackman their supporting actor plaque. Apparently a scheduling error did not allow one of the critics to vote, and the fact that she had named *Unforgiven* the best film of the year in her column made it clear the votes would have gone to Eastwood's film. As it was, she was unable to vote, and *The Player* (1992) won best film from the New York scribes.

The Hollywood Foreign Press honored the film with awards for best director and best supporting actor, while the Directors Guild of America gave Eastwood their highest annual award for best director.

When the Academy Award nominations were announced, *Unforgiven* led the pack with nine, including best film, best actor, best director, best supporting actor, best screenplay, and best film editing. For best film, the Western would compete with the courtroom drama *A Few Good Men* (1992), *The Crying Game* (1992), *Howard's End* (1992), and a bizarre choice, *Scent of a Woman* (1992), which, for reasons known only to the Academy, was nominated in place of Robert Altman's scathing black comedy about Hollywood, *The Player.*

Having won the Directors Guild Award for best director, *Unforgiven* seemed a lock, though there was growing support for the upstart independent film *The Crying Game*, which had stunned audiences and critics with its infamous twist ending. In the best director category with Eastwood was Robert Altman for *The Player*, Martin Brest for *Scent of a Woman*, Neil Jordan for *The Crying Game*, and James Ivory for *Howard's End.*

Nominated for his first Academy Awards, Eastwood, though he would never admit to it, was very pleased, in particular with the attention he was receiving for his acting (for the first time in his long career). The other four nominees for the Oscar for best actor were Al Pacino, the sentimental choice for *Scent of a Woman*, Robert Downey Jr. for *Chaplin* (1992), Stephen Rea for *The Crying Game*, and, for the performance of the year, Denzel Washington in *Malcolm X* (1992). Though Eastwood had won the L.A. Film Critics Best Actor Award, the New York scribes went with Denzel

Washington's powerhouse work in *Malcolm X*, and the Golden Globe went to Pacino.

On Oscar night it was clearly Eastwood's night, as *Unforgiven* won four Academy Awards, including best picture, best director, best supporting actor, and best film editing. Eastwood lost best actor to Al Pacino for his wildly over-the-top performance in *Scent of a Woman*, which was widely known to be a make-up Oscar for an award he should have won years earlier for his mesmerizing work as Michael Corleone in *The Godfather Part II* (1974).

Upon winning the best director Oscar, presented to him by Barbra Streisand, Eastwood humbly walked to the stage and said to the live audience and the billions watching the telecast, "This is pretty good . . . this is all right. I've been around for 39 years, and I've really enjoyed it. I've been very lucky. I heard Pacino say he was lucky, but everybody feels that way when you are able to make a living in a profession you really enjoy. That's an opportunity I think a lot of people don't have."

He went on to thank the crew, the writer, and the producers, and then stunned the audience by thanking "the film critics for discovering this film. It wasn't a highly touted film when it came out, but they sort of stayed with it throughout the year."

The award for best director made clear Eastwood was now among the elite directors in the business and, better yet, thought of as such. Despite all the controversies surrounding the Academy Awards, with its bizarre choices and nominees, an Oscar is still the major film award to win—a validation or some sort of acceptance of artistry in the industry. Though he had long been thought of as a strong director, the Academy Award for *Unforgiven* stated to the world that Eastwood was a world-class director to be taken most seriously.

Within two years, two Westerns had won the Oscar for best picture, which was nearly miraculous considering the last Western to win the award before Kevin Costner's *Dances with Wolves* (1990) was *Cimarron* (1931). How strange that *Red River* (1948), *Shane* (1953), and especially *The Searchers* (1956) were ignored by the Academy. At long last the Western seemed to be back and better than ever.

Eastwood's *Unforgiven* explores how men living with violence and murder lose themselves bit by bit as their deeds cause their morality, their humanity, and their soul to decay. William Munney knows this at the beginning of the film, which is perhaps why he has buried himself in family life, hanging on for dear life to the memory of his wife, who placed him on the path of right. While he does return to this life, it is only when he is beaten within an inch of his life and his good friend Ned is killed and left on display, that he commits cold-blooded murder. Does Little Bill—himself haunted by his own ghosts, justifying them with his sense of being on the side of the law—realize what he is doing when beating this man? Does he know the demon he is setting free? Munney can kill these men easily because they are no more than him—they too have killed, they too are unforgiven—and Munney will remain forever unforgiven by all of society with the exception of his wife, who knew what he was and found it in herself to forgive him. Their love must have been all-powerful.

In the years since its release, *Unforgiven* has earned a reputation and standing in the industry as one of the greatest films ever made and, arguably, the finest Western of the genre, battling with and discussed in the same breath as *The Searchers* for that coveted number one position.

Without question, *Unforgiven* is an American masterpiece. If Eastwood is to be remembered for a single film, this is it, his greatest achievement as a director.

17

A Perfect World (1993)

By the time shooting began on *A Perfect World* (1993), both Kevin Costner and Eastwood were Academy Award–winning directors, with best picture awards for their Westerns, and awards from the Directors Guild of America and several critics' organizations. Costner was the hottest actor in the business, with huge success in Oliver Stone's fiery *JFK* (1991) following his Oscar glory.

Kevin Costner is an interesting case study in a talent gone awry in the business, undone perhaps by his own ego and too much too soon. After being edited out of *The Big Chill* (1983), in which he was the corpse and seen in flashback, he knocked around doing substandard work until Lawrence Kasdan cast him as the wild man in *Silverado* (1985), a popcorn Western. This would lead Brian De Palma to cast him in *The Untouchables* (1987) as Elliott Ness, and a star was born. His easy-going style made him a favorite with men and women alike, and before long he was dominating the box office with *Bull Durham* (1988) and *Field of Dreams* (1989), the classic male-bonding film known as the "male weepy." By the time he approached Orion to make *Dances with Wolves* (1990), his dream project about a white man's integration into the Lakota Sioux tribe, he was a legitimate star with great ambition. Imagine pitching a three-hour Western, with more than a third of the film in Sioux dialogue and subtitled, in a generation where Westerns were widely considered box office poison. Further, Costner not only wanted to star in the film, he wanted to direct and produce it as well.

To the shock of everyone, including the cruel critics who dubbed the film *Kevin's Gate* before a frame had been seen, *Dances with Wolves* was a stunning success. It was a massive hit at the box office and was nominated for a whopping 12 Academy Awards (actor, director, and producer for Costner), winning seven, including best film and director. Costner left the ceremony having conquered Hollywood and no less than Martin Scorsese and *Goodfellas* (1990).

When Costner agreed to portray Butch for Eastwood in *A Perfect World*, he was at the height of his popularity and power within the business, having won two Oscars (director and producer) and been in one box office hit after another. He could have made virtually any film he wanted to make. Coasting on the success of Stone's controversial and Oscar-nominated *JFK* (1991) followed by the romantic story *The Bodyguard* (1992) with singer Whitney Houston, Costner had his pick of roles, but he was a serious actor, choosing to continue challenging himself.

In the years that followed, box office failures such as *Waterworld* (1995) and *The Postman* (1997) had a great impact on the star's status in the industry, and by 2000, he found himself labeled box office poison. To his credit Costner simply reinvented himself as a character actor, giving a fine supporting performance in *The Upside of Anger* (2005) and directing his second Western, the underappreciated and quite excellent *Open Range* (2003) opposite Robert Duvall.

In his younger days, Eastwood might have portrayed Butch, the escaped convict Costner portrays, but as a director in his sixties, he understood he could no longer tackle that sort of role and make it believable to the audience. There was initial concern that Costner would not be able to bring the sense of menace and unpredictability required for the part of the dangerous criminal, but after meeting with him, Eastwood was convinced. He was quite pleased when Costner agreed to take the role, and after some mild arm-twisting from Costner, he agreed to take the supporting role of the sheriff on the hunt for him, with their pasts linking them together.

While there was a mutual respect for one another, both men worked in almost completely opposite ways. Eastwood liked to shoot and shoot fast, often printing the first or second take and using that in the film. Costner liked to talk about the character, discuss the motivation, and focus on what Eastwood often considered minute details. During the early days of the shoot, Eastwood realized that Costner needed to discuss the character and was more comfortable when he knew precisely what was going on in the scene. Eastwood had not counted on this and became frustrated with it very quickly because he sensed the production was falling behind schedule, something that rarely happened to him.

Eastwood's biographer, Richard Schickel, tells a now famous story about an incident on the set that came to a head, with Costner angrily stomping off the set and Eastwood making clear precisely who was in charge. The scene required an extra to wave back at Costner's character, but for some reason the man kept missing his cue. Angered by the mistake, Costner tossed down what he had in his arms and walked to his trailer, slamming the door. Looking around, Eastwood spotted Costner's double in costume and motioned him into the shot. With the camera behind the man, no one would know the difference, so he shot it and printed it. Now calmed down, Costner returned to the set and asked what was happening. Eastwood stated they had shot everything. Stunned by this, Costner asked how, and Eastwood explained he had used his double; and should Costner stomp off the set again, he would use the double for the entire film.

"Daly and Semel pay me to shoot film. If you walk off, I'll shoot closeups of this double . . . I'm not here to jerk off," Eastwood seethed at his younger costar. With the disarming smile of a little boy caught doing something wrong, Costner replied, "OK," and it never happened again, without any apparent grudges between the two.

In the film Costner portrays Butch, an escaped convict on the run with his partner, the homicidal Terry, who operates in a manner Butch finds repulsive. Bursting into the home of a family, Butch prevents his partner from raping the mother, but does not hesitate to take a young boy, Phillip (T.J. Lowther), along as a hostage. From the beginning there is an unspoken connection between the two, as the boy sees Butch as the father he does not have, as well as the door to another world that his mother keeps closed to him.

Upon fleeing, Butch comes to understand that the child is a Jehovah's Witness, and therefore does not celebrate Halloween or other such events important in a child's life. His father, who is absent, has left without explanation, much like Butch's had. When Terry attempts to molest Phillip, Butch kills his partner without hesitation, refusing to see a child injured in any way. The two hit the road fleeing the law, but Butch is smart enough to realize how it is seen through the eyes of the child, and makes every effort to show the boy a good time. A bond is forged between them because they are both fatherless.

In hot pursuit is Red (Eastwood), who is tracking the criminal from a metal trailer and slowly letting the audience in on the fact that he and Butch had crossed paths years earlier, when the man was just a boy. He knows Butch is brilliant, with an above-average IQ, but is not sure whether he will harm the boy.

Phillip certainly is given a front row seat in seeing Butch's agonized, dark side during their stay with a black family who has taken them in for the night. Max and Lottie are grandparents to Cleve, a child who Max bats in the head, which angers Butch. Butch befriends the child, flipping him upside down in a playful game as he has done with Phillip. However, when Max hits the child much harder the second time in front of Butch, something inside of the convict snaps. He prepares to kill the old man in front of his wife and grandson, but first he makes Max—at gunpoint—tell the boy how much he loves him. Obviously Butch has seen something all too familiar from his past: a father who struck him rather than loved him. Before Butch can kill the old man, Phillip retrieves the gun and shoots Butch, as tears of fright stream down his face.

With the law closing in, Butch, now mortally wounded, takes to the fields but knows he is finished. With Red talking to him, he makes Phillip's mother promise to let up on him and allow him to practice Halloween. Apparently content to be taken to the hospital before jail, Butch dies from a single shot by an FBI sharpshooter.

For the first time in his career, Eastwood had given himself the secondary role; and though it was a plum one, he was aware that the film was firmly carried on the shoulders of Costner. The younger actor responded with what many consider to be the finest performance of his career, and one for which he most certainly should have been nominated for the Academy Award.

There is an edge in Costner's acting that had never been there before. There is a sense of danger, of a seething rage borne of abuse as a child that has never been addressed for him as an adult. While he kills his partner for attempting to hurt Phillip, it is with the older couple that his explosive rage manifests itself. With memories burning in his mind, once Max strikes Cleve, the match is lit; and the second time it happens—harder and without any sort of hesitation or warning—he can no longer contain himself. Perhaps he does not want the child to turn out as he has, or to go through what he has, living with the demons as he so obviously does. Costner conveys this beautifully to the audience through his eyes and body language, taking risks with this character that he would not take again for many years.

While his is very much a supporting performance, Eastwood anchors the film, portraying a lifetime lawman who has been connected to Butch for a very long time. It was Red who first encountered Butch on his path to becoming a career criminal, sending him away the first time as much for the crime as to get him away from his father, who was a habitual child and wife abuser. Eastwood brings wisdom to the role, as well as a sense of sadness and of a lost opportunity to save someone he believes is worth saving, perhaps because he never really had a chance. There are some nice moments of verbal sparring with Laura Dern, but ultimately the film belongs to Costner, and Eastwood is generous enough to understand and accept this.

Of all of Eastwood's films, *A Perfect World* may be the most underappreciated and misunderstood. Warner Brothers had enough confidence in the film to rush the release in hopes Costner would earn an Academy Award nomination for best actor, as his reviews were some of the finest of his career; however, the Academy failed to notice the film in any category.

Critics, however, took note of the work and celebrated Eastwood once again, with Janet Maslin writing in the *New York Times* that she believed (oddly) he had surpassed his achievement in *Unforgiven*: "*A Perfect World*, a deeply felt, deceptively simple film that marks the high point of Mr. Eastwood's directing career, could never be mistaken for a young man's movie. Nor could it pass for a reckless, action-packed tale of characters on the run. A lifetime's worth of experience colors the shifting relationship between Butch, superbly played by Kevin Costner with an unexpected toughness and passion, and Phillip (T.J. Lowther), the little boy who starts out as Butch's prisoner and winds up his surrogate son.

"Mr. Costner's performance is absolutely riveting, a marvel of guarded, watchful character revealed through sly understatement and precise details; . . . this is Mr. Costner's most vigorous screen performance since *No Way Out,* and an overdue reminder of why he is a film star of such magnitude," raved Maslin for the nation's most important and most read newspaper.

"This is a movie that surprises you," wrote Roger Ebert in the *Chicago Sun-Times.* "The setup is such familiar material that you think the story is going to be flat and fast. But the screenplay of John Lee Hancock goes deep, and, in the direction of Clint Eastwood, finds strange, quiet moments of perfect truth in the story.

"You may be reminded of *Bonnie and Clyde, Badlands,* or an unsung masterpiece from earlier in 1993, *Kalifornia,*" continued Ebert. "Not because they all tell the same story, but because they all try to get beneath the things we see in a lot of crime movies and find out what they really mean."

"Costner turns in a subtly nuanced performance that is by far the best work he has ever done," raved Mark Savlov in the *Austin Chronicle.*

"Star Kevin Costner and director Clint Eastwood deliver lean, finely chiseled work in *A Perfect World,* a somber, subtly nuanced study of an escaped con's complex relationship with an abducted boy that carries a bit too much narrative flab for its own good," griped Todd McCarthy in *Variety,* though he had high praise for Costner. "The film's major surprise is Costner's performance, which is undoubtedly the best of his career to date. Costner skillfully indicates the glimmerings of good instincts buried somewhere deep in Butch that have rarely, if ever, been articulated or brought to the surface," he stated, obviously thrilled with Costner's electrifying performance. "For once Eastwood the director has served other actors significantly better than he serves himself . . . a director brings strong tact and intelligence to the human story and elaborates it with many grace notes," continued McCarthy.

Not as impressed with the film was *Entertainment Weekly*'s Owen Glieberman, who wrote, "Beneath its road movie surface, the film has a daytime talk show squishiness—it's Eastwood's version of 'Violent Criminals and the Fathers Who Don't Love Them.'"

The film turned in a tepid $30 million at the box office, but truth be told, Warner Brothers expected a great deal more from a film starring Kevin Costner and their number one draw, Clint Eastwood. They had positioned the film to draw attention from the Academy of Motion Picture Arts and Sciences, believing the combination of Costner and Eastwood, merged with the strong reviews, could mean Academy Awards, at the very least a nomination for Costner for best actor. Disappointment prevailed, leaving Eastwood and Warner Brothers puzzled by the film's North American failure.

"I always felt this movie was high risk," Eastwood would tell the *New York Times* early in January of 1994. "I just liked the story. Sure, a lot of people are disappointed. But if you don't grow, you just get in a rut. You can make sequels and imitations and make some dough. But you've got to make a wide variety of things so someday people look back and say, 'Hey, he tried. He did this; he took some risks.'"

Writer John Lee Hancock perhaps summed up best the reasons for the film's failure to find an audience: "In some ways it's discouraging. Perhaps people had expectations of either a buddy movie or a nail-biting, edge-of-your-seat thriller. Perhaps people wanted lots of great scenes of Clint and Kevin drinking beers, looking at each other, giving each other a hard time. This movie just isn't that. Kevin and Clint and Warner Brothers liked it for what it was. Some people just would not accept Kevin as an antihero. The really nice thing is his reviews have been outstanding."

Hancock is very likely right in assuming that audiences expected something radically different from a tender story between a criminal and little boy being pursued by a cop linked to the criminal. Sadly, through the eighties and nineties audiences were less inclined to take chances on films, preferring to stay with mainstream Hollywood.

In hindsight, the film is among the finest of Eastwood's career, and certainly among the best performances of Costner's career. Placing the story above his own character, Eastwood made clear to the industry that he was a director who was most generous, and who was slowly readying his audiences for the fact that he was no longer the star of his films. Never before had Eastwood taken the second role or given over a film so completely to a costar. His obvious talent with actors allowed Costner to do the finest work of his career, and Eastwood was free to create this powerful statement about absent fathers and the inherent damage that results. In both their own ways, Butch and Red are perhaps trying to make up for what their fathers did not give them, but each proves a poor substitute for the real thing, linking them on the road to tragedy. It seems from the moment they first encountered one another, years before the opening of the film, they were linked on a path toward death, something the intuitive Red seems to understand from the moment he discovers Butch is involved. Almost like a regretful father dealing with a wayward son, Red treats Butch with respect, somehow knowing that his behavior is all that he has ever known in life. One of society's misfits, Butch was doomed from birth, and only Red seems to understand that.

18

The Bridges of Madison County (1995)

It was not the directing job that initially attracted Eastwood to the film adaptation of Charles Waller's love story *The Bridges of Madison County* (1992), which had long been a massive best seller, but the role of *National Geographic* photographer Robert Kincaid that piqued his attentions. Eastwood saw in the role a natural fit to his own screen persona, as well as a chance to flex his acting muscles in a role in which audiences did not necessarily expect to see him. He discovered that his friend Steven Spielberg, who was long a champion of Eastwood's, controlled the property. Eastwood approached him about the part, seeing it as a chance to do a role he was truly interested in playing and further offering him a chance to work with the esteemed Spielberg.

The trouble seemed to be in the adaptation, as the bad metaphors of the book would not transfer to the screen, and the sappy storyline had to be streamlined. Writer Richard LaGravanese wrote the screenplay that was eventually shot, managing to actually make a great story out of a shockingly weak book that somehow became part of pop culture despite being, as actress Meryl Streep stated, "a crime against literature."

When Spielberg was forced to back off directing, he turned to Bruce Beresford who had helmed the Oscar-winning picture *Driving Miss Daisy* (1989), a gentle character study with Jessica Tandy and Morgan Freeman that found an audience a few years earlier. Beresford had a solid reputation with actors, going back to the independent film *Tender Mercies* (1983), which had won Robert Duvall an Oscar for best actor in addition to earning nominations for best picture and best director. Eastwood was fine with the decision to give the picture to Beresford, finding him an agreeable man, though that opinion would change rather quickly. Knowing that Eastwood was attached to the project as Kincaid, Beresford began his search for an actress to portray Francesca. He seemed to ignore Eastwood's suggestions of

Angelica Huston, Jessica Lange, or Meryl Streep, and headed off to Europe to find someone younger. This annoyed Eastwood, who assured the production that they may be looking for a leading man as well, which would have killed the film.

Spielberg intervened and let Beresford go from the project, then offering the directing reins to Eastwood who, despite misgivings, took the job.

Wasting no time in casting, he obtained the phone number for Meryl Streep, who was his first choice for the role, and placed a call to her. Not knowing Eastwood, she made clear her concerns about the book, not believing initially that a writer could lick the many problems in the book in creating a screenplay. After reading the finished script, she conceded that the writer had indeed done well, eliminating everything she found offensive in the book to create a very real, very adult love story.

After watching *Unforgiven* (1992), which she found to be a "wholly directed work," and *In the Line of Fire* (1993), which she admired because she had never seen an actor take the chances Eastwood did at his age, she committed to the role, thereby green lighting the production. Very quickly *The Bridges of Madison County* went from a production in limbo to a production in progress with an Academy Award–winning director at the helm and the greatest English-language actress in a leading role.

In Streep, arguably the greatest actress in the history of the cinema, Eastwood would have the ideal Francesca, but also faced his greatest challenge as an actor, acting opposite Streep. Her reputation was made early in her career, winning an Academy Award for best supporting actress in *Kramer vs. Kramer* (1979) before giving the performance widely considered to be the single greatest ever given by an actress in *Sophie's Choice* (1982), which won her every single acting award available to her, including the L.A. and New York Film Critics Awards, the National Society of Film Critics, the Golden Globe, and the Academy Award. Through the eighties and early nineties, she furthered her reputation with an array of thrilling performances in films, such as *Silkwood* (1983), *Out of Africa* (1985), *Ironweed* (1987), *A Cry in the Dark* (1988), *Postcards from the Edge* (1990), and *Death Becomes Her* (1990). There was little doubt that Eastwood had cast the first lady of the American silver screen, and there were whispers that he was not up to the challenge of acting opposite Streep.

It was rather easy to understand why the role of Robert Kincaid so appealed to Eastwood: it offered him something different to do as an actor. He had never in his long career portrayed the flat-out romantic lead in a classic romance. Nor had he ever been given the chance to play someone this nakedly emotional, which may have been where critics were waiting for him to fall down. Did he have the acting chops to go opposite the best there was? Certainly he had grown as an actor over the years, giving a stunning performance in *Unforgiven* (1992) that was good enough for both an Oscar nomination and for the L.A. Film Critics to name best of the year, but the

Western also was familiar ground to him. This was something entirely different.

His friend and longtime film editor made it clear on the special features for the special edition DVD of the film that the secret in Eastwood's performance was not so secret after all, explaining, "I can tell you that Clint's performance is based on one thing, and people don't know this—that's who Clint Eastwood really is, that character."

Eastwood was most aware that the screenplay told the story through the point of view of Francesca, and that this was very much her story, thus he would be serving her story at all times. Not that that would diminish in any way his role in the production, but his acceptance of this was crucial. Not only did he accept this as a director, he embraced it. Trusting in his strengths as a storyteller, he made the decision to support the Streep performance every step of the way.

Streep, who had a strong background in theatre, had hoped the film would fill her need for that style of acting, and she was not disappointed, later calling the production "one of my favorite things I've ever done in my life," which is indeed high praise from this artistic icon. She enjoyed Eastwood's pace, the easy-going atmosphere on the set, the near-hushed manner in which he commanded his cast and crew, and of course that first-take spontaneity.

"We'd be making up as we went along," Streep would explain to Richard Schickel, "exploring its evolution," which for an actor is exactly the sort of shoot they want. Eastwood had always treated his actors very well, believing he hired them to do a job, and therefore he did not feel the need to lay everything out for them, asking instead only that they showed up prepared and ready to work. Streep had a reputation for being a sublime professional, and never did she disappoint him.

"This is heaven," she would say of the shoot. "Clint's very instinctual. If it feels good he says, 'We're outta here,' and we move on," she stated happily.

"It's about their dreams. I really understood who she (Francesca) was. There was a war bride in my neighborhood in New Jersey," explained the actress, "who lived up the street from us. Her name was Nucci. I was in love with her; I loved the way she spoke.

"She (Francesca) was rooted—four square. I worked hard on imagining a physicality for her, and this is part of the actor's fun—sort of a full-bodied transformation," Streep finished in interviews for the special edition DVD release of the film in May 2008.

Throughout the shoot there was genuine affection and constant admiration between the two actors, working as close as two actors could with one another. For Eastwood, in particular, this marked the most intimate performance of his career, as never before had he tackled a role that required him to be so close, physically and emotionally, with a woman on screen. The chemistry between the pair would explode on the screen when the film opened, bringing to the screen a sizzling eroticism absent from so many adult romances these days. One watches a film like *The English Patient* (1996), which was absolutely devoid of any such chemistry or heat, and wonders how and why it was so lavishly praised while Eastwood's film slipped curiously under the radar?

As production wrapped, Eastwood admitted to being thrilled at having worked with the screen's greatest actress, believing that the two of them had created something rather special. It must have been a vindication of sorts that he kept pace with Streep's brilliance throughout the film, creating a full-bodied character in Robert Kincaid. The promise of the evolving actor in *White Hunter Black Heart* (1990) and *Unforgiven* (1992) had been borne out, as Eastwood gave one of the year's best performances.

The film is about regret, lost chances, and sacrifice for those loved deeply. On an Iowa farm, Francesca (Streep) is preparing dinner for her family. She is slightly out of sorts as they eat without speaking, focused on the meal. The family, her husband and children, will soon be departing for a fair in another county, leaving her alone for four days of much-needed tranquility. Distracted, Francesca needs the time for herself.

Into her life comes Robert Kincaid, a photographer shooting the covered bridges in Madison County. He is lost and in need of directions. With nothing to do, rather than simply telling him how to find the bridges, she takes him there and begins a relationship that catches both of them by surprise in its depth and meaning. They have, quite by accident, found their soul mates, though the timing could not be more wrong. For the next few days, they never leave one another's arms, finally making love and finding the sort of passion that comes along once in a lifetime. He offers her the chance to leave the farm and live an exciting life with him, but she knows she cannot do that to her children or her husband. Upon the family's return, they encounter one another across a street in the town, and they stare knowingly at one another as she fights the urge to open the door and run to him, forever leaving the life she has forged with her husband . . . but she does not. She leaves Robert standing on the street in the rain, tears cascading down his cheeks, forever alone, forever without her.

After her death, her children learn of the affair and that their mother has asked that in death she be permitted to belong to Robert, something she had denied herself in life.

"Streep wonderfully embodies Francesca Johnson, the Italian woman who finds herself with a husband and children," began Roger Ebert, the nation's most famous critic, in his high praise for the film. "There is a tendency to identify Eastwood with his cowboy or cop roles and to forget that in recent years he has grown into one of the most creative forces in Hollywood, both as an actor and director. He was taking a chance by casting himself as Robert Kincaid, but it pays off in a performance that is quiet, gentle, and yet very masculine," Ebert raved. "*The Bridges of Madison County* is about two people who find the promise of perfect personal happiness and understand with sadness and acceptance that the most important things in life are not always making yourself happy," he finished.

Janet Maslin at the *New York Times* wrote, "Clint Eastwood, director and alchemist, has transformed *The Bridges of Madison County* into something bearable—no, even better. Mr. Eastwood locates a moving and elegiac love story at the heart of Mr. Waller's self-congratulatory overkill.

"Ms. Streep rises . . . to embody all the loneliness and yearning Andrew Wyeth captured on the canvas," Maslin continued in her praise for the leading lady.

Writing for the *Austin Chronicle*, Marjorie Baumgarten astutely deduced, "The real stroke of genius, though, was casting Meryl Streep as the story's Italian-born Iowa housewife. Through her body language, Streep conveys just as much through what she doesn't say as through what she does. Through her gestures, her facial expressions, the way she holds her body, and her stolen glances, we learn the depths of the currents flowing through her still waters. She is a lonely woman, though she is surrounded by family; she is someone whose dreams of coming to America have not been fulfilled by the dull reality of her life in Winterset, Iowa. . . . She's ready for that handsome stranger to come to her door seeking directions.

"With *Unforigiven*, Clint Eastwood was grandly given credit for single-handedly reviving the moribund genre of the Western. Such hyperbole may also come his way for *The Bridges of Madison County,* which can be seen as breathing fresh life into the genre of women's melodrama," finished Baumgarten.

"Meryl Streep and Clint Eastwood as Waller's tenderly plaintive heartland lovers are so visually and spiritually right, they seemed to have walked right off the page," raved *Entertainment Weekly*'s Owen Gleiberman. "To say that Eastwood, who directed, has done a first-rate job of adaptation does not do him justice. What he's brought off is closer to alchemy. He finds the core of sincerity in Waller's novel—an ordinary woman's romantic dreams—and purges the material of its treacly poetic showmanship."

Gleiberman was among many critics to state the obvious about Eastwood's direction in writing: "His most rewarding feat, however, is turning *The Bridges of Madison County* into a showcase for Streep, who, for the first time in years, succeeds in acting with her heart."

Variety's Todd McCarthy reviewed the film saying, ". . . a handsomely crafted, beautifully acted adult love story. Given the restraint of the treatment, this is about as fine an adaptation of this material as one could hope for . . . longtime Eastwood fans may have divided reactions to seeing their hero in his most sensitive, touchy-feely role to date. . . . It's Douglas Sirk–type female weepy material handled by Eastwood with the utmost tact, maturity, and restraint, so much so that there is a noticeable distance between the story and its emotional effect."

While McCarthy, like many critics, struggled with the film, he had nothing but praise for the performances, writing, "It's impossible to imagine anyone but Eastwood as Kincaid, so it follows that he's perfect in the part—charming, confident, amusing, sexy in a low-key way. Even better is Streep, who has never been so warm, earthy, and spontaneous. Sporting an Italian accent that adds a welcome flavor to the otherwise cornfed ambience, the actress radiantly delineates the late flowering of a neglected heart."

Despite so many strong reviews for the film and the performances, not all critics were as enamored by the film as those aforementioned.

"In one sense, Clint Eastwood's film version was doomed before it started, for the book's readers had played the movie version in their heads, cast the roles, lived the love scenes. In the age of facetiousness, could any director film this without giggling?" asked *Time* magazine critic Richard Corliss, who dismissed the film with a few kind comments but nothing more.

The esteemed Stanley Kaufmann, writing in *The New Republic*, believed the film's troubles began and ended with the casting of Eastwood in the role of Kincaid. "Eastwood, who directed the picture adequately, is inadequate in the role (of Kincaid). He has done a lot of impressive acting in films, but none of it has been sexually romantic, and the age of 64 was not the right time to take up that line of work," wrote Kaufmann.

"While this adaptation of Waller's treacly bodice ripper leaves out a lot of the lurid excess, it is not altogether free of pomposity," wrote Rita Kempley for the *Washington Post* in a somewhat snide review.

Despite strong box office sales, obviously from adults starved for a believable and realistic love story, the film was not the blockbuster the studio hoped it would be, though it was a solid hit for the company in a time of romantic comedies—films that see the stars together at the end of the film after going through the long tried-and-true formula of "boy meets girl, boy loses girl, boy gets girl back." Walking into a film starring Tom Hanks and Meg Ryan, both fine actors, there is simply no doubt they will be together by the film's conclusion because that is what people have paid to see.

The Bridges of Madison County was more along the lines of the very successful seventies' film *The Way We Were* (1973), directed by Sydney Pollack and featuring outstanding performances from Robert Redford and Barbra Streisand as two lovers who marry and find, though they adore one another, they are not compatible as a couple and, to the sobbing of the audience, part company. Real, honest, and powerful, one has to think that is where Eastwood was going with this film. Love stories are a tricky type of film to make work because they depend completely on the chemistry between the actors; the audience must believe in the love or the film will fail.

Eastwood found the project enormously rewarding as an artist, as he was able to challenge himself as an actor as never before acting opposite the great Streep, and as a director creating a tale of great erotic beauty. We, the audience, understand and feel the longing the characters have for one another before they have touched each other; it is in every glance, every gesture, and every movement. Quietly and effectively, Eastwood captured adult lust in an authentic manner, without resorting to cheapness. His performance as Kincaid was one to be proud of, capturing the heartache of a man who knows with every fiber of his being he has found the one woman right for him, but also knowing that they cannot be together because of what fate has dealt them. Rarely had he ever risked this much before as an actor, and never had he been this emotionally naked on screen.

Streep received the lion's share of rave reviews and, come the end of the year, was nominated for best actress by the Hollywood Foreign Press Association, the Screen Actors Guild, and the Academy of Motion Picture Arts and Sciences. Sadly, it was not to be, despite the fact the performance is one of the finest of her career, she lost the Academy Award to Susan Sarandon for her career-best performance in *Dead Man Walking* (1995). In the aftermath of the shoot, and years later for the DVD special edition, she had high praise for her director and costar.

"It's my experience that the really great directors don't let you know when they're directing you or how. At the end of the shoot you think, 'I got to do whatever I wanted.' You don't realize you were subtly manipulated— I felt completely free," she said in honoring Eastwood.

Time is both friend and foe to film, eroding away those that have no lasting impact or preserving the brilliance of films ignored by the generation upon which they were released, but to be rediscovered by the future generation of filmgoers and appreciated for the gem it always was. The *Bridges of Madison County* (1995) strikes me as such as film, for I cannot remember an adult love story with so much pure overwhelming power and truth in every single frame. There is a purity in the performances that comes out of the authenticity of the story, as though a slice of life had been filmed and presented to audiences around the globe. In its deceptive simplicity, *The Bridges of Madison County* has remarkable depth.

19

Absolute Power (1997)

Of the two films Eastwood released in 1997, *Absolute Power* was the one in which he chose to act, finding a strong role for himself in this political thriller based on a novel written by David Baldacci. Known for involving the various government agencies, including the Federal Bureau of Investigations and Central Intelligence Agency, Baldacci's works were popular even in the White House, where President Bill Clinton professed to be a fan of *Simple Truth*. Oscar winner William Goldman would adapt the book to the screen, bringing to it his gifts for strong dialogue and excellent character development; something Eastwood knew was needed to make the book work on film. His work as master thief Luther would be one of the finest performances of his career, elevating an otherwise ordinary film to greater heights, as the story was, in a word, ludicrous. It was well written, but simply impossible.

"I guess it was Lord Acton who said that absolute power corrupts absolutely," Eastwood told the *Rocky Mountain News* in discussing his new film *Absolute Power*, which deals with shady dealings in the White House that stretch all the way to the President of the United States. The film poses the question: Is anyone above the law? "The moment I read the script, which was adapted by William Goldman, I thought, 'This guy's a really interesting character,'" Eastwood explained to the *Boston Herald*. "He's obviously a thrill criminal and does it for the kick of it, running the numbers down to the end and then he gets caught in this wild situation with the President.

"I tend to pick offbeat characters like that because they're fun to play, and yet he has some real concerns in his life, such as the relationship with his daughter," he continued. "He has his own moral code, and in his own way, he's a moral person. He's a thief, yes, but he's not a murderer."

Though not out to make any sort of political statement, Eastwood could not deny that the subject matter of the film would hit a nerve in America in the years after Nixon and the Clinton-Lewinsky affair. First and foremost, he was making a piece of entertainment, but he could not deny the sense of mistrust the American people had for their government.

"We want to believe that our government has our best interests at heart. When I grew up, we thought the government was on our team. We idolized the government agencies. The FBI, for example, was very romanticized. It was there to protect us. Now these agencies have another image . . . the trust of power has been lost. It reflects from the top down. I'm sure the writer of the novel based it on several presidents that were rumored to be philandering. I'm not going to accuse anyone. I'm not interested in that kind of stuff," he explained with some genuine regret to the *Rocky Mountain Post*.

After Eastwood's long and fruitful relationship with Warner Brothers, this film was set up over at Sony Pictures, the first time Eastwood had directed a film for another studio since the seventies. The first major challenge for the company was locking down suitable locations in Washington, D.C., as the city has a definitive look that Eastwood wanted for the film.

"The big problem was finding locations that looked like Washington D.C. because shooting there is so tough. There are a lot of streets you can't use because of all the security. We shot there for *In the Line of Fire*, and it worked pretty well—but we filmed a minimum of scenes. So for *Absolute Power* we ended up getting our establishing shots in D.C. and then moving on to Baltimore. The rest of the logistics were pretty straightforward," he explained to Ian Blair.

The picture allowed Eastwood to work again with Gene Hackman, whom he had loved working with on *Unforgiven* (1992), and Hackman did not hesitate this time when Eastwood offered him the role of the President.

"I like working with great start-up actors like Gene who walk on the set all ready to roll, because I'm not big on rehearsal," Eastwood explained. "I like to try a scene just raw to see where it goes and what the first impression brings to me."

With himself cast as Luther, the world-class thief, and Hackman as the President of the United States, Eastwood rounded out the cast with up-and-comer Laura Linney in the key role of his estranged daughter; Ed Harris, one of the top actors in the business, as Detective Seth Frank, who investigates the crime; Judy Davis as the President's fire-breathing Chief of Staff; and veteran actor E.G. Marshall as billionaire Walter Sullivan. Character actor Scott Glenn would portray one of the Secret Service men who protects the President and is part of the cover-up and corruption within the White House.

Once again Eastwood ran a quiet set, surprising some of his actors, including Ed Harris, who is known for being an actor's actor and often giving various directors a difficult time in the past. Harris's greatest complaint has been directors giving him too much direction; he prefers to be hired for his talent and then permitted to do his job, which of course is precisely what Eastwood allows and, frankly, expects.

"Clint didn't say a lot when we were shooting. He creates an atmosphere of ease on the set. There's no yelling; no one's out of sorts," Harris explained to the *Rocky Mountain News*.

Laura Linney, who was thrilled to be a part of an Eastwood film, praised the director for his manner of working, calling the shoot something like a "wonderful, long sunny day—not bland but easy."

The story is almost Hitchcockian in tone, with Luther Whitney, a master thief, breaking into the home of billionaire Walter Sullivan (Marshall). When Sullivan's much younger trophy wife comes home, interrupting the theft, with company no less, Luther is forced to hide behind a one-way mirror where he can see everything going on. He sees her guest is Alan Richmond, the President of the United States, and they are going to engage in rough sex. For her, however, Richmond gets too rough, and she is forced to defend herself with a letter opener. Richmond's screams bring in the Secret Service, who shoot the defenseless woman to death. Luther watches this in horror, as they then clean up the crime scene to make it look like a burglary gone terribly wrong. Luther is then discovered, but not before he steals the letter opener, which contains both the dead woman's fingerprints and the President's blood. Forced to go on the run, and now hunted by agencies far more powerful than the police, he vows to bring the murderous President down after hearing a speech by Richmond in which the hypocrisy of the corrupt leader standing beside his friend, the husband of the dead woman, sickens Luther. Knowing he is being hunted by the most powerful police force on the globe, he bravely returns to help expose the corrupt President, who is responsible for the death of an innocent woman, the wife of the President's good friend, no less. The investigating detective, Seth Frank (Ed Harris), is slowly piecing the evidence together, and deduces that though there is little doubt Luther is a thief, he is certainly not a killer.

The film moves along at a brisk clip, with strong performances in particular from Ed Harris, who spars brilliantly with Eastwood. Hackman again portrays the nasty character in an Eastwood film and does well enough as the President, though in the years since winning the Oscar for *Unforgiven,* we had seen that sort of character again and again, yet never as strong as he was in Eastwood's Oscar-winning Western. Revealing the President as the villain of the film so early certainly made an impact on the story development—a fact many critics pointed toward when discussing the film's weaknesses. Once revealed as a crook, Hackman is given very little to do except create an arrogant and smarmy man who clearly believes he is above the law and will get away with this crime. Laura Linney made a nice impression as Eastwood's daughter, an interesting foreshadow of the father-daughter relationship that would play out in *Million Dollar Baby* (2004) in years to come. Linney would go on to become an Oscar and Tony Award nominated actress, one of the best and most respected of her generation. And Eastwood was as reliable and as wily as ever as Luther, drawing some good notices for his acting, in fact more so than for his directing this time.

"Mr. Eastwood's own performance sets a high water mark for laconic intelligence and makes the star seem youthfully spry by joking so much about his age," wrote Janet Maslin in the *New York Times*. "Without the heft or seriousness of recent Eastwood films, like *A Perfect World* or even *The Bridges of Madison County*, the more contrived *Absolute Power* is best watched for its strong cast, lively rejoinders, and moments of discreet panache," she continued in praise of some of the cast, while hitting some of them hard with "Once *Absolute Power* has introduced and discredited Mr. Hackman's President Alan Richmond, it doesn't know what else to do with him. Mr. Hackman languishes in the smallish role of a White House buffoon, with Judy Davis equally cartoonish as his witchy chief of staff."

Todd McCarthy of *Variety* wrote, "*Absolute Power* is a high-toned potboiler, a reasonably engrossing and entertaining suspenser for most of its running time that is undercut by too many coincidences and some whoppingly far-fetched developments in the home stretch. Clint Eastwood has delivered a clean, unfussy, and straightforward piece of old-fashioned narrative filmmaking . . . as Luther, Eastwood is in good, sly form, once again delighting in a character's splendid solitude and singular skill at what he does. A major improvement in his work, generally since *Unforgiven*, is that, unlike before, he now readily surrounds himself with other fine actors, who bring the pedigree of the films up several notches."

"Clint Eastwood's *Absolute Power* is a tight, taut thriller with a twist: it's also about a father and daughter, estranged for years, who are finally able to become friends. Most thrillers depend on chase scenes and shootouts. Some of the best scenes in *Absolute Power* involve dialogue. Eastwood as director is usually eclipsed by Eastwood the actor; he has directed almost 20 films good enough and successful enough to make him one of Hollywood's top filmmakers, and yet his stardom overshadows that role," stated Roger Ebert, writing in the *Chicago Sun-Times*.

"Sleek and satisfying, almost a drawing room thriller, unhurried and genteel, but enlivened with suspense and surprising bursts of sly, even biting, humor," wrote Kenneth Turan in the *Los Angeles Times*.

Desson Howe of the *Washington Post* probably understood the film better than any other major film critic. "*Absolute Power* is a hoot, a riot, a kick in the funny pants. Unfortunately these are not the qualities you seek in a Washington D.C. conspiracy thriller . . . the film devolves into such ludicrousness, the best response is to laugh . . . the only saving grace is Eastwood the actor who has a peculiar ability to glide through the worst of his films with his granite-hewn dignity intact."

Actor Ed Harris in 2008 told me that "working with Clint was like working with a well-oiled machine. He's got these guys he's worked with for so long. I mean, I honestly cannot remember working past 4 p.m. any single day.

"And we never did more than two takes," he recalled. "The man knows what he wants; he hires his actors, trusts us, and we're off to make a movie. He just is so clear in what he wants from us and himself."

The film was not a strong hit with audiences, though everyone who viewed the picture admitted to being impressed with Eastwood's continued growth as an actor. There was a gravity to his work that had not been present in his youth. There was something comfortable about him on screen; something real and honest. Yet Eastwood was becoming more and more disenchanted with acting, believing his place in film was now behind the camera. Though he would have one more great performance in him, he would soon be recognized more as a director than an actor.

He was about to enter the single most artistic and productive stage of his career as a filmmaker who would see three Academy Award nominations for best director, and one win come out of the next six films he directed.

Midnight in the Garden of Good and Evil (1997)

In the tradition of the great novels to explore the American South, John Berendt's *Midnight in the Garden of Good and Evil* (1994) brilliantly captures the flavor of the South in its portrayal of the characters and the town of Savannah, which is rich in history and culture. Mark Twain, Tennessee Williams, and William Faulkner had written extensively about the South and the characters from that area, educating and entertaining readers for more than 100 years, so when Berendt's book emerged, written in that same tradition, it was welcomed with open arms by a public that seemed to be waiting for it. For more than 220 weeks the book appeared on the *New York Times* best seller list, an extraordinary feat for a modern novel, and initially there was no need to even consider a paperback edition because readers were snapping up copies of the hardback, more than happy to pay the higher price.

Drawing on characters and themes familiar to readers of literature by those great writers, in Berendt's book were the familiar Southern touchstones, including grotesque characters, racial issues, gothic settings, North and South dichotomies, Southern heroes and belles, and those impeccable Southern manners that always seemed to hide something twisted and sexually sinister underneath. While Scarlett O'Hara may appear to be a lady, we know by now that steel exists under that pretty face and genteel upbringing, and it is no secret that black magic and voodoo is very much a practiced dark religion south of the Mason-Dixon Line. Tennessee Williams created a flawed Southern belle in Blanche du Bois in *A Streetcar Named Desire*, a lady clinging to the old South while struggling with the guilt of nymphomania, unable to come to terms with her illness and consumed with shame. So many characters from the South try to conceal what they really are, and the characters in *Midnight in the Garden of Good and Evil* are no exception.

Berendt spent five years in Savannah, without a publishing contract or book deal, to research the various characters surrounding Jim Williams, a well-to-do antique collector accused of murdering his lover. The more he and Williams got to know one another, the closer friends they became, yet there was little doubt that again, underneath the gentle and well-mannered exterior, a murderer's heart beat. Berendt wrote all of this down, including himself in the book's narrative, and within weeks of hitting the stands, the book became a runaway best seller, stunning the American publishing world. The moment there is any sort of buzz on a book about to be published, the natural instinct is to seek a movie deal, and though Berendt himself was not interested in a film version, his publishers were and actively sought one out. The novel was bought for the outrageously low price of 20 thousand dollars, though Berendt would make much more based on built-in incentives within the contract. Though asked to write the screenplay, the author deferred, believing he could not possibly capture what he had in the book and transfer that to cinema.

In the manner of Truman Capote's seminal nonfiction novel *In Cold Blood* (1966), which altered the face of modern American literature, Berendt's story was based on a true one, though he changed some of it for legal reasons. While Capote's book was a landmark piece of writing, Berendt's tended to be embraced more for being a great story with interesting characters than anything else. No one believes the work to be a soaring work of art like Capote's, but the similarities cannot be denied.

"People love the way the story transports them into the Savannah mindset," the author explained. "Everybody's life is like a work of art and is regarded that way. People gossip a lot, and the stranger an individual's behavior, the better the gossip about them. The people who are gossiped about know that they're appreciated for that reason, so it encourages them to be stranger."

John Lee Hancock was hired to adapt the massive book and streamline the story. The four trials within the story were condensed to one with many characters combined, and at least one character was created specifically for the film, a love interest for the Berendt character that was renamed Kelso. Hancock managed to keep the tone of the book within the film, believing the rest would be up to the director and actors to bring to life. Berendt, of course, and many others would later state that the book had been gutted, but no such complaints were heard initially.

Arnold Stiefel bought the book with Eastwood in mind for the role of Jim Williams, though Eastwood had no interest in the role at all. He already had read the screenplay written by John Lee Hancock who had penned *A Perfect World* (1993) for him years earlier.

By the time Eastwood's name was mentioned as Jim Williams, he had read the screenplay and was interested in directing the film. Despite having won the Academy Award and the Directors Guild of America Award for best director for *Unforgiven* (1992), he was not the first choice for the film. The producers were not convinced Eastwood had the "stuff" to direct the film and to bring the Southern eccentricities to the screen. However, Warner Brothers intervened, and within a few days Eastwood was given the assignment to direct it, though he had by then made clear he would not appear in the film, seeing no role for himself.

"I read the script before I read the book," he confessed, "and I thought it was just plain, good storytelling. That's what I want in a movie—storytelling. I didn't cast myself in it because, frankly, I didn't think I was right for any of the parts. I do feel that my best performances have been in movies I have directed. But the part wasn't there in this one," Eastwood told Mal Vincent of *The Virginian Post*.

Knowing the pressure on him to create a film based on a much-loved book, Eastwood made clear the fact he knew he was not filming the book as it was written.

"A movie is a different kind of storytelling. Moviemaking is a strange business. It's full of both fakery and intelligence. Sometimes the two mix," he explained in the same article. "The characters, who are interesting just because they are so diverse, and then in Savannah, a very unusual city which we wanted to make into a character in its own right," Eastwood stated. "This isn't the South the way it's portrayed most of the time, with an over-abundance of clichés. In Savannah you can encounter elderly black home-less women who perform voodoo rites at night in the cemeteries on behalf of people who are sophisticated, cultured, intelligent, and very much in the public view; people no one would ever think would ever be interested in sorcery.

"I think in the beginning, the stage of filmmaking I liked best was the editing. To work with just one or two people in the editing room, I loved that. I still do, but now I take more pleasure in the shooting itself. On every film, I discover something new; I want to try new things out. That's also why I loved making *Midnight in the Garden of Good and Evil*. This kind of story was something new for me. In fact I'd like to try out all the genres. I'd like to attempt every time to do something new," Eastwood explained.

The decision to shoot on location was a natural, and casting was relatively easy. Recent Academy Award winner Kevin Spacey won the plum role of Jim Williams, fresh from his win for his role as crime lord in *The Usual Suspects* (1995) and his brilliant cameo in *Seven* (1995). John Cusack was cast in the Berendt role as Kelso, while newcomer Jude Law would portray Billy Handon, the murdered lover of Williams. For the role of Mandy, the singer who catches Cusack's attention, Eastwood approached his daughter Alison, though he refused to play favorites and made her take a screen test.

"Last Christmas I was on holiday with him, and he said, 'I have this script. Would you read it and tell me what you think?' So I read it and liked the role of Mandy, but I never asked him if I could read for it, and he didn't lead me to believe there was a part for me. A couple of months later my agent called saying, 'You have an audition in a few days for this movie *Midnight in the Garden of Good and Evil*.' I said, 'Oh, that's my dad's film!' So I went in and read for it and was put on tape. He wasn't there, but I called him afterwards and said, 'I'd like to know what you thought.' I didn't hear anything for six weeks. Then I get a callback and went in and read again, but didn't hear anything for another month. Then my agent called and said, 'You go in next week for fittings.' I was ecstatic. I called my dad and said, 'This is going to be great—I can't wait to work with you.' Then it dawned on me; I had an incredible amount of work to do," explained the younger Eastwood to *Interview* magazine.

"The biggest challenge was to be true to my instinctual choices as an actress," she explained when asked about the challenges of the role. "I'm just starting out in this business and oftentimes as an actor, if you're not 100 percent confident about yourself, you tend to hold back or stay in a safe place. I wanted my performance to be natural, to have some color and strength, yet to be vulnerable and funny. I had to make sure I pushed my mind aside and just let my heart tell me what to do," she finished.

Kevin Spacey, a stage-trained actor, learned very quickly that on Eastwood's sets, the camera could be rolling at any time. Eastwood would call him and John Cusack in for a rehearsal, and often without knowing it, their rehearsal would be the master shot printed for the film. "You learned to be prepared at all times," he said with a smile. "Clint is the Zen master."

For the key role of Lady Chablis, the cross-dressing singer who plays a huge part in the book and film, Eastwood considered many actors in Hollywood before making the daring decision of casting the real thing. Though Lady Chablis had never acted in a film and had never done anything this important, suddenly he was cast in a Clint Eastwood film.

"Yes, I considered using an actor," Eastwood explained about the casting of Lady Chablis. "But a lot of times when you do drag in a movie, the actors camp it up, just go overboard with the lipstick and the women's clothing, and play up the comedic element of it. I wanted her to be just what she is. I met Chablis, and I saw a person who's rehearsed a particular role all her life. There's no reason to deny that, so I thought, 'Why not just let her roll?'

"I wasn't comfortable with Chablis at first," Eastwood boldly told the *Virginian Post*, "and I don't think she was entirely comfortable with making a movie, but she caught on fast. She's something of a chippy. I had to tell her to behave herself."

The film follows the story of Kelso (John Cusack), a writer for *Town and Country* magazine who is sent to Savannah to cover the Christmas party of Jim Williams (Kevin Spacey), a rich antique dealer whose parties have become one of the most sought after invites of the social year in old Savannah. Residing in the historical Mercer House, once home to the relatives of famous crooner Johnny Mercer, Williams holds court with his guests in the manner of the old masters of the plantations surrounding Savannah. After the party, Williams is apparently accosted by his lover, whom he shoots dead, leaving him charged with murder. Smelling a story, Kelso asks to be left on assignment and begins to follow the trial, studying all things Jim Williams, who may be a murderer but is a most charming one. Into the nightlife of Savannah he is drawn, where he encounters voodoo, sorcery, and the belief in all things evil, which to say the least startles the writer. Charmed by Williams, he slowly peels back the root of the story and comes to find that Williams is a homosexual, though not publicly, even though virtually everyone who knows him knows it, with the exception of his mother. One of the things bothering him most at the trial is that his mother may find out. The friendship between Williams and Kelso ends when Williams lies in court, thus getting off the murder charge and leaving the courtroom a free man. However, that night in his home, he suffers what appears to be a massive heart attack and drops dead on the floor, almost as though the spirits that walk the streets of Savannah had cursed him.

Like all Eastwood shoots, this one went without incident on location, and the film, the second of the year for Eastwood, was ready for the fall of '97 as Warner Brothers' major Oscar contender. Before the film was released, the campaign for Academy Awards attention had begun, but when the reviews began rolling in, the campaign's horns were quieted.

While most reviews were at least appreciative of the artistry with which the film was created, the consensus seemed to be that Eastwood's film was but a pale shadow of the dense and superbly detailed book. John Berendt made the foolish public statement thanking Eastwood for making a 50 million dollar commercial for his book, which enraged Eastwood and the executives at Warner Brothers to whom the author apologized, recognizing his arrogant mistake.

"*Midnight in the Garden of Good and Evil* is an outstanding, lean film trapped in a fat film's body. Clint Eastwood's screen version of John Berendt's phenomenally successful non-fiction tome about a sensational murder case in genteel, eccentric old Savannah vividly captures the atmosphere and memorable characters of the book. But the picture's aimless, sprawling structure and exceedingly leisurely pace finally come to weigh too heavily upon its virtues," wrote Todd McCarthy in *Variety*.

"Clint Eastwood's film is a determined attempt to be faithful to the book's spirit," wrote Roger Ebert in the *Chicago Sun-Times*, "but something is lost just by turning on the camera: Nothing we see can be as amazing as what we've imagined. In a way the filmmakers faced the same hopeless task as the adapters of Tom Wolfe's *The Bonfire of the Vanities*. The Berendt book, on best seller lists for three years, has made such an impression that any mere mortal version of it is doomed to pale. Perhaps only the documentarian Errol Morris, who specializes in the incredible variety of the human zoo, could have done justice to the material."

Perhaps the most stinging comments came from Owen Gleiberman in *Entertainment Weekly*. "By the time *Midnight in the Garden of Good and Evil* is over, it may send more than a few viewers scurrying off to the bookstore. They'll surely want to see what all the fuss was about."

"Listless, disjointed, and disconnected, this meandering two-hour and 30-minute exercise in futility will fascinate no one who doesn't have a blood relative among the cast or crew," penned Kenneth Turan for the *Los Angeles Times*.

The performance of Kevin Spacey drew the most praise for the film, and indeed Spacey was terrific, bringing to the role the smarmy, intellectual arrogance that quickly became his trademark. Hiding behind those manners and genteel attitudes, Williams really *is* the sort of man who can get away with murder, leaving Kelso walking away in disgust.

The Lady Chablis character drew some strong notices; however, one has to wonder if it was more because she did not ruin the film. Alison Eastwood was barely mentioned, not even for her singing on the film's soundtrack, which also was populated by Spacey and Clint Eastwood. Like the film, it seemed no one really noticed it.

21

True Crime (1999)

This crime thriller represents possibly the single greatest miscalculation of Eastwood's career as both an actor and a director in terms of his casting. Understand by that statement I do not mean that *True Crime* (1999) is the worst film of his career—it most certainly is not—but rather his choice of casting himself was a grave error.

At the age of 70, he chose to cast himself as Steve Everett, a rogue journalist with a past that haunts him and a confirmed horndog willing to bed virtually any woman he sees. He is a lousy husband and father, a drunk, and in the middle of an affair with his boss's wife that he does not even attempt to hide. Though once considered a great reporter, he is on the downside of his career, seeing most of it through a whiskey bottle. What is interesting about Everett is that deep down inside he knows he is a rotten father and husband, but he truly does not care. The issue is not that Eastwood was beyond playing the role. He certainly possesses the range, which he had proven in *Unforgiven* and again in *The Bridges of Madison County*, but rather the type of role it was and whether he ever asked himself if he was really the right actor for the part. Clearly written for a younger man, and Eastwood, for the first and only time in his career, miscast himself in the role, not seeming to see that his age had finally caught up to him. For one of the first times in his career, he looked sadly out of place in bed with a much younger woman, and when he hits on a pretty young thing at the film's end, he looks like a dirty old man, and frankly a little silly. One has to wonder why he did not step behind the camera and allow another to take the part, perhaps James Woods who was in the film, or Alec Baldwin, a vastly underappreciated actor.

"Richard and Lilli Zanuck had the project and sent it to me. I read it and thought it was a very interesting story," he explained. It was the character of Steve Everett that drew Eastwood to the project.

"The character I play, Steve Everett, is a guy who's on the road to self-destruction. This job he's got is his last shot. He's been slowly demoted through the ranks of journalism to where he's now working, a smaller newspaper in a small city. His life is all screwed up. He destroyed his marriage, and he's jeopardizing his relationship with his daughter. He believes a man on death row is innocent so he goes on a tangent," the actor explained to Robert J. Emery.

"Though he has a family that adores him, he can't . . . that doesn't seem to be enough. He has to destroy it, and the thing that makes the story interesting is that the victim who is falsely accused, at least we think he is, is very much a family man who is trying to keep his family in order and do all the things our hero isn't," he continued. "But our hero's tenacity sort of carries him through to make him successful. Even though in the end he's not a totally successful person, he seems to have accomplished what he wanted to do, his doubts about this person's guilt," finished Eastwood.

The screenplay was based on the book by Andrew Klavan, which in turn was based on a true story of a newspaper reporter who helped a man prove his innocence of a crime for which he had been convicted. Ray Herndon was a reporter working in Dallas, Texas, when he received a letter from an inmate in prison proclaiming his innocence, which the writer took with a grain of salt, knowing not an inmate alive admits to the crime. But his research into the crime put a hook in Herndon, and as he dug further, he found that the inmate was indeed very likely innocent of killing a store clerk because he had been miles away when the crime took place. The key to the case was finding a truck driver, known only as Kangaroo, who had given the convict a ride that night to get to his sons in St. Louis. That and that alone would provide him with his alibi. Through his extraordinary efforts and extensive research, Herndon was able to locate Kangaroo and overturn the conviction, thus freeing an innocent man. For his efforts, Herndon was awarded the Pulitzer Prize, the highest honor in professional journalism.

One can understand why Eastwood the actor would find the character of Steve Everett interesting to portray, as he is a man seeking redemption for the mistakes in his life (though he may be unaware of it), and trying to find some decency in his life to perhaps justify the manner in which he has allowed his marriage to fall apart. Perhaps ashamed of his actions towards his family, he sees a chance to allow another to remain together. However, it becomes problematic as to why Eastwood as a director, believed he was the best choice for the role. Obviously confident of his skills as an actor, it would be difficult for any producer or studio chief to second-guess the actor, yet casting himself would prove the weakness of this film.

Everett is a writer for a small, insignificant newspaper, formerly a hotshot for the *New York Times*, who has made far too many major mistakes in his career and life. We first encounter him in his favorite hangout, a bar, where he is putting the moves on a much younger woman who is more than a tad bored by him. The death of a colleague and friend lands him a death row interview, where he will first encounter the Beachum family. Frank Beachum (Isaiah Washington), by all accounts an upstanding citizen, has been convicted to die of lethal injection for the murder of a store clerk, though he and his family have always maintained his innocence. Everett's colleague also believed in Beachum's innocence and had been researching the investigation for quite some time before her death. With his career on the line, Everett knows he cannot ruin this chance and is warned by his editor that indeed he is on shaky ground at the paper.

When this selfish, self-absorbed writer encounters the Beachum family for the first time, he is deeply affected and stunned by what he encounters. This tightly knit family, even in this darkest of times, is filled with love and affection for one another. With his writer's nose, Everett recognizes that something about the case is off, not right, and begins his own investigation, working against the clock to prove the man's innocence. Following his dead colleague's tracks, he tries to gain an understanding of why she, like he, believed Beachum was innocent. Interviewing witnesses that already have been spoken with, poring over police files and reports, and exploring unturned leads, Everett finds a fact that everyone has missed and races against time to save the man.

But this is where we really have to suspend our disbelief as an audience and accept the conceit that Everett would find what police investigators and lawyers would miss, that his colleague had not found yet, and somehow, with near superhuman ability, prove the man's innocence all in a 24-hour span. He must do all these things and still attempt to live his life. So close does he cut it, that the death sentence has begun and the first injection administered when the phone rings in the death room to stop the killing of Beachum.

In the next scene Everett is back to his old ways, trying to pick up a pretty young girl played by a pre–*Kill Bill* Lucy Liu who knows and is impressed that he has been nominated for a Pulitzer Prize for his efforts in freeing Beachum. Leaving the store, he spots Beachum together with his family, and they gently acknowledge each other with a nod, before moving on to their lives.

Again, it takes a great leap of faith to believe everything we are asked to accept in this film, and the critics had a difficult time doing that.

"Say it ain't so Clint. Please tell me that tired old man, directing his tired old self in a tired old flick, is not the real Clint Eastwood but some rank imposter," wrote Rick Groen of the *Globe and Mail*. "As an actor, of course, Eastwood has always possessed what might be charitably described as a narrow range. But as a director, he's often been able to transform those same minimal instincts into a visual asset, giving his best work an elliptical and sparse efficient quality, a keen edge. Yet here, both before and behind the camera, he just seems to have lost it."

"It's a gritty story made in the director's more elegiacal mode; a confusion of style and content that is not in the film's best interests," wrote Kenneth Turan in the *Los Angeles Times*.

Not all the reviews were as harsh, though, with Todd McCarthy of *Variety* weighing in with "Clint Eastwood's latest picture boasts tight storytelling, sharp acting, and an eye for the unexpected, enlivening detail that spells strong viewer involvement and solid early spring box office among adult mainstream audiences. . . . Eastwood takes evident delight in applying the fine brush strokes to his portrait of a sympathetic but amoral scoundrel."

Roger Ebert, writing as always for the *Chicago Sun-Times,* stated, "*True Crime* has a nice rhythm, intercutting the character's problems at home, his interviews with the prisoner, his lunch with a witness, his unsettling encounter with the grandmother of another witness. And then, as the midnight hour of execution draws closer, Eastwood tightens the noose of inexorably mounting tension."

There were strong performances given by Washington as the convicted Beachum, and, best of all, Lisa Gay Hamilton as his anguished wife who knows in the pit of her gut her husband is incapable of killing someone. Best known for her work on television's *The Practice,* she gave a ferocious performance that outshone her better-known costars. James Woods, as always, is great fun to watch, while Dennis Leary was given so little to do it was criminal. Diane Venora, who was so fine for Eastwood in *Bird,* was wasted as his wife, leaving us to ponder why she even took the role.

Critics were split on their opinions, though the general consensus was that the film was among the weakest of Eastwood's career. It did tepid business and is rarely discussed when one discusses the films of Eastwood. In fact, all it has in common with his other work is that his character, like so many other Eastwood characters, is haunted by his past actions, dogged by his history, and seeks some form of redemption.

2000 AND BEYOND

22

Space Cowboys (2000)

"Team Daedalus was a bunch of guys who were ahead of their time in the fifties," explained Eastwood. "They had the pioneering mentality. They pioneered early spaceflight, breaking through the sound barriers and going up to the substratosphere. Chuck Yeager and the other great pilots of the fifties never actually got into space, but they wanted it badly. And when they were ready to go, and the whole world was ready to see them go, they got replaced by a monkey."

"Cowboys were the pioneers of the American frontier. The new frontier is space, so astronauts are the cowboys of space. So it's timely. And when Warner Brothers gave me this script, I could see right away it was a story about four old guys who blackmail their way into a chance they missed 40 years ago. This movie deals with the Americans and Russians cooperating in space," Eastwood told Prairie Miller. "I actually started working on *Space Cowboys* before NASA sent John Glenn back into space. I like to say that NASA heard we were making this movie and decided to send Glenn up there to give us some credibility. It certainly proved convenient for us that he made the trip. It proved a person in decent shape could go up there and perform."

Films exploring the American space program had been rare on movie screens, with just two high-profile films to speak of since 1983, only one of which found an audience in movie theaters. Ironically Phillip Kaufman, the man Eastwood had fired from *The Outlaw Josey Wales* (1976), directed and cowrote *The Right Stuff* (1983), an American masterpiece about the Mercury space program and the first astronauts, John Glenn, and his partners. The film had been released in the summer of 1983, facing off against mindless blockbusters such as *Trading Places* (1983), *Flashdance* (1983), and the third installment of the Star Wars trilogy, *Return of the Jedi* (1983), and while bearing some substance, never had a chance. Filmed like a glorious epic, the film was many things, including an adventure, a biography, a science fiction thriller, and knockout entertainment on every level, leaving the entertainment world stunned when it failed at the box office after receiving rave reviews from North American film critics. Nominated for seven Academy Awards, the film won four in the technical categories and is now, years later, considered one of the great American films of the decade, and stands as one of the greatest American films ever made.

Twelve years later the electrifying *Apollo 13* (1995) was widely considered the best film of the year before *Braveheart* (1995) swooped in and collected the Oscars for best film and director. Released in the summer to extraordinary reviews, *Apollo 13* was directed by Ron Howard, who drew enormous suspense out of an event to which most audiences knew the ending, giving moviegoers a tension-filled work that kept them on the edge of their seats throughout the picture. Superbly acted by Tom Hanks, Kevin Bacon, Bill Paxton, and in particular Ed Harris, the film was the picture perfect mixture of blockbuster and masterpiece, which was something quite rare in movies after the seventies. The Academy of Motion Picture Arts and Sciences, in their infinite wisdom, nominated the film for nine awards, but snubbed the creative force behind the picture, Ron Howard. Despite the fact that he was not nominated for an Oscar, Howard did win the Directors Guild of America Award for his work, which considering the lack of an Oscar nomination was astounding, though just.

The screenplay for *Space Cowboys* (2000), by Ken Kaufman and Howard Klausner, had begun initially as an idea from producer Andrew Lazar who thought it might be interesting to see a film about aging astronauts finally getting their chance to go into space after being passed over. Kaufman, who had written *The Muppets in Space* (1994), took the idea and ran with it, bringing in longtime friend Klausner to work on the script with him.

"Just to see Clint Eastwood and Tommy Lee Jones becoming these people you created was the main reason to do this job," smiled Klausner. "And the guys are such icons, starting with Clint Eastwood," smiled Kaufman in discussing the film. "Just having the fortitude to work on a project with someone like him who was a hero for both of us growing up; then to actually be involved in an artistic endeavor with this giant is really remarkable. To have him trust ideas we would come up with—we had to pinch ourselves."

"These guys are the keys to getting this done on time and on budget. They've seen it all," Eastwood explained to *The Boston Globe*. "And they have reputations as guys who just come to work to do this job with a minimal amount of screwing around. Like a lot of other older guys, they're not fighting any insecurities. They reminded me of a friend of mine when we were sitting around talking one time. He told me, 'You know there's one good thing about being past 60. When you get this far what else can you do? It doesn't matter what anyone says; it doesn't matter what anybody does. You can just do what you want and do it for yourself.'"

Eastwood knew going into *Space Cowboys* that the effects would tax him, having gone through the nightmare that *Firefox* (1982) became. Knowing he lacked the patience to do a film in which two or three shots were completed a day, Eastwood consulted with effects artists to understand exactly what was required to make the film the way he wanted. There had been massive advancements in the art and technology of visual effects since 1982, largely through computer-generated images, in which effects are composed within a computer and blown up for the big screen. They first made their appearance as a visual effect tool in *The Abyss* (1989), *Terminator 2: Judgment Day* (1991), and *Jurassic Park* (1993). Later entire films were created within the computer with *Toy Story* (1995), *Shrek* (2001), and *Monsters Inc.* (2001). These new effects allowed the creators to do anything, later astounding audiences when used in Peter Jackson's triumphant *The Lord of the Rings* trilogy and his underappreciated remake of *King Kong* (2005). Assured the effects would not compromise the story, Eastwood moved on with production. It was essential to the director that the film remain character driven and that the story be at the forefront, not the effects.

"We've all watched movies change a lot in the last decade or two. We've gotten away from storytelling and into a lot of razzle-dazzle, probably due to the fact there is so much fantastic technology out there," he explained to *Urban Cinefile.* "You can put computer-generated characters into a movie. . . . It works terrifically, but sometimes the toys start running the factory and that's what has happened now. I think people have fallen in love with the toys, in my opinion anyways, and the consciousness of the stories and the writers have been set aside as a secondary part of production in favor of more razzle-dazzle. I'm not sure if that is the demands of the audience, the MTV generation, or whether it's just newer directors being raised on television and with computers and that has become the most dominant factor for them."

To the visual effects artists and the artists operating the computers, Eastwood made it very clear that he was interested first and foremost in the story. As important as the effects were in making the film realistic, without a strong story he had nothing and he knew that better than anyone.

With the full support of NASA, the American space agency, in itself a huge accomplishment, Eastwood would be able to shoot segments of the film at the Johnson Space Center in Houston, Texas, and others at Cape Canaveral, which is part of the Kennedy Space Center near Cocoa Beach, Florida. Used as the site of the launches for all spacecraft, including the space shuttle, the Kennedy Space Center is both an operational government facility under high security as well as one of Florida's top tourist attractions.

"We were very lucky to have NASA helping us out with almost everything. And we had astronauts who had been in space visiting us on the set all the time. Sometimes they would come up and say, 'Well, we wouldn't say that,'" Eastwood told Prairie Miller. "Without NASA's help, this film would have been more expensive and far less accurate. They couldn't have given us more assistance on this project."

Having just come off three consecutive adaptations of novels, Eastwood was thrilled to be working on an original script with some basis in reality.

Astronaut and one-time presidential hopeful John Glenn, one of the Mercury astronauts and the first American to orbit the earth, had been sent into space on the space shuttle at the age of 77, perhaps being the inspiration for the film. The picture would allow actors of an advanced age to have plum roles in a film that was story driven, with the characters being the most exciting quality of the script, although strong effects were needed to capture the realism Eastwood sought. As always, he went for the best cast available, with the screenplay needs allowing him to go after some people he had admired for years and had wanted to work with for a very long time.

Eastwood would portray team leader Frank Corvin, and Oscar winner Tommy Lee Jones, one of the greatest character actors of his generation, would portray Hawk Hawkins, a daring test pilot who is willing to risk his life to push the envelope on the performance of whatever aircraft he is piloting. An aggressive pilot, the military considers him a high risk. When he joins Eastwood's team of elderly astronauts, he does not divulge the fact that he has cancer and is dying.

Canadian actor Donald Sutherland, one of the busiest actors working in movies and vastly underappreciated, was cast as Jerry, the astrophysicist, ladies' man, and wise guy, who keeps the others amused with his antics. As the fourth member of the team, James Garner was cast as Tank Sullivan. Eastwood and Garner had worked together years earlier on television when both were young actors on the way up. Garner was a major TV star on *Maverick*, making the odd film here and there over the course of his career. In 1985 he was nominated for an Academy Award for best actor for his sensitive performance in *Murphy's Romance* (1985) with Sally Field. Garner was cast as a man who has found God after his life in the military and becomes a minister in a small town, living a peaceful life.

"It's a terrific cast," smiled Eastwood. "They are people whose work I've always admired. I worked with Jimmy years ago when we were both starting out in one of his *Maverick* episodes, and I've known him for years."

"If any of these guys had turned me down, I wouldn't have done the film. If they had refused, we just wouldn't have done the picture," Eastwood stated clearly and with customary brutal honesty.

James Cromwell was cast as Bob Gerson, the nemesis of the team and the man who grounded them so long ago but who needs them now; and Marcia Gay Harden would portray NASA mission director Sara Holland, a love interest for Jones.

The actors were put through the same training as the astronauts would go through before being sent into space, including the shuttle simulator, the shuttle simulator control booth, the virtual reality room, and the neutral buoyancy lab.

"I wanted to make the film as believable as possible," Eastwood explained. "In order to do that, we needed NASA's help to get as close as we could to the circumstances surrounding a launch. It's a complicated process, and it requires careful planning and teamwork on all levels. Bringing a film crew in to simulate the whole thing was probably an even bigger headache for NASA, but the agency really came through for us. I couldn't be more pleased with the results."

"We've done it, I suppose in every way it can be done," mused Tommy Lee Jones after the filming. "We've hung people from ceilings. We've had people stand around holding onto walls as if that were necessary to keep yourself from floating off, and then we have had ballpoint pens and clipboards floating by suspended filament lines. We've been on little stools that have casters to move them around. It really presents no challenge to an actor; all you have to do is stand there and take these various rides, but it's a group effort for the whole company."

To experience the weightlessness of space, Eastwood and his cast, like Ron Howard and his cast for *Apollo 13*, went up in what is known as the Vomit Comet, a giant cargo plane that allows those on board to be weightless for a few seconds, with all the bizarre results.

Many of the sequences in space combined the use of miniature spaceships photographed using motion-controlled cameras, digitally painted backgrounds, computer graphics astronauts, and live action actors. The integration of these new and old techniques actually mirrored the story within the film, as the old dinosaurs were suddenly thrust into a brand new world of technology and science that had been invented while they had been retired.

The film opens in the past as young actors portray the roles of the older men, yet speak with the voices of Eastwood, Garner, Jones, and Sutherland, as they go through their nightmare of crashing yet another plane that will end their dream of going to the moon. Years later, long after the men have retired, NASA comes calling when a Russian satellite suffers a system breakdown that the Russians insist will cause a complete communications breakdown in their country should it not be repaired. Gerson stumbles onto the solution of sending the members of Team Daedalus into space to repair the satellite. With the system having the same guidance system as the early American satellite Skylab, the designer of the Skylab, Frank Corvin, should know how to fix it. Offered this chance, Frank (Eastwood) is stunned to think that after all these years he can finally go into space. He agrees with a single condition— that he be permitted to reassemble his old team to go with them. Going through the extraordinary training for space travel hits the older men hard, yet they stun the administration by doing everything asked of them, passing training with flying colors. The younger men sent on the mission with them are a tad resentful they are sharing the shuttle with men they consider to be dinosaurs, but the two groups gradually develop a mutual respect. Upon arriving at the satellite, they discover to their horror that the instrument is armed with nuclear missiles, suddenly making the mission a matter of national security and its success all the more vital. The men are, without warning, thrown onto the stage of world politics where their work could determine the future of the United States, much to their cha-grin and the embarrassment of Bob, who knew the entire time what they were going to find when they got there. The story takes a dramatic turn, leading to the sacrifice of one of the team, who selflessly gives his life for the greater good yet oddly is able to accomplish something in his death he never could in life. The last image of the film, haunting in its quiet power, shows Tommy Lee Jones's character on the moon—dead, but finally on the moon—achieving in death what he could not in life. The song on the soundtrack is Bobby Darin's *Fly Me to the Moon*, which earlier in the film, 40 years previous, Jones's character sang as they saw the outreaches of space beyond the stratosphere.

Opening in the late summer, the film provided Eastwood with his strongest opening up to that date, with more than $18 million at the box office. Those were impressive numbers for a summer film that was story driven and in which actors over 50 starred. Though Eastwood remained popular with movie audiences, his box office appeal had slipped measurably over the years, while neither Jones, Sutherland, nor Garner had ever had box office appeal, but rather were recognized for their substantial gifts as actors.

Critics liked the film, finding in it a film that was both an adventure and exciting, with enough of a story to give it substance and strength. Eastwood had not allowed the visual effects to overpower the actors or the story, but rather guided the effects to enhance the film and the story, which is precisely what good effects should do.

"Mr. Eastwood is ordinarily a rather earthbound director, more interested in the efficient (and somewhat graceless) conveyance of story and character than in visual beauty, but here, the special effects by Industrial Light and Magic add depth and richness to the movie without distracting from the greater pleasure of watching four great actors reclaim their prime," cele-brated A.O. Scott in the *New York Times*. "Over the course of his directing career, Mr. Eastwood has quietly advanced a revisionist notion of masculinity, a critique from within of the brutal individualism that made him famous as an actor. His films explore the possibility that the best parts of the old code of manly virtue—loyalty, good humor, a certain reckless bravado—might be retained even as its less attractive features are abandoned."

"While his overlong *Space Cowboys* is not a portrait of cinematic perfec-tion, it is consistently engaging, features likable irascible characters, and does not descend into the shoot-and-scoot idiocy that has marked far too many outer space endeavors," wrote Jami Berardinelli with plucky honesty at *ReelViews.com*.

Roger Ebert of the *Chicago Sun-Times* liked the film, but also noted its shortcomings, stating, "Great swatches of *Space Cowboys* are constructed, indeed, out of generic expectations. But the stuff in outer space is unex-pected, the surprise waiting out there is genuine, and meanwhile there is an abundance of charm and screen presence from the four veteran actors. There is a reason Eastwood, Garner, Sutherland, and Jones have remained stars for so long, and the movie gives them all the characteristic scenes. *Space Cowboys* lacks the urgency of *The Right Stuff*—it's too secure within its traditional story structure to make much seem at risk—but with the structure comes the traditional pleasures as well."

"So breezy and half-hearted that it barely exists, Clint Eastwood's new film is nevertheless a welcome change from his prior triptych of strained melodramas. Calling the movie light is an understatement, calling it weightless is also on the nose. But it is impossible to deny that it does indeed have a certain charm, and it's no surprise from whence it came," wrote David Luty for Screen International, pointing to the film's weaknesses (in his opinion), but also its obvious strengths.

"This is the stuff of geezer comedy and throughout the middle section of the movie, it is a superior example of this rather worn-out genre. There's a lot more going on, however, with some real pros—including Tommy Lee Jones, Donald Sutherland, and James Garner—who know how to bring it off. As *Space Cowboys* progresses from comedy to adventure to fable about settling old grudges, Eastwood does something amazing. He not only sidesteps the trap of turning himself into an old fool, he reasserts himself as the movie icon audiences for decades have come to expect," raved Bob Graham in the *San Francisco Gate*, perhaps understanding the film better than any other critic in North America.

Kenneth Turan of the *Los Angeles Times* praised the film, and Eastwood, for telling a story with older characters and allowing them to be older characters. "It's also pleasant to see a movie where—shall we say—mature stars work with, instead of trying to hide, their age. The Ken Kaufman and Howard Klausner script includes numerous *The Ripe Stuff* references to bad eyes, false teeth, and friends who have died. Where Eastwood's character once said things like "Go ahead, make my day," he now mutters, 'I've got Medicaid, take your best shot,' when ruffians cross his path. No actor, with the possible exception of Paul Newman, has aged better on film than Eastwood, who turned 70 in May, and whose lined and weathered face makes Mount Rushmore look like the Pillsbury Doughboy."

The film was a grand entertainment from beginning to end, which is precisely what Eastwood was going for. He did not want to make any sort of statement about politics, the arms race, the Cold War, or even aging for that matter (and he did not), but rather a film that thoroughly entertained audiences with its story of four old warriors who finally through a fluke get their chance to go into space.

Watching the four actors together in the film was the greatest special effect anyone could have hoped for.

23

Blood Work (2002)

With the strong box office success of *Space Cowboys* (2000), his first major box office hit in some years, Eastwood again turned to the written word for his next film, finding himself interested in the book *Blood Work* (1998) by author Michael Connelly. It would be a crime thriller, which concerned Warner Brothers after the tepid reception of *True Crime* (1999), *Absolute Power* (1997), and *Midnight in the Garden of Good and Evil* (1997). Eastwood assured the studio the film would be much different than *True Crime*, even though in fairness, *True Crime* had many admirers and, like *Blood Work* (2002), was essentially a detective story in that the narrative focused on finding a killer.

What he seemed to like most about *Blood Work* was the fact that the lead role was of a man struggling to find himself after a heart transplant that has forced him to retire from his job as a Federal Bureau of Investigations profiler. Now 72, Eastwood was aware that audiences would not accept him as anything less than such, and so for the first time in his career he would play close to his age.

"As an actor, you have two philosophies; one is that you are afraid to let go of what you once were, or you are not afraid but you have to let go anyway," he explained in *Urban Cinefile*. "I have no other choice. They don't make enough shoe polish for my hair, and they don't have a belt sander for my face! At some point you have to say, 'This is who I am, and this is an opportunity to play roles that I couldn't play before.' I couldn't play that vulnerability factor 30 years ago. You have to view it as an opportunity and not worry about it. If your ego is to the point where you always have to look like a matinee idol, it'd be over. I always thought of myself as a character actor, even though some people viewed me as a leading man.

"You know it's very difficult to figure out why you do any project—at this particular time the script seemed like an interesting detective story with a degree of vulnerability, both physically and psychologically, for the guy to overcome," explained Eastwood. "Any time an actor can find a role where there's more than obstacles to overcome, then it becomes a much more interesting project, rather than just a guy solving a case or chasing around a villain."

FBI profiler Terry McCaleb is on the trail of an infamous serial killer known as the Code Killer, when he is stricken with a massive heart attack that will end his career. Flashing ahead two years, luckily doctors have been able to perform a heart transplant, but he is now unable to work, slowly recuperating from the life-altering and life-giving surgery. Watched closely by his cardiologist Dr. Bonnie Fox (Anjelica Huston), he is on the mend, though frustrated with the 34 pills he is taking daily, the very real fear that his body may still reject the donor heart, and the restrictions Fox is trying to enforce upon him. He instead spends a great deal of time on his boat hanging out with his friend Buddy Noone (Jeff Daniels), a lazy though likable man, who has had a far greater impact on McCaleb's life than the retired cop realizes.

Into his life comes Graciella Rivers (Wanda De Jesus) who has heard about McCaleb's mastery of investigative talents and wants to ask him to help her. Her sister Grace was recently killed, the victim of a murder who seemingly was in the wrong place at the wrong time. With the police getting nowhere, she wants McCaleb to look at the case and see where he can get with it. Initially, McCaleb refuses, knowing the state of his body and the fact that he must take things easy so as not to stress the new heart beating within him, but his mind is forever changed when he is told that the heart keeping him alive is that of Grace, the murdered sister.

As he digs into the killing, he is met with furious opposition from Mexican cop Ronaldo Arrango (Paul Rodriguez), who seems to hate McCaleb just for being McCaleb, yet finds support in Jaye Winston (Tina Lifford).

McCaleb and Graciella become close friends and then lovers, as he continues to explore the murder of her sister, becoming increasingly close to the dead woman's son, now in the care of Graciella.

The further he digs into the case, the more frustrated he becomes with the lack of help from the police force and his own physical limitations. However, a chance glance at a check will answer all his questions, and he realizes the man he seeks, both the killer of Grace and the Code Killer he has long been seeking, is his neighbor Buddy Noone. However, when he confronts Buddy about this, he does so with the knowledge that the killer has snatched Graciella and the boy, hiding them somewhere from where they cannot escape, with just him holding the answer as to their whereabouts. Despite the taunts from Noone, McCaleb shoots him, wounding him, and demands that he be taken to them. Noone does so, leading McCaleb to a rundown barge that he calls his own "little shop of horrors." On the way there, McCaleb gains insight into the twisted mind of Noone, who believes that he and McCaleb are friends forever and somehow linked by these deeds of murder, which include Grace, whom Noone claims he gave to McCaleb. The killer goes so far as to state he gave McCaleb life by killing Grace.

The shootout on the barge ends with Graciella holding Noone's face underwater and drowning him, exacting the revenge she so desperately needed to atone for her sister's death.

Audiences seeing Jeff Daniels in the film were startled by the character he portrays, in particular when it becomes clear he is the killer Eastwood has been seeking all those years. Daniels had broken through with a performance in *Terms of Endearment* (1983) and *Something Wild* (1986), and since then had become popular as a sort of "every man" in films. He was never a hero but never anything less than a reliable and very fine character actor. A stage-trained actor, adept at both comedy and drama, Daniels proved he could handle lead roles with ease, but seemed better used as the character actor in strong support of the leading man. He was outstanding for Woody Allen in *The Purple Rose of Cairo* (1985), but even with that acclaimed performance, he never broke through as a full-fledged star. His work in Disney films made him very recognizable, and his performance as Ontario artist Bill Lishman in *Fly Away Home* (1996) made him enormously popular with young audiences. For every box office hit, such as the spider thriller *Arachnophobia* (1990), there was a *101 Dalmatians* (1996) or an *RV* (2006). His work in the Civil War epic *Gods and Generals* (2003) received rave reviews, noted for being by far the most moving element of the film, and strong reviews came for his performance in *Pleasantville* (1998). In the years after *Blood Work*, his first role as a bonafide villain, Daniels was nothing less than astonishing in *The Squid and the Whale* (2005) as the father in a dysfunctional family struggling with a divorce. Eastwood felt Daniels was among the finest actors he had worked with, and did not hesitate to cast him as a killer in the film despite the fact that he had never played one.

"You know Jeff Daniels can play a wide variety of roles. He's very underrated on the American scene, capable of complete buffoonery in *Dumb and Dumber* (1994)," Eastwood explained on the special features section of the *Blood Work* DVD, "or very serious, bordering on psychotic, roles. He's got the scale and scope that makes him very interesting. I've been a fan of his work for years. He is one of the lowest-maintenance actors I have ever worked with. He was always there and always ready to go."

Daniels had met Eastwood years before at the Pebble Beach Pro-Am when, much to Daniels's shock, Eastwood walked straight over to him and told him how much he liked *Dumb and Dumber*.

"It was not the words you expect to hear coming out of Clint Eastwood's mouth," smiled Daniels in remembrance. "He really enjoyed what improvisation we did do," explained Daniels in the *New York Times*. "There's stuff that never made it into the movie where he would start doing things like he was thinking he was in *Dumb and Dumber*. I'm bouncing back with him, and he's having a ball. So there I am as the funny sidekick, but I think I was also on the set for entertainment purposes. "He wants it to happen the first time," explained Daniels in discussing Eastwood's directing style. "He wants that initial attack so once you figure out that's what he's looking for, you learn not to pre-plan everything but to be open and react. You may shoot the rehearsal, or you may shoot one take. I've been with other directors where it's been 25 or 30 takes. But if you're on take three with Clint, he'll turn and apologize for taking so long."

Academy Award winner Anjelica Huston, whose father Eastwood had portrayed in *White Hunter Black Heart* (1990), saw many similarities between Eastwood and the legendary John Huston, which led to high praise for Eastwood.

"*Blood Work* was one of the more relaxed, extremely operational, and good-humored sets that I've ever been on, and I think that's due to the fact so many of the crew have worked with Clint for many years. There's a kind of shorthand between them and a wonderful camaraderie and interest in the work," she explained. "Also," she continued, "Clint's a funny guy and he keeps everyone in a good mood. He makes it look simple. My father had an expression whenever I came to him with big questions, which was: "Just do it, honey." And Clint seems to just do it beautifully. I spent many years with my father in Intensive Care Units and watched him undergo a heart aneurysm operation. He was not well for the last 12 years of his life. So the combination of my experience with my father (an Oscar in *Prizzi's Honor*) in the hospital and Clint having played him in *White Hunter Black Heart* was strangely convergent. In terms of the man Clint is, his way of being, his ease and calm, reminds me a lot of my father. He has a wonderful way of slow talking and slow moving that just makes you feel right at home. His style really lends itself to a relaxation on set that is tremendously useful and calming for an actor, particularly when you come in nervous to work with Mr. Eastwood."

Eastwood, choosing to portray his age, gave a solid performance as a man being betrayed by his own body—at the beginning suffering a near fatal heart attack, and then later in the film weakened by a heart transplant, struggling to stay healthy, still fragile but obsessed with finding the killer because he knows in his gut they are linked. The firm belief that he owes the memory of the dead woman whose heart now keeps him alive burns bright in his eyes throughout the film. The moment he gets that knowledge, we can see the eyes change and a shift in his very being. Suddenly he has found a reason, which is to find the killer of the woman whose very death and whose murder gave him life. Can one even begin to imagine the guilt that the recipient of a heart harvested in this manner would feel? It is that guilt that fuels the obsession that drives McCaleb, and the very thing that no doubt put the hook in Eastwood for the story.

Blood Work would mark the last film of a weak period in Eastwood's career, which would be followed by four consecutive masterpieces, three of which would earn Academy Award nominations for best picture, one of which would win him his second Academy Award for best director, and the reasons Eastwood is now among the greatest living directors in modern film.

24

Mystic River (2003)

Clint Eastwood is the least disappointing American icon.

—Sean Penn

In the years since winning the Academy Award for best director and best film for *Unforgiven* (1992), which also won Eastwood the coveted Directors Guild Award for outstanding achievement in direction, his output of films had ranged from the excellent, with *A Perfect World* (1993) and *The Bridges of Madison County* (1995), to the erratic, with *Midnight in the Garden of Good and Evil* (1997). Yet even when a film failed, as some did, Eastwood was growing considerably as a filmmaker, honing his storytelling skills and work with actors. While both *A Perfect World* (1993) and *The Bridges of Madison County* (1995) deserved far more attention than each received, it is a fact of life in the film business that some films need time to allow their greatness to be seen. In many ways *Mystic River* (2003) would be a comeback of sorts for Eastwood.

After reading a book review for Dennis Lehane's novel *Mystic River* (2001), Eastwood became interested in the novel, believing it might make a good film. He read the book and immediately believed that he could make a fine film out of the dark parable so beautifully created on the pages by Lehane. He hired Brian Helgeland to write the screenplay and began the process of finding his actors. "I've always been fascinated with the stealing of innocence. It's the most heinous crime and certainly a capital crime if there ever was one," Eastwood explained. "I think anything to do with crime against children is something strong in my mind. So it was that that attracted me to do the story, the fact it comes back in adulthood and things just keep coming around," he stated.

Eastwood also believed that this "street opera" might be a fine piece for actors, as it brilliantly merged the classic elements of Greek tragedy and Shakespearean tragedy with the modern elements of today's cinema.

The first and only person Eastwood approached for the key role of Jimmy Markum, the father who loses his daughter to murder, was Sean Penn, who read the script and committed with a simple "I'm in." Eastwood had long wanted to work with Penn, who was widely considered the greatest screen actor of his generation and certainly the most purely talented. There was a purity in Penn's acting, something that was seen in the early work of Marlon Brando, as though he were speaking the lines for the very first time and totally immersing himself in the character until all trace of the person, of Sean Penn, was gone. Penn had established himself through the eighties and nineties as a major force in the acting world, but was often in trouble with the law due to his hot temper, which made him prone to snapping and landed him in hot water. He spent time in jail in the eighties for an assault on a photographer, and remained as surly as ever. His performance in *Dead Man Walking* (1995) earned him his first Academy Award nomination, and though he lost the Oscar, many felt he should have won the award for his electrifying performance directed by Tim Robbins, who would actually allow the audience to feel sympathy for a repellant character. Ironically, Robbins would join the Eastwood cast as Dave Boyle, the adult living with the memory of being molested as a child.

To gain a frame of reference for how extraordinary an actor Penn is, one only has to view *Fast Times at Ridgemont High* (1982), in which he portrayed Spicoli, the stoned surfer dude who defined a generation of eighties filmgoers. Was it possible that the same actor could follow this performance with the one in *The Falcon and the Snowman* (1983), surpass that one in *At Close Range* (1986), and continue the amazing trajectory into *Dead Man Walking* (1995)? It is virtually impossible to connect the actor Penn with Spicoli, that goofy, surf-loving student who orders pizza to class and is genuinely hurt when his teacher fails to understand, or with any character he has portrayed since with. That he became an actor willing to explore such dark areas of the soul was something of a surprise to anyone who saw and admired that early film. Penn alone seems the heir apparent to Brando, and certainly is the only working actor who seems to possess Brando's gifts.

Kevin Bacon would portray the detective investigating the murder, his partner portrayed by Laurence Fishburne, while Laura Linney would portray Penn's wife, and Marcia Gay Harden would take the role of Celeste, Dave's wife.

The shoot in Boston was like all Eastwood shoots, quick and quiet. He made the set comfortable for his actors to create their characters, with the actors bringing their best to the set every day. The actors loved the experience of working with Eastwood, enjoying the freedom he offered as a director and often gathering to work on the script and their characters on their free time. "We wished the shoot would never end," explained Tim Robbins. "It was that incredible."

Though the subject matter was dark and troubling to the actors, Eastwood, by allowing the space to create, drew the very best out of them as artists, creating one of the greatest ensembles in film history.

"Clint's vibe is very productive," explains Sean Penn. "He's not the director as disapproving father. Clint is the approving rascal, older brother. You are not inclined to rebellion unless you want him to laugh at you."

Working with real actors, and not necessarily movie stars, allowed Eastwood to plumb the depths of despair with the film, taking his cast on a journey into the darkest recesses of the human psyche to explore what we are capable of. The results would be quite extraordinary and lead some of the actors to do the finest work of their careers.

The film opens 25 years in the past on a street in blue-collar Boston. Three young friends, Jimmy, Dave, and Sean, are playing street hockey in the neighborhood, taking time out to scrawl their names in wet cement. A sedan pulls up behind them, and a large man gets out of the car, claiming to be a police officer, and begins interrogating the boys. He grows watchful when two of the boys make clear they live close by, within eye shot, but when Dave tells him he lives on the next street, he is targeted by the man. It is Dave that he decides to take home and tell his parents what the boys have been doing. Ordering Dave to get into the car, there is something terribly wrong, something horribly sinister about the entire situation that strikes the boys as wrong. Terrified, Dave gets into the back of the car, noticing at once it is messy, and the gentleman in the passenger seat turns to give him a strange smile. As the car pulls away, Dave looks out the back window, giving to his friends the last stare of his childhood, which will soon be taken away. The other two boys tell their fathers about the incident, and a search is launched for Dave, who was never taken home. Instead he became a sex "toy" for the two men, held and raped repeatedly for several days before managing to escape and return home, forever impacted by the incident.

Twenty-five years later the boys are now men, and once again a tragedy will bring them together. Jimmy is an ex-con having done time for robbery several years ago before turning his life around and now running a small corner variety store in the neighborhood in which he grew up. Sean is a homicide detective, struggling with a separation from his wife, who will call and say nothing, while Dave, still haunted by his childhood abduction, is married and a father himself, but is a stooped and beaten-down man.

When Jimmy's daughter is found brutally murdered, their existence once again is disrupted by an act of violence against a child. Jimmy erupts like a wounded animal when he realizes the body in the park is Katie (Emma Rossum), later vowing vengeance to find her killer and make him pay with his life. Using contacts from his criminal world, from which he has never really lost contact, Jimmy begins his own search for the killer. Meanwhile, on the night Katie was killed, Dave returns home covered in blood, telling his wife he was mugged. His story will later change several times, at one point becoming a tale of a child molester that he found and the fight that ensued. So bizarre is Dave's behavior that Celeste comes to believe that her husband, whom she now fears, may have killed Katie. Making good on his vow to his dead daughter to find her killer, Jimmy takes Dave to the spot where he once killed another man and allows him to bargain for his life. Knowing that Jimmy will indeed kill him, Dave makes a false confession, at which point Jimmy plunges a knife into his stomach mortally wounding him, which he follows with a shot to the head, killing Dave. In the meantime, Sean has discovered that Katie was killed by two young boys, one of them the brother of her lover, out of jealousy. He finds Jimmy the next day sitting in the street and informs him of his finding, telling him that the murderers have confessed. Jimmy is stunned, telling Sean he wished he had gotten to him sooner. Sean, who has received a call from Celeste about Dave's disappearance, knows at once what Jimmy has done and, though he has no proof, he makes clear to Jimmy that he will find some. They share a last look during a parade in which both men are there with their families, and watch a frantic Celeste try to get the attention of her son who is sitting on a float, dour and sad, just as Dave had lived his life.

Like a secondary character in the film throughout is the Mystic River, hiding and washing away the sins of the characters. Through Jimmy's past we understand that the river holds secrets of terrible deeds done, but just as time heals, so the river cleanses.

The director superbly captures the agony of losing a child—that sense of loss for what will never be, for when a child dies, the parents perish. We feel in every fiber of Jimmy Markum his grief and pain, and his growing rage at what his daughter experienced in the final moments of her existence. This is a primal violation of innocence, as the order of life is forever altered and will never be set right again. With his rage comes an understanding that there is a darkness within his soul that will seek vengeance and will not be still until he has found it.

There is neither redemption nor forgiveness offered to the characters, as the crimes are forever seared into their minds, forever haunting the landscape of the subconscious. Eastwood superbly merges the modern day tale with that of the tragedies of the ancient Greeks, allowing Penn's terrible scream of despair to become almost mythological in its raw and visceral power.

The film was first seen at the Cannes Film Festival in May of 2003, where reaction was hugely positive with critics falling over themselves trying to find superlatives for the film. It would open commercially in North America in the fall of the same year, and with its opening, bolstered by the rave reviews out of Cannes, it would become an immediate Oscar favorite.

The performances in the film drew the most attention, in particular those of Penn and Robbins. Penn was cited often by critics for his astounding performance as Jimmy, with many haunted forever by the scene in which dozens of police officers pile on top of him to keep him from seeing his dead daughter. With Penn appearing like a wounded animal, a cry of horribly wronged rage erupting from his very soul, the scene is among the most powerful ever committed to film. That simmering rage he carries with him throughout the film, and the very matter-of-fact way he makes the decision to kill Dave—a man he has known since childhood—leads to the terrible decision that what he believes to be true is without a doubt correct. Penn's performance was not just the finest of the year; he gives one of the great screen performances of all time, moving into the class occupied by Brando's best, Nicholson's strongest, Duvall's greatest, and De Niro's most remarkable work.

Laura Linney brilliantly complements Penn's performance with a quietly terrifying scene in which, even when it has become clear that he did the wrong thing in killing the wrong man, she, like Lady Macbeth, becomes complicit in the killing by knowing of it and approving of it. We do not see her true colors until close to the end of the film, but when we do, it is an unsettling scene of remarkable, quiet power.

Tim Robbins, a massive presence at 6'5", somehow shrinks himself as Dave becomes smaller throughout the film. There is something terribly off about Dave, as though he had been through something terrible in his life and forever carries that with him, which of course he does. Long after the film ends, we are haunted by Dave, by the manner in which he carries himself and speaks, and in particular by that final line, "I wasn't ready," before the trigger is pulled, exploding the screen to shocking white.

As Dave's shell-shocked wife, Celeste, Oscar winner Marcia Gay Harden captures the frayed-nerved woman living a lie, knowing that her husband may be a killer, faced with the awareness that her life is unraveling around her and she is helpless to do a thing about it. To her eventual horror she will wrongly implicate and condemn Jimmy, and her final look of utter defeat is forever haunting.

A.O. Scott of the *New York Times* would rave, "Jimmy Markum is not only one of the best performances of the year, but also one of the definitive pieces of screen acting in the last half century, the culmination of a realist tradition in the old Actor's Studio that begat Brando, Dean, Pacino, and De Niro.

"What gives the movie its extraordinary intensity of feeling is the way Mr. Eastwood grounds the conventions of pulp opera in an unvarnished, thickly inhabited reality," he finished.

Roger Ebert raved, "Directors grow great by subtracting not adding, and Eastwood does nothing for show, everything for effect."

"To see strong acting like this is exhilarating," he added.

"*Mystic River* echoes Eastwood's previous exploration of true life violence, *Unforgiven* (1992), by tracing how death and depravity stain over one's life for generations, leaving seeds to take root in each branch of a tainted family tree," wrote film critic K.J. Doughton at *Film Threat*.

With few detractors, the film was a heavy favorite to win the Academy Award for best picture, but it would run into the juggernaut that was *The Lord of the Rings: The Return of the King* (2003), the final chapter in the massive trilogy by director Peter Jackson. It had long been believed that the Academy was waiting to honor Jackson for his entire achievement after the first two films in the series had earned best picture nominations.

Kicking off the award season, *Mystic River* earned five Golden Globe nominations, for best film, best actor (Penn), best director, best supporting actor (Robbins), and best screenplay. A huge harbinger of the Academy Awards, the Globes honored the film with awards for best actor and best supporting actor. A short time later, Penn would shockingly lose the Screen Actors Guild Award for best actor to Johnny Depp for his swishy Captain Jack Sparrow in the blockbuster *The Pirates of the Caribbean* (2003), which threw a curve into the Oscar predictions.

Eastwood would win the best director award from the prestigious National Society of Film Critics, as well as earn his second nomination from the Directors Guild of America. The Broadcast Film Critics Association would honor both Penn and Robbins for their lead and supporting performances.

Nominated for six Academy Awards, including best picture, actor, director, supporting actor and actress (Harden), and screenplay, *Mystic River* went into the Oscar race as a potential spoiler, ready to knock *King* off its throne. Nominated for a whopping 11 Academy Awards, *The Lord of the Rings: The Return of the King* wound up winning every single award it was nominated for, tying the record for most awards won with *Ben-Hur* (1959) and *Titanic* (1997).

Yet *Mystic River* did not come away empty-handed, as the first award of the night went to Tim Robbins for his haunted performance as Dave. Stepping to the podium, Robbins said, "Oh boy! Wow! Thank you so much members of the Academy. This is a really lovely, lovely honor. I'd like to thank my fellow nominees who are all spectacular, and I want to work with all of you on a movie at some point. Dennis Lehane, Brian Helgeland for the writing of this amazing script. Clint Eastwood, you're so great. You're an amazing director, and you're making my mantel very crowded. Thank you. It's due to you, sir."

Robbins went on to thank his cast members and the usual family members and legal folks. He tells the story of watching the reading of the best actor nominees and the announcement that cast member Sean Penn had won. "And Sean's walking to the stage and does not see yet that the entire audience is standing. So he turns around and sees this extraordinary tribute . . .," said Robbins. Humbled and deeply moved, Penn, who is notoriously private, was suddenly in front of more than one billion people. "Thank you. If there's one thing that all actors know—other than that there weren't any WMDs— it's that there is no such thing as best in acting. And that's proven by the actors I was nominated with as well as the Giamattis, Cages, Downey Jrs., Nicholsons, etc. that were not nominated. We know how great all of you are. My daughters Dillon and Hopper find it presumptuous and embarrassing to write speeches, and so I'm gonna go without. God, I really thank Clint Eastwood, professionally and humanely, for coming into my life."

In the years following *Mystic River* (2003), Eastwood seemed to move into one of the most productive periods of his career. Just one year later he would find himself back in the Oscar circle, and this time it was he who took the stage as a winner . . . again.

25

Million Dollar Baby (2004)

One year after watching the Australian director Peter Jackson return to the stage again and again to collect Academy Awards for his extraordinary fantasy epic *The Lord of the Rings: The Return of the King* (2003), Eastwood would find himself in the enviable position of arriving at Oscar night with the film many felt would win the Oscar for best picture, *Million Dollar Baby* (2004). The film arrived late in the season as a contender, though there had been whispers as to just how good the film was since late summer. Shot in 37 days on a small budget, the film had been the critics' darling during award season, with Eastwood winning the highly coveted New York Film Critics Award for best director. Walking the red carpet as a triple nominee, having been nominated for best director, best producer, and best actor, Eastwood was typically modest about his chances. He and his film had been nominated, as had Martin Scorsese's Howard Hughes epic *The Aviator* (2004), which featured a stunning performance from Leonardo di Caprio as the legendary billionaire who during his heyday in Hollywood made millions with his obsession with aviation and conquest of air space. Nominated for 11 Academy Awards, the film had won the Golden Globe for best picture, and the Academy deeply wanted to honor Scorsese, who was widely considered to be the greatest living American director. Many, however, felt *The Aviator* was neither his best film nor vintage Scorsese.

The race would come down to the two films, each of which had a remarkable genesis. *The Aviator* was a multi-million dollar production with no less than Michael Mann—himself a fine director—producing, and an all-star cast, whereas Eastwood's picture had been a low-budget, gritty affair with strong actors. Little was known about the film when it was released in December, but by Oscar night, there was no one in the film business who was not aware of the film. Going into Oscar night Eastwood had the advantage of having won the Directors Guild Award for best director, which is often a telltale sign of who is going to take home the Oscar.

When the awards were handed out, *Million Dollar Baby* became a part of history, winning best picture, earning Eastwood a second Oscar for best director, and generating acting awards for Hilary Swank (her second Oscar for best actress) and Morgan Freeman (his first).

The script came to Eastwood from writer Paul Haggis, a Canadian who arrived in Los Angeles 20 years earlier and had made a strong living in television. Adapting the story from a collection titled *Rope Burns*, he carved out a unique story that struck Eastwood deeply upon reading the script.

"I read the stories and particularly liked *Million Dollar Baby*. I thought it would be relatively simple. *Mystic River* had done reasonably well. So I went to Warner Brothers, and they said, 'We don't think boxing pictures are really that commercial now,' and I said, 'Well, I don't quite see this as a boxing movie.' I said it was a love story between a surrogate father and his surrogate daughter, and it's the next picture I'm going to do. They all thought it was interesting material but not commercial," Eastwood explained.

Despite his success as a movie actor and an Academy Award–winning director, he had a difficult time getting anyone in Hollywood interested in the project, including Warner Brothers, long his home studio. What eventually happened is that Warner Brothers and Lakeshore Entertainment financed the film at the rather tiny budget of 30 million dollars, an incredibly low amount given today's standards and soaring budgets.

He tackled the role of Frankie himself, perhaps the last role we will see him play on screen. The role of the tough old trainer who finds a young woman and makes a champion of her was tailor-made for Eastwood, but in the screenplay's latter half there would be demands made on him as an actor that had never been made before. There was no doubting his talent as an actor, not after that exceptional performance in *Unforgiven* (1992), but did he have the dramatic chops to handle this and go toe-to-toe with two formidable talents? He believed he did, and that was enough for his cast and crew.

Hilary Swank had burst from out of nowhere five years earlier in a small independent film called *Boys Don't Cry* (1999), in which she portrayed real-life character Brandon Teena, a young woman who was struggling with her sexuality and believed herself to be a man, thus passing herself off as such. Eventually found out, she was brutally raped and murdered. Directed by Kimberly Pierce, the film was made on a shoestring budget, and Swank, having been cast in *The Next Karate Kid* (1996), which flopped, needed the work. No one could have expected what would happen with *Boys*, as it turned to gold and earned rave reviews from the critics in North America, and Swank began winning award after award for her exceptional transformation. Eventually she won the Academy Award for best actress, but in the subsequent years she had a hard time finding the right role for herself. She had managed just one strong performance, in a Home Box Office film titled *Iron Jawed Angels* (2004), since winning the Oscar. Eastwood offered her the second role of a lifetime as Maggie Fitzgerald. In many ways, Swank could connect to Maggie, because she too had arrived in L.A. dirt poor and lived out of her mother's car for a time between auditions. When Eastwood called, she took the part in order to work with Eastwood, and was often heard stating she would have worked for free.

For the crucial role of the film's narrator, Scrap, Eastwood turned to an old friend, Morgan Freeman. Once called the greatest actor in American film by no less than the esteemed critic Pauline Kael, Freeman had become beloved to audiences for his performances in *Driving Miss Daisy* (1989) and *The Shawshank Redemption* (1994). There was something wholly authentic about each of his performances, something real and oddly comfortable.

The shoot was grueling for Swank in particular. She had to get herself in peak shape to portray boxer Fitzgerald, and worked long and hard with trainers to whip her lithe body into a muscle machine. She gained 30 pounds of pure muscle for the part, and became quite a lethal presence in the ring.

The story is that of Maggie, a Southern girl who has come to Los Angeles looking for an escape from her trailer park roots and welfare-supported family. Though she wants to fight, she has no training and no one is willing to train her, but she comes in time after time to the rundown gym owned by Frankie, where Scrap ekes out a living as a cleanup man. They used to be fighter and cut man, but Frankie allowed Scrap to keep fighting once and it cost the man his eye, something that Frankie feels enormous guilt over. Scrap let go of it a long time ago because he knows that Frankie has greater ghosts hanging around him. His daughter, who abandoned him a long time ago, returns the weekly letters he writes unopened, leading Frankie to church day after day seeking an answer.

In Maggie he finds one.

Initially he refuses to train her but sees something in her that he likes, so he agrees that until she is ready for another to take her to the next level, he will be her trainer. She proves to be a superb student who is brilliant in the ring—almost too good, as she wins fights quickly and almost always with a knockout in the first round, causing others not to want to fight her. She becomes his surrogate daughter and he her father, as an uncommon love develops between the two of them. There is no hint of romance here, just a deep bond between two people who need to find love, and who need to know there is one single person they can count upon.

Maggie rises swiftly through the ranks, becoming wealthy in the process, and purchases a home for her welfare-stealing mother who throws the gift back in her stunned daughter's face. Witnessing this, Frankie comes to understand how far Maggie has come and the life she sought to escape so as not to fall into the trap of her mother.

Dubbed "Mo Cuishle," a Gaelic phrase that Frankie will not translate for Maggie, she rises to the top of her profession and finally is given the chance to fight for the championship of the world. The opponent fights dirty and she knows this, as she is always told by Frankie to watch out for herself. Sucker punched by the other fighter, Maggie falls onto a chair placed too soon in her corner and fractures her neck, leaving her paralyzed from the neck down for the rest of her life.

Frankie sits with her constantly, reading to her and trying to raise her spirits, while haunted by the fact that once again someone he cares about has been injured due to him. Maggie holds no regrets, knowing that Frankie took her as far as she could go and more, and she has achieved everything she dreamed of. She does not wish to remain "frozen," as she calls it, for all of time and asks that Frankie allow her to die, help her to die, and put her out of her misery as her father once did to her pet dog. Horrified by the question, Frankie refuses, and Maggie tries to swallow her tongue, finally having to be sedated. Loving her enough to let her go, Frankie one night creeps into her room and disconnects the breathing tube, then injects adrenaline into Maggie to stop her heart, setting her free. In her final moments he tells her what Mo Cuishle means—"my darling, my blood"—and gently kisses her goodbye, sitting with her as she slips away. A single tear slips down her face.

And as Scrap tells us on the track, they never saw Frankie again. He left the gym, leaving it to Scrap to run, and disappeared, though a final shot suggests that he bought a diner in the South, a spot where he and Maggie once stopped for pie. He finishes the letter to Frankie's daughter, letting her know that he thought she might want to know the sort of man her father is.

Who knew that Clint Eastwood had such a performance in him? True, he was brilliant in *Unforgiven* (1992) and *The Bridges of Madison County* (1995), but here he is called upon to be as dramatic as some of the greats of movie history, and he answers the call. His final moments with Maggie as she passes into eternity are utterly heartbreaking. The moment she asks him to do this deed, there is such dawning horror on his face at the prospect of losing this girl he has come to love, he cannot bear the burden of what she has asked. Yet he does as she asks, though it tears him apart. There is such gentle sweetness with which he administers the lethal injections that will end Maggie's suffering. Never before has Eastwood been so heroic on screen.

Upon accepting her Golden Globe for best actress, Swank remarked, "If I may, this is simply the finest performance of your career, Clint," and she was precisely right. As previously stated, Eastwood became a greater actor with age, and though it is often not obvious just how powerful an artist he may be, viewing this film makes it quite clear.

Hilary Swank is a revelation as Maggie, capturing the essence of a girl who separately knows she is on the path to nowhere unless someone believes in her and gives her a chance. The ferocity with which she throws herself into the role is matched only perhaps by that of Maggie in the ring, beating back the life she dreads should she stop doing what she does best, which is of course fighting. All she seems to need is someone to believe in her, just once.

When Frankie does, she puts her faith in him and hands him her heart, doing exactly as he teaches her and rising to the top of the boxing world. The bond between the two of them is unbreakable, each knowing that they can count on the other. She tells Frankie after a nasty incident with her mother, "You're all I got Frankie," to which he replies without hesitation, "Then you've got me." We come to realize that when Maggie fights in the ring, the opponent is often herself and the life she left. The life she does not want for herself is that of her mother relying on welfare. She fights this back with every fiber of her being, and moves farther and farther from her roots, until she has at long last escaped from where she came.

Swank is the sort of actress who will always have to choose her roles carefully, but in the right part she is a formidable and powerful talent with a knack for pulling the audience into her, allowing them to feel her joy and pain, and is most generous with her fellow actors. She has mastered what many actors never do: that ability to listen, to be still and listen to the dialogue being spoken to her and react. Reaction is so much a part of her performance here. Her transformation into the boxer was a very real process, brought on by hard work, training, and the gaining of 30 pounds of muscle.

"I have an enormous amount of respect for boxers as athletes because boxing is the most physically challenging thing I have ever done," she explained to Brad Balfour of Pop Entertainment.com. "Yes, I went to boxing matches. I lived, slept, ate, breathed, and drank boxing."

Her admiration for Eastwood was boundless, as she made clear, speaking of her director and costar in glowing terms.

I love Clint. Everything you hear about him is true. I had such high expectations because he's Clint Eastwood and had been making movies longer than I've been alive. I have such enormous respect for his talent. I've heard from Laura Linney, Kevin Bacon, and people who've worked with him; it's the best experience you'll have in your career. That's some high expectations. And when we make expectations, usually things can't live up to it because our imaginations are really powerful. But he exceeded them and more. The man is an anomaly. There will never be another Clint Eastwood. He is so multifaceted; his talent runs the gamut, and he creates an environment in which everyone feels comfortable. He says he gets people he feels are right for the job, and he lets them do it. He's the most amazing collaborator. When all is said and done, and you've watched the movie, his fingerprints are all over it. And you didn't even realize the gentle guidance and color that was happening in every moment because he's so subtle and so simple.

"He's so moving in this movie," she continued. "I just sit in awe. It just gives us all hope. He's 74. I have a few years to catch up. It's an extra dimension because it's Clint being this emotional. It's so powerful because you really haven't seen him do that. He does that, and he's so confident, not in an arrogant or egotistical sort of way. He's just so calm because he's done it.

He knows what he wants and how to do it. His suggestions were always poignant; as a man of few words, when he talks, it's important or hilarious," she finished.

Watching Morgan Freeman together with Eastwood on screen is like watching two great jazz musicians go toe-to-toe with one another, not one-upping each other but complementing the work of the other. They put these characters on like a well-worn glove, and their friendship seems as old as they are. Note the scene in which Frankie catches Scrap airing his feet, his socks full of holes, knowing that money he gave him got gambled away, but he cannot be angry because he knows they know each other so well. Freeman was simply superb in the film, and richly deserved the Oscar that came his way. Having worked with Eastwood before, he knew what to expect from his friend as a director, but he was very surprised at the film's reception.

When the little film, which was shot in a mere 37 days, opened in late December, the critics were stunned by the film and began writing rave reviews, which in turn drew audiences to the film.

Roger Ebert called the film, "by far the best of the year," going on to state, "*Million Dollar Baby* is a masterpiece, pure and simple, deep and true.

"These three characters are seen with a clarity and truth that is rare in movies. . . . Some directors lose their focus as they grow older. Others gain it, learning how to tell a story that contains everything it needs and absolutely nothing else," continued Ebert in the *Chicago Sun-Times.*

He finished with "Hilary Swank is astonishing as Maggie; every note is true," making clear his adoration for the film, though clearly Ebert was not alone in his admiration for Eastwood's latest effort, which was taking the continent by storm.

Once again A.O. Scott at the *New York Times* found himself writing another rave review for an Eastwood film. "Clint Eastwood's *Million Dollar Baby* is the best movie released by a Hollywood studio this year and not because it is the grandest, the most ambitious, or even the most original. On the contrary: it is a quiet, intimately scaled, three-person drama directed in a patient, easy-going style without any of the displays of allusive cleverness or formal gimmickry that so often masquerade as important filmmaking these days," he wrote. "With its careful unassuming naturalism, its visual thrift, and its emotional directness, *Million Dollar Baby* feels at once contemporary and classical, a work of utter mastery," he continued in one of the film's strongest reviews.

"*Million Dollar Baby* is," wrote Peter Travers for *Rolling Stone* magazine, "a stunningly drawn map of the human heart disguised as a boxing yarn." He held especially high praise for Eastwood, writing, "The knockout punch comes from Eastwood. His stripped-down performance—as powerful as anything he's ever done—has a rugged haunting beauty. The same goes for the film."

Entertainment Weekly film critic Owen Gleiberman wrote, "a movie of tough excitement . . . even grace." David Denby at *The New Yorker* posted,

"Joins the honor list of the great boxing films . . . a beautifully modulated sadness."

Despite rave reviews and a general consensus among film writers not to expose the film's shocking twist—Maggie becoming paralyzed, which takes the film off in a shocking direction—Eastwood found himself under attack from some writers for seeming to support euthanasia in allowing Maggie her right to die. Conservative commentators, such as Michael Medved and Rush Limbaugh, attacked the film and Eastwood for what they perceived to be the film's right-to-die agenda, claiming that Eastwood had sneaked that message into what audiences believed would be a feel-good boxing film. Roger Ebert lashed back that the critics had no right to reveal such a crucial plot point, so why did they do so?

When the year-end critics' groups started handing out their awards, Eastwood collected his first award from the prestigious New York Film Critics Circle for best director, an honor that eluded him for *Unforgiven* (1992) due to a critic's lateness and missing the vote.

The National Society of Film Critics named *Million Dollar Baby* best film and Swank best actress, and the lithe actress found herself awarded best of the year by the Boston Society of Film Critics, the Broadcast Film Critics Association, and the San Diego Film Critics Society.

The Screen Actors Guild honored the film with two awards, for best actress and best supporting actor for Morgan Freeman, as well as a nomination for outstanding ensemble.

When the Hollywood Foreign Press Association announced its nominations for Golden Globe Awards, *Million Dollar Baby* was nominated for five in all, including best film (drama), best actress, best director, best supporting actor, and best musical score (Eastwood). On the evening of the awards, Eastwood and his film went up against Martin Scorsese and his Howard Hughes epic *The Aviator*, and at the end of the night, while *The Aviator* had won best picture, Eastwood had collected his third Globe for directing, Swank another award for best actress, and Morgan Freeman had taken best supporting actor. And there was more to come.

In yet another harbinger of the Academy Awards, Eastwood won his second best director award from the Directors Guild of America, and he watched while *Million Dollar Baby* was nominated for 6 Academy Awards, up against 11 for *The Aviator*. Oscar history dictated that the film with the most nominations, by and large, would emerge the winner, though there had been exceptions over the years. Still, even with that bit of history against him, he walked into the Oscars the favorite to win. While *The Aviator* won the lion's share of the early awards, including best cinematography, best editing, and best supporting actress, the tide turned in the final awards of the night.

Morgan Freeman was the first winner of the *Million Dollar Baby* crew for best supporting actor. The revered actor strode to the stage with his well-known cool demeanor and spoke to the nearly one billion watching the show. "I want to thank anybody and everybody who ever had anything to do with the making of this picture, but I especially want to thank Clint Eastwood for giving me the opportunity to work with him again and to work with Hilary Swank. This was a labor of love. And I thank the Academy. I thank you so much," he said in a heartfelt acceptance speech.

Later in the evening, the previous year's best actor winner, Sean Penn, announced that this year's best actress was another actor directed by Eastwood, Hilary Swank, who found herself in the incredible position of having won her second Academy Award for best actress, something not accomplished by even the great Meryl Streep. The lithe young actress would join an elite group of artists having won twice or more for best actress, including Jane Fonda, Luise Rainer, Elizabeth Taylor, Olivia de Haviland, Ingrid Bergman, Glenda Jackson, Vivien Leigh, and the great four-time winner Katharine Hepburn.

"I don't know what I did in this life to deserve this! I'm just a girl from a trailer park who had a dream. I never thought this would happen, let alone be nominated. . . . Well, the ever-amazing Morgan Freeman . . . and then Clint. Clint Eastwood, thank you for allowing me to go on this journey with you. Thank you for believing in me. You're my 'Mo Cuishle.' Thank you," she told the many who had worked on the film with her.

Eastwood had again brought with him his mother, now in her nineties, to watch the awards with her son. She had been with him in 1993 when he took home the prize for *Unforgiven* (1992), and she now watched her boy win his second Academy Award for best director over the revered Martin Scorsese.

Julia Roberts tore open the envelope to announce that Eastwood was named best director for the second time by the Academy of Motion Arts and Sciences. He ambled to the stage and accepted the award before speaking.

> Thanks, thank you very much. I'd like to thank my wife, who is my best pal down there, and my mother, who was here with me in 1993. She was 84 then, but she's here tonight. So at 96, I'm thanking her for her genes.
>
> It was a wonderful adventure. To make a picture in 37 days, it takes a well-oiled machine, and that well-oiled machine is a crew—the cast, of course, you've met a lot of them, but there's still Margo and Anthony and Michael and Mike and Jay and everybody else who was so fabulous in this cast. And the crew: Campanelli and Billy Coe, and of course Tom Stern, who is fantastic. And Henry Bumstead, the great Henry Bumstead, who is head of our crack geriatrics team. I'm just lucky to be here. Lucky to still be working. And I watched Sidney Lumet out there who is 80, and I figure, "I'm just a kid, and I've got a lot of stuff to do yet." So thank you all very much. Appreciate it.

Ironically, just three years later, Sidney Lumet, whom Eastwood references in his speech, made a huge comeback with his film *Before the Devil*

Knows You're Dead (2007), making clear that at 83 he was still a force to reckoned with.

But of course Eastwood was far from finished, and had in fact already begun his next adventure that would again land him in the Oscar circle. A conversation the year before with Steven Spielberg had set Eastwood on the path to his largest canvas yet: the Second World War.

26

Flags of Our Fathers (2006)

Of all the films Eastwood has directed, *Flags of Our Fathers* (2006) is perhaps the most misunderstood, and the one most deserving of attention it did not receive. In years to come I have every confidence that this film will come to be appreciated as the masterpiece it always was.

There is a sequence towards the end of Clint Eastwood's *Flags of Our Fathers* that is startling in its subtle power, perfectly conveying what the director is seeking to convey. An old man is speaking with his son about his memories of the war. He tells his boy about going swimming in the ocean after a battle, and we flash back in time to see the old man as a young man at the beginning of adulthood, his entire life ahead of him. The men around him are stripping down and running joyously into the ocean, splashing around like school boys at play, forgetting the battle that has been waged that day, and forgetting for just a few moments that just a few feet away lie the bodies of their friends and foes, cut down that day in war. The director makes clear that this was a war fought by young men—very young men—many of whom survived to become old men and share their remembrances with the generations behind them, though often it was difficult to discuss those remembrances. Perhaps the scene packs such an enormous punch because the men we know to be veterans of the Second World War are now very old, time having carved deep lines in their faces, their hair (if any) snow white, and their eyes misty at the mention of the war years. Many would not discuss what they did over there, or what they saw, choosing instead to let that battle wage across the landscape of their subconscious, return to life in North America and leave behind the death and mayhem of combat. Some were called heroes, and indeed some were just that, but many died, sometimes fast deaths, sometimes terrible deaths, crying out in the mud as their blood leaked out of their bodies and their lives slipped away as they were held by their buddies. There was a bond forged between these men during this war like no other I can recall; whether they know one another, they know instantly and understand the ghosts each carries around. It is a bond understood only by men who have been to war.

Throughout the film we see the horror of war, the brutality, the violence, and the inhumanities done to man, and yet it is the smiles and silly playing in the sea that we will take away with us. Do we really realize how young these men were when they went over to fight the most important conflict of the last two hundred years? Barely out of high school and some not yet shaving, they were boys on the cusp of manhood. They were boys who would become men all too quickly, exposed to life-and-death situations that brought on premature maturity, and forced to do and see things no man should ever be exposed to.

We see many powerful images throughout Eastwood's massive war epic, yet none stayed with me as long as those final moments of these smiling young men frolicking in the ocean, their cares momentarily put aside. Perhaps the moment is so great in its power because we, the audience, like God for a few moments, know what will become of these men—the ones who will die within days, and those who will grow old, with this single memory etched into their minds forever, to be recalled on their death bed. To them, their buddies never aged, because their memories of them are always going to be as young men.

Iwo Jima is a volcanic island 650 nautical miles south of Tokyo, 700 miles north of Guam, and roughly halfway between Tokyo and Saipan. It is a small island of just 5,200 acres, with looming Mount Saribachi at its southern tip being by far its most notable landmark along with its black volcanic rock that resembles the surface of the moon. The island became famous in 1945 when Joe Rosenthal snapped an iconic photograph of a group of U.S. Marines lifting the American flag, a photograph that almost at once became one of the most famous ever taken and that was responsible for rallying those at home around the men fighting overseas. As of 2008, Rosenthal's photo may be the most reproduced snapshot in history, its image conjuring up patriotism in one glance.

From February through March of 1945, one of the Second World War's fiercest battles was raging on Iwo Jima between U.S. Marine forces and 21,000 Japanese dedicated to defending the small island. All but abandoned by their superiors, the Japanese were instructed to fight to the death, knowing that the Americans outnumbered them, had greater weaponry, and, some would believe, had the advantage geographically. What should have been a short skirmish ended up lasting 35 bloody days during which nearly all of the Japanese fighting for the island were killed, either by the Americans or by their own hand.

The story of Iwo Jima had been told many times through history, but never so eloquently, as in the book *Flags of Our Fathers* by James Bradley and Ron Powers, with Bradley writing about his father's experiences on the island and after. The author had not been aware of his father's military history until after the man passed away. The book became a national best seller, and was purchased for a film by no less than Steven Spielberg.

Eastwood was celebrating the Academy Award wins for Sean Penn (best actor) and Tim Robbins (supporting actor) in *Mystic River* (2003) at the Governors Ball when he encountered his friend Steven Spielberg at the massive party. Spielberg had presented the Academy Award for best picture to Peter Jackson for *The Lord of the Rings: The Return of the King* (2003), quipping, "It's a clean sweep," in reference to the film winning all 11 awards for which it had been nominated, joining *Ben-Hur* (1959) and *Titanic* (1997) as the most winning films of all time.

The two men chatted, and talk came around to *Flags of Our Fathers*, which Eastwood had wanted to direct since reading the best-selling book by James Bradley and Ron Powers. Without batting an eye, Spielberg told him to come over and direct it, with Spielberg acting as producer. The successful director had perhaps shied away from directing the film himself after helming the Academy Award–winning *Saving Private Ryan* (1998), which is arguably the greatest film about the war ever made. Spielberg may have been worried about repeating himself, or perhaps just had nothing further to say on the subject, so he handed it to someone he trusted to make an excellent film from the book.

Eastwood had just begun work on *Million Dollar Baby* (2004) and thus was committed to finish that first, but he had decided that night to make the film. Smiling as he walked into the Malpaso offices the next day, he was thrilled with the news he had for his associates as to what their next project was going to be.

Steven Spielberg by this point in his career was without question the most famous director in the history of the cinema, and although he had matured as an artist through the nineties, he was not recognized as one of the finest. His Academy Awards for directing *Schindler's List* (1993) and *Saving Private Ryan* were both well earned, with the former being widely considered among the greatest films ever made.

"I had originally bought the book because I felt that the photograph was one of the most iconic images in all of American history next to some of the Lincoln portraits," Spielberg explained to AP Television during the film's opening. "That photograph really launched a really amazing campaign that located three survivors of the Iwo Jima flag raising and put them on a public relations tour that, in many ways, was harder than fighting alongside their buddies on the island of Iwo Jima," he went on.

When asked why he took the project, Eastwood smiled and stated simply, "Because he asked me to," making clear his admiration for Spielberg in the process.

Though said with a smile, Eastwood's reasons clearly ran deeper. "One, there's never been a story on Iwo Jima, even though there have been pictures that have been entitled—using it in the title—but the actual invasion, it was the biggest Marine Corps invasion in history, the most fierce battle in Marine Corps history," Eastwood explained to Rebecca Murray at About.com.

"I've always been curious about families who find things out about their relatives after the fact," he stated. "I just wanted them to get to know these people, know what they went through. Maybe give the audience a feeling of what it was like in that time, what these people dedicated their loves or donated their lives for," the director went on. "We live in a time now where it's different. We have a voluntary military. The country's a lot more comfortable now as far as economically . . . war is more of an inconvenience now where then it was an absolute necessity. "At the end we just try to show these guys; really what sums it up is these guys are just a bunch of kids who were sent off to fight for their country. And if you watch the ending credits, we tried to show the real people, and you realize that these 19-year-olds looked 45 in a matter of a two-week period, a three-week period, or something. It shows how much you can change a person and how appreciative they are to have made it through," explained Eastwood.

Always interested in a great story, he found it in both their experiences on Iwo Jima in combat and in the manner in which the three young men were used by the U.S. government to raise money through war bonds. In a campaign that was admittedly manipulative and rather shocking, for several months they were treated like rock stars or presidents, moving in a few days from the battlefield to the bright lights of celebrity, where they often struggled with what was happening to them. Hayes, in particular, did not feel worthy of the attention, believing that the real heroes of Iwo Jima were back there fighting and dying on the field. Told in a nonlinear fashion, the film would move effortlessly back and forth between Iwo Jima and the United States, exploring the experiences of the men.

Eastwood turned to Paul Haggis, who had earned an Oscar nomination for his *Million Dollar Baby* screenplay, to handle the massive adaptation of the Bradley-Powers book, with the writer deciding that the story worked best when told in flashbacks.

His cast was made up of young actors on their way to stardom, none of them major players in Hollywood, which Eastwood justified through his research, making clear that the men who fought in the war were young men just out of their teens and in their early twenties. Of the actors cast, the best known was Ryan Phillipe, who was seen shortly before the film in *Crash* (2005), which collected the Oscar for best picture. Canadian actor Adam Beach would portray Ira Hayes, a folk hero sung about by no less than Johnny Cash; and Jesse Bradford would portray Gagnon, the third member of the party credited with the flag raising and sent home to help in the war bond drive.

"I read that Eastwood had optioned this book in the newspaper, and I immediately went out and bought it and read it in two days. I just thought to myself if there was one thing I could do in it, be involved with it in any capacity, the smallest role, I wouldn't have cared. I just wanted to be a part of it, if at all possible," explains Ryan Phillipe. "I very much tried to make it accurate. I had pictures of him, a lot of pictures of John Bradley . . . to inspire me," stated the young actor.

Cast in the pivotal role of Ira Hayes was Canadian native Adam Beach, who recently had been in John Woo's war epic *Windtalkers* (2002). Portraying a man who had been the subject of a film called *The Outsider* (1961) with Tony Curtis, was daunting to the young actor. "Eastwood has given me confidence, my creativity, and courage to give my all, and I've never felt that before," Beach told About.com, lavishing praise on his director.

The film unfolds in a nonlinear fashion, with scenes on Iwo Jima that show us the nightmares these young men experienced. The scenes are cross-cut with the sequences back in the United States as they were paraded from city to city and treated as heroes, but obviously irritated by what was happening to them. Hayes, in particular, struggled with the hero applause and sense of adulation, believing the real heroes were back on the island, where he longed to be. He battled the bottle, and often appeared drunk in front of thousands, who were oblivious to his actions. Gagnon loved the rock star treatment, believing he was setting up his future, whereas Doc Bradley, like Hayes, struggled with the moral question of the whole operation; he believed that the United States needed funds to win the war, but he was deeply confused at being used as a pawn in the bond drive.

The film is seen largely through the eyes of Doc Bradley, portrayed with quiet stoicism by Ryan Phillipe, who does the finest work of his career for Eastwood, creating a man struggling with his own demons but always thinking of the men around him and how he can come to their aid. When Ira Hayes is constantly drunk during the bond drive, it is Doc Bradley who helps him, sobers him up, and holds him up in front of the audiences. It is Doc who returns to his quiet life after the war, whereas Ira dies in a ditch in 1955 and Gagnon struggles to find himself, hoping to cash in on the success of the bond drive.

Flags of Our Fathers is a melancholy film tinged with a deep sadness throughout, as though the memories that are Doc's become our own. We see the nightmare of battle and hear the screams in the darkness from wounded men seeking help. We see Doc frantically calling for Iggy, his friend who dies in the battle, feeling for the rest of his life that he let him down. Whereas Steven Spielberg's *Saving Private Ryan* brought a new heightened sense of realism to war films and scenes of combat, Eastwood does not attempt to one-up his producer, choosing instead to find his own sense of realism, making the scenes authentic but not possessive of the same frenetic power as Spielberg's film.

Beautifully capturing the time and place, *Flags of Our Fathers* takes audiences back in time to the so-called Greatest Generation, a time when things made sense. The film was considered to be a major Academy Award contender from the moment the release date was announced, and Eastwood was now an Oscar favorite, having won his second Oscar for best director on *Million Dollar Baby*.

When the film was released, there were indeed rave reviews, but certainly not from all critics, many of whom found the film cold, distant, and tedious. Those who loved it, however, truly loved it.

"A narrative like this requires a measured, classical style to be most effective, and it couldn't have found a better director than Clint Eastwood," praised Kenneth Turan of the *Los Angeles Times*. "After two best picture Oscars, 26 films behind the camera, and more than 50 years as an actor, Clint Eastwood knows a gripping story and how to tell it. He found this one in James Bradley's book about the celebrated February 23, 1945, flag raising on Iwo Jima, a narrative that was nearly a year on the *New York Times* best seller list and has 3 million copies in print.

"As he did with *Unforgiven, Mystic River,* and *Million Dollar Baby,* Eastwood handles this nuanced material with aplomb, giving every element of this complex story just the weight it deserves. The director's lean dispassion, his increased willingness to be strongly emotional while retaining an instinctive restraint, continues to astonish. We are close to blessed to have Eastwood still working at age 76, and more fortunate still that challenging material like *Flags of Our Fathers* is what he wants to be doing," wrote the veteran *L.A. Times* critic.

"Clint Eastwood just keeps getting better. At 76 his skill for directing films that mine the human experience for truth and emotion continues to astound. He seemed at the top of his game in 2003 when he made *Mystic River,* then reached a new peak the following year with the emotionally wrenching *Million Dollar Baby.* Who would have thought he could best himself with an epic and unflinching film about World War II, especially after so many noteworthy war films have already been made," said *USA Today* film writer Claudia Puig. "It is one of the year's best films, and perhaps the finest modern film about World War II," completed Puig.

"Clint Eastwood's *Flags of Our Fathers* does a most difficult and brave thing and does it brilliantly. It is a movie about a concept. Not just any concept, but the shop-worn and often wrong-headed idea of heroism," said Kirk Honeycutt, raving in the *Hollywood Reporter.*

Stephen Hunter in the *Washington Post* believed the film to be among the finest released in the last few years, writing, "Stands with the best movies of this young century and the old ones that precede it. It's passionate, honest, unflinching, gripping, and it pays respect."

"Clint Eastwood's tough, smart, achingly sad *Flags of Our Fathers* is about three anointed heroes of World War II—three of the men who appeared, backs to the camera, in the legendary Joe Rosenthal photograph of six soldiers hoisting the American flag on Iwo Jima . . . an epic both raw and contemplative," commented David Ansen in *Newsweek.*

In *The New Yorker*, former stomping ground of Eastwood detractor Pauline Kael, critic David Denby considered, "an accomplished, stirring, but, all in all, rather strange movie. It has been framed as a search for the truth, yet there isn't much hidden material to expose. . . . The movie has a fine, sensitive temper, but it lacks an emotional payoff."

Manohla Dargis, writing in the *New York Times*, focused not only on the film, but also on the career of Eastwood, and the fact it seemed to take film critics a long time to discover his skill as a director. "Here, at age 76, is Clint Eastwood saying something new and vital about the war in his new film, and here, too, is this great gray battleship of a man and movie icon stating something new and urgent about the uses of war and of the men who fight it," she wrote.

"One view of Mr. Eastwood is that he has mellowed with age, or at least begun to take serious the measure of the violence that has been an animating force in many of his films. In truth, the critical establishment caught up with the director, who for decades has been building a fascinating body of work that considers annihilating violence as a condition of the American character, not an aberration. *Flags of Our Fathers* is an imperfect addition to that body of work, though its flaws are minor and finally irrelevant in a film in which ambivalence and ambiguity are constituent of a worldview, not an aftereffect," finished the critic.

However, not all the critics felt the same about the film, with others finding it meandering and awkward and lacking the focus of Steven Spielberg's *Saving Private Ryan*, to which it could not help but be compared, that Oscar-winning film being the greatest war film of this generation.

"You come out of the theater impressed by the scope of Eastwood's reach and frustrated by how little remains in his grasp . . . brutal, elegiac, caustic, noble, sentimental—a World War II film that tries to be all things American to all Americans," complained Ty Burr in the *Boston Globe*.

Writing for *Film Threat*, critic Pete Vonder Haar was brutally honest in stating, "What *Flags of Our Fathers* is not, however, is moving, evocative, or very unique."

Initially the film had been widely considered a shoo-in for Academy Award attention, but weak box office sales hurt its chances greatly. Eastwood and Spielberg were somewhat stunned by the lack of audience for the film, considering Spielberg's epic *Saving Private Ryan* had been a massive box office hit. However, Spielberg's film had Tom Hanks as its star, which was something to be considered. As fine a film as *Flags of Our Fathers* was, it lacked a major star.

Finally the film was a box office failure, forcing Warner Brothers to rush *Letters from Iwo Jima* (2006) into theaters in hopes of drawing some attention to *Flags of Our Fathers*. Quite the opposite happened: it drew attention to itself with its majesty and excellence.

Oddly in 2008 the film was back in the news when director-writer Spike Lee lashed out at Eastwood for not including any black characters or soldiers in the film, despite the fact that African American soldiers had a presence at that crucial battle. Lee, known for making statements about other directors who do not serve the interests of blacks, had previously attacked Norman Jewison for daring to think he could direct *Malcolm X,* and later had a go at Quentin Tarantino for what Lee termed "excessive use" of the word "nigger" in his films, which Lee felt demeaned the black characters in those films, even though it was the black characters speaking the word. In the case of Jewison, Lee ended up directing *Malcolm X* (1992) and did a very fine job of it, though it was Eastwood's film *Unforgiven* (1992) that took the lion's share of awards that year. Hardly new to Cannes, Lee had famously lashed out in 1989 when his film *Do the Right Thing* (1989) was bested by *sex, lies, and videotape* (1989), leading Lee to state, "we wuz robbed." Attacking one of America's most iconic filmmakers as he was promoting his new film *Changeling* at Cannes seemed to be sour grapes. Eastwood took the news in stride initially, stating that he used history for his story, and though there were indeed black soldiers at Iwo Jima, none were close to the flag raising, which involved just one munitions company—hence their absence in the film. Interviewed by the *Los Angeles Times,* he was a tad more clear in what he thought about the verbiage from Lee. "He should shut his face." Lee immediately back-pedaled, stating he meant no ill will towards Eastwood and was simply asking a question as to why the director would deviate from history. He did, however, throw in a comment in which he stated he felt Eastwood was coming off as an angry old man. By now angry with the whole situation, which threatened to pull focus from the premiere of his new film *Changeling* at Cannes, Eastwood reminded Lee once again that he was working from a book, an eyewitness account, and though there were black soldiers at the island, they had no part in the raising of the flag. Of course the press is going to jump all over an American director known for controversial statements attacking another, and in the end it really meant nothing except some bad press for Lee and a glimpse of Eastwood being his authentic, honest self.

When Lee's film *Miracle at St. Anna* premiered at the Toronto International Film Festival in September 2008, it was among the most disappointing films of the festival. Once again Lee went overboard in trying to explore racism, and within the film there is not a single decent American white man; all are prejudiced rednecks. Terence Blanchard's overbearing score telegraphs each moment like a large neon sign, and there is a central performance so awful, so intensely terrible, that one wonders what Lee was thinking. His attack on Eastwood only draws attention to the fact his film is not on the level of Eastwood's films and, sadly, is a failure.

Flags of Our Fathers was nominated for just two Academy Awards, best sound and best sound editing, though curiously Eastwood was nominated for best director twice by the Hollywood Foreign Press Association, for both Iwo Jima films. In years to come I believe that *Flags of Our Fathers* will come to be appreciated for the haunting, melancholy study of the war it is.

27

Letters from Iwo Jima (2006)

With the shocking failure at the box office of *Flags of Our Fathers* (2006) and the somewhat tepid critical reception, Eastwood approached Warner Brothers about releasing *Letters from Iwo Jima* (2006) in 2006 rather than 2007 as originally planned. His reasoning was that the release of the second film might entice viewers to see the first and come to a greater understanding of the entire Iwo Jima experience. There were accusations in the industry that Eastwood's ego was stung by some of the weak reviews for *Flags of Our Fathers*, and that releasing *Letters from Iwo Jima* was merely a ploy to ensure his place in the Oscar race; but given his long career and reputation for being who he is, the attacks seemed wildly out of place.

Flags of Our Fathers had been considered a major Oscar contender even before filming began. Certainly the fact that Eastwood was directing and Spielberg was producing made the film attractive and important, and on the Internet, Oscar predictors buzzed about the film. However, upon release, the film's stock fell sharply, some believe unjustly, and Eastwood sought a remedy. Releasing *Letters from Iwo Jima* so soon after the other film made sense to him as a businessman, because he knew *Letters from Iwo Jima* was the better film, and therefore might bring audiences back to the first film.

The genesis for *Letters from Iwo Jima* began during the shoot for *Flags of Our Fathers*, when Eastwood became interested in the Japanese general who dealt with the massive American onslaught on the tiny island. The Japanese were badly outnumbered and outgunned, yet patriotic to the end in defending their soil. These men had been sent there and told not to expect to come home, and only a very few would survive, with the death toll higher than 20,000. The American attack numbered more than 70,000, and there was no reason to believe the attack would last more than two or three days. The Americans greatly underestimated the Japanese, and themselves would suffer more than 6,000 casualties.

Once Eastwood became interested in the story from the Japanese side, he began to feel he could not tell the entire story of Iwo Jima without telling the story of the enemy. He approached producer Steven Spielberg about the idea and was told to do it.

"These men donated their lives to defend their country for what their superiors [said] would delay any invasion of mainland Japan," stated Eastwood to Emmanuel Levy. "I think it's important for audiences not just in Japan, but everywhere to know what kind of people they were.

"In most war pictures I grew up with, there are good guys and bad guys," explained Eastwood in his approach to making two films. "Life is not like that and war is not like that. These movies are not about winning or losing. They are about war's effects on human beings and those who lose their lives much before their time."

Eastwood's fascination with General Kuribayashi had led to this film, and he explains how that strange obsession began. "I wondered what kind of person he was to defend this island in a ferocious way, but also in a very clever way. By tunneling and putting everything underground, he did it differently from most Japanese defenses at that time. Most of them were beachhead defenses and used a lot of artillery from the sea. You couldn't do that effectively with this particular battle. He had a lot of resistance among his own troops about the defense of the island. A lot of his fellow officers thought he was crazy doing this whole tunneling thing."

Once his interest started, Eastwood sought to have several Japanese books translated into English. Among them was a book of letters by the general titled *Picture Letters from Commander in Chief.* "The letters were to his wife, his daughter, and his son. A lot of them were mailed from the United States when he was there as an envoy in the late twenties and early thirties. He was a very sensitive man, very family oriented, and missing his family very much. In those letters you got a feel for what he was like. General Kuribayashi was a unique man; by all accounts he was a man of great imagination, creativity, and resourcefulness."

The decision was made to scale the film down in budget from what *Flags of Our Fathers* had cost, and upon finishing that massive shoot, Eastwood would start the second film right away. He called Paul Haggis about the project and, though interested (and thinking his friend insane), Haggis knew he was not qualified to write the screenplay on his own. He began searching the United States for a Japanese writer, but could find no one, and he knew that the budget did not allow a search in Japan. Luckily, his agency also represented Iris Yamashita, a film professor who had written several scripts but had nothing produced. Haggis was sent her work and liked it; thus a meeting was set up between the pair. Yamashita prepared some preliminary notes about the story that impressed Haggis, and at their second meeting he made it clear she had the job. Like Eastwood and Haggis, she focused on the character of General Kuribayashi for her story, studying the letters that Eastwood had read and become obsessed with.

"The letters to his family certainly drew out his character for me. I didn't have concerns about making him a sympathetic character because I only portrayed what was based on reality. My main difficulty with his character was ensuring that he was active despite being a high-ranking officer and therefore mostly on the sidelines rather than in the heart of battle," she explained to the *Japan Times Online*.

Yamashita had written a script about Japan on the eve of the Second World War; therefore much of her research about the war and Japan's involvement was done prior to starting the work for Eastwood. Her mother had been a child in Japan during the war, and during the time Iwo Jima was falling, her family home was burned to the ground during the Tokyo fire raids. After reading Haggis's first draft, she wrote her own screenplay titled *Red Sun, Black Sand*, which she gave to Eastwood, who loved it. "He read the first draft and said, 'Let's go with it' and immediately he started into preproduction and he shot it in something like six weeks," she explained.

"Paul found Iris Yamashita to come and write the screenplay," explained Eastwood. "She wrote a screenplay that both honors and illuminates the souls of the men whose story we are trying to tell. There are 12,000 unaccounted for Japanese soldiers on Iwo Jima. I think those lives deserve a spirit, a certain respect, just as I feel the American forces deserve respect. I feel terrible for both sides in that war and in all wars. There are an awful lot of innocent people that are sacrificed in those situations, and if we can show something of their lives through these young men now, it will be a tribute to these people who gave their lives for their country."

One thing Yamashita accomplished in the work was the undemonizing of the Japanese, making them very much human beings with the same fears and loves as the American soldier. Having grown up in the United States, she was acutely aware that in American schools it is taught that the Japanese started the war with their attack on Pearl Harbor. In most American films about the war, the Japanese are portrayed as unfeeling monsters who follow their emperor and believe whatever he tells them. Only in a handful of films, one of them being Steven Spielberg's criminally underappreciated *Empire of the Sun* (1987), are the Japanese treated as people rather than "evil beings." It was most important for Yamashita to write a truthful screenplay, and she believes that she has accomplished that.

Though just a teenager when the war was raging, Eastwood remembers clearly when it was over. He remembers that those around him were yearning for a peaceful state again, and he himself was quite pleased when it finally ended.

With a low budget, Eastwood decided to shoot much of the film in California on the beaches of Malibu, with one trip to Iwo Jima with a skeleton crew and actor Ken Watanabe for some crucial scenes. He had long ago made the decision that the actors would speak in their native tongue (Japanese) and the film would be subtitled, his first such, giving the film a greater sense of authenticity. Assembling a cast made up of strong Japanese actors and a pop star, the film was shot very quickly—just 35 days for a complicated war film—though in fairness, shots not used from *Flags of Our Fathers* could be utilized for the smaller film. Much more intimate than *Flags of Our Fathers*, this was very much a series of character studies about men at war and how they deal with what they know is impending doom. How would American soldiers react if they were told before being sent into conflict that they should not expect to be returning? Can we imagine what that must do to one's mind? Already dealing with war, which tracks and tears at the psyche, they enter into that arena knowing that their superiors fully expect them to lose their lives for their country.

The story of the film is deceptively simple. It opens long after the war, when a group of archeologists are digging on the island and find a bag of what later will be discovered to be the letters of the men who fought and died there. We flash back to the happenings on the island with the arrival of the general (Ken Watanabe), a brilliant man who has a sensitive side for his soldiers, understanding their fears and terrible loneliness. He orders the troops to dig a vast series of caves underground so that when the American forces strike on the beach, they will not see the Japanese until it is too late, and the Japanese can fire on them. His colleagues think this to be an act of a madman, but he insists, and the men dig the caves that will become their home. Not aware of what has happened to the Japanese navy in terms of losses, the general believes that the men will be backed up by the rest of military until he is told otherwise. Obliterated at the battle of the Philippine Sea, the Japanese fleets will not be backing up the general on Iwo Jima because they are all but gone. The men are to defend the island to the death, which he understands at once, knowing they are doomed to die on Iwo Jima. He evacuates the civilians from the island, knowing that should they stay they would likely be killed. Recognizing that the poor nutrition and dreadfully unsanitary conditions are weakening his men, Kuribayashi does his best to rally the men, who take to eating the insects and worms they find in the caves and sand. When the Americans attack, they do so in waves, outnumbering the Japanese army four to one with massive air and navy support that tilts the battle in favor of the Americans. Yet the Japanese hold firm in their caves, fighting by sheer will, it seems, to hold onto the tiny island, a sacred bit of Japanese soil.

The script allows the audience to get to know the men on the island much in the manner of the classic American war films, where a platoon of soldiers is usually a cross section of Americana. Here the culture is radically different; the will to live, the love for family, and the fact that none of the men wish to die unites them and brings a familiarity to the audience. Saigo is the character the audience best connects with. He is a timid baker with a child he has not seen back on the mainland, clearly hoping to see to see the baby and to be reunited with his wife. It is Saigo who buries the letters, and Saigo who recognizes that the general's weapon has been taken as a trophy by an American soldier, and who then frantically attacks him with his only weapon, a shovel used to bury the dead.

As the Americans close in, the general will order his own beheading, and very few of the Japanese soldiers will survive.

When the film opened in the United States in late December of 2006, it already had opened in Japan, where it was enjoying a strong run and rave reviews. North American critics responded strongly to the film, admiring Eastwood's courage in making not only a foreign language film, but also a stunning study of war and of the enemy, something never before attempted in such a fashion by an American director.

"*Letters from Iwo Jima* is the only American film of the year I will not hesitate to call a masterpiece," stated CNN critic Tom Charity boldly in his review.

"The word masterpiece costs nothing to write and means less than nothing in an age when every third picture and each new Eastwood project is proclaimed such," raved Michael Phillips of the *Chicago Tribune*. "After two viewings, however, *Letters from Iwo Jima* strikes me as the peak achievement in Eastwood's hallowed career."

"*Letters from Iwo Jima*, a Japanese language film from a director steeped in Hollywood tradition, is not just an exercise in cross-cultural sympathy, but also a work of cultural synthesis. The behavior of the characters may be shocking at times, but it rarely feels exotic or strange because the codes that govern their actions are so clearly articulated," raved A.O. Scott of the *New York Times*, going on to name the film the best of 2006.

"It takes a filmmaker of uncommon control and mature grace to say so much with so little superfluous movement, and Eastwood triumphs in the challenge. *Letters from Iwo Jima* enthralls in the audacity of its simplicity . . . profound and magisterial," wrote Lisa Schwarzbaum in *Entertainment Weekly*, also naming the film the best of the year.

"Clint Eastwood's latest film *Letters from Iwo Jima* takes audiences to a place that would seem unimaginable for an American director. Daring and significant, it presents a picture from life's other side, not only showing what wartime was like for our Japanese adversaries on that island in the Pacific, but also telling the story in their language," wrote Kenneth Turan in the *Los Angeles Times*. "What Eastwood seemed to sense intuitively was the connection between his own themes of men being men and the challenges of masculinity, and the notions of honor, duty, and heroism that are embedded in Japanese culture and tradition," Turan continued, also naming the film the year's best in his year-end article.

Todd McCarthy, the film critic for the industry bible *Variety*, wrote in his review of December 7, 2006, 65 years after the attack on Pearl Harbor, that "*Letters from Iwo Jima* represents something rare in the history of war movies—a case of a filmmaker from one country sympathetically telling the combat story from the perspective of a former enemy. Elegantly, but with dramatic bite, Eastwood unfolds the story of some of the men who put up the resilient fight, emphasizing the way their personalities were expressed through crisis rather than ideology or stock notions of bravery and heroics."

"It's unprecedented—a sorrowful and savagely beautiful elegy that can stand in the company of the greatest antiwar movies," stated *Newsweek's* David Ansen.

Peter Travers of *Rolling Stone*, like many critics, cited Eastwood's direction as the film's primary strength, comparing Eastwood to two masters of Japanese cinema in his review, which said, "Eastwood's direction here is a thing of beauty, blending the ferocity of the classic films of Akira Kurosawa (*The Seven Samurai*) with the delicacy and unblinking gaze of Ozu (*Tokyo Story*)."

One of the boldest reviews came from Stephen Saito, writing for *Premiere* magazine of both the film and producer Steven Spielberg, "*Letters from Iwo Jima* isn't just the film that Eastwood wanted to make, but the one producer Steven Spielberg had tried to make twice with *Empire of the Sun* (1987) and *Saving Private Ryan* (1998). While the latter film had the brutality of Eastwood's film, and the former had its compassion, *Letters from Iwo Jima* reminds us how redemption can be found in the most interesting places, whether it's for the filmmakers in real life, or on screen for those we used to fight against." When award season began, the National Board of Review awarded *Letters from Iwo Jima* best picture of the year, though in truth it was the best picture prize from the Los Angeles Film Critics Association that started the journey to Oscar glory. Eastwood found himself nominated twice by the Hollywood Foreign Press Association for best director for each Iwo Jima film, though oddly neither was up for best film. *Letters from Iwo Jima* had been nominated for best foreign language film by the Foreign Press and would win the Golden Globe for that category.

The announcement of the Academy Award nominations thrust Eastwood back into the Oscar race with four nominations, including best picture, best director (his fourth nomination), best screenplay, and best sound. There was some surprise that the film had been snubbed for its breathtaking, dark, and desaturated cinematography and film editing; however, it was an odd year at the Oscars, with nominations spread around. The most nominated film, *Dreamgirls* (2006), was not up for either best film or best director, a genuine rarity that left insiders shaking their heads in disbelief.

The best director category again became fodder for the press in that it again appeared to be a showdown between Eastwood and Martin Scorsese, who was nominated for his Boston crime saga *The Departed* (2006). Much had been made of Eastwood besting the best with *Million Dollar Baby* over *The Aviator* (2004) two years before, and now again, with the Academy very much wanting to honor Scorsese, here was another small battle.

Eastwood played it down, making it clear how much he admired Scorsese and his work, and stating that he believed Scorsese should win the Oscar for the film. When the Directors Guild of America failed to nominate Eastwood for either Iwo Jima film, his Oscar chances seemed over. And, true enough, come Oscar night it was Martin Scorsese who won the long overdue Academy Award for best director. Eastwood himself had been championing Scorsese through the awards season, content with the knowledge he had made a movie masterpiece that would be watched and discussed for ages to come.

2006 may be remembered as the year Scorsese finally won his Oscar, but in years to come I also believe it will bring back memories of Eastwood's staggering accomplishment of two films dealing with the same subject matter seen from different sides, each presented with dignity and honesty.

28

Changeling (2008)

On March 10, 1928, in Los Angeles, California, a young, single mother went off to work at her job as a telephone operator, leaving her young son, Walter, at home with enough money to go to a movie. Being a single mother at this time in history was something of an oddity, but Christine Collins had watched her husband be convicted of running an illegal operation. She returned home to find her son missing, and she frantically reported her missing son to the police. The missing boy's story was reported in the *Los Angeles Times*, and the police spent days combing the area, dragging Lincoln Park lake, and investigating every lead they were given in search of the missing nine year old. Through all of this, Christine pushed the police department to do more because she believed her boy was alive somewhere. In August, 1928, the police reported to Christine that they had found her son, alive, in Illinois, and arranged for her to be reunited with him at a train station with the press watching.

Upon seeing the boy, Christine announced to the police that the boy was not her son, but she was then pressured into taking the boy home, allowing the police department to save face. Three weeks later with her son's circumcision records and documentation from witnesses who knew this boy in hand, she returned the boy to the police, demanded that they resume their search for her son, and stated that the child returned to her was not Walter. Though she did not mean to do so, she created a media nightmare for the police who lashed back by promptly declaring her unstable and had her taken to a mental asylum.

Like a mother lion defending her cub, Christine never quit fighting the Los Angeles Police Department that was known for its corruption across the United States. Eventually the case broke, and Walter was declared a potential victim of a serial killer in Wineville, California.

This story came to Eastwood in the form of a screenplay titled *Changeling*, written by screenwriter J. Michael Straczynski who had stumbled across the case while going through old records of the *Los Angeles*

Times. Although he was best known for his science fiction scripts, Straczynski was quickly fascinated and obsessed with the story and spent more than a year studying records of the story, piecing together the tragic story of Christine Collins.

"I was so caught up by the raw, naked courage she showed, that she fought so hard for her son, and nobody remembered this. It was outrageous," he told Rachel Abramowitz of the *Los Angeles Times* in 2008. His research told him that Collins was treated this way because she simply refused to give in to the men working on the case and would not conform to the image they had of what a woman, a mother, should be. The police department wielded enormous power at this time in American history, having the sheer power to place people in mental hospitals if they saw fit to do so.

"At the time it was very easy for the police to throw anyone they didn't like into the asylum for causing problems," Straczynski continues, "They did it more with women than men. The reality is had Christine been a single dad, this never would have happened."

"The driving force of the movie is a mother's love," stated Eastwood to Kennth Turan in May of 2008, shortly after the film was seen for the first time at the Cannes Film Festival, where Academy Award talk began almost as soon as the closing credits had run.

Producers Ron Howard and Brian Glazer gave the screenplay to Eastwood hoping that he would direct the film. Eastwood then agreed to do the film because he saw in the work the potential to tell a strong story and perhaps bring to the screen a strong female protagonist, which was typical in movies of the 1940s.

"You had a lot of women protagonists in stories that were dramatic," he told the *Los Angeles Times,* recalling the memories of Bette Davis, Katharine Hepburn, and Ingrid Bergman. "I always liked those stories, and we got away from them over the years. This was a chance to do one of those kind of stories."

The subject matter also intrigued him, having dealt with crimes against children before, such as in his masterpiece *Mystic River* (2003), and individuals scarred by a life-altering event, such as in *Million Dollar Baby* (2004) or *A Perfect World* (1993). Here was a chance for Eastwood to make a film that was a throwback to the great pictures featuring strong women he remembered seeing when he was a boy, and to explore the impact of crimes against children, which is one of the only criminal activities he believes justifies the death penalty.

"Crimes against children are the most hideous of all. I think they would be on the top of my list of justification for capital punishment," he explains to the *Los Angeles Times.* "It's hard to think about. When you're doing the movie, you're just using your imagination to figure out what the trauma was like. Angelina Jolie was very affected by it because she is a mother. You don't have to be a mother to be affected. I never cease to be amazed how blasé people can be about victims of crime."

Eastwood saw the film as a modern day horror film as it tapped into the worst fear of every parent, including himself. He understood as a father that monsters did not have to be supernatural to be terrifying, because for a father or a mother the most frightening monster of all is a predator of children.

Angelina Jolie, the daughter of Oscar winning actor Jon Voight, had made a name for herself in the late nineties as a strong actress, willing to go out on a limb for the right role. She won the Academy Award for best supporting actress for her fine performance in *Girl Interrupted* (1999) and had earned strong reviews for other performances as well early in her career. Her marriage to Billy Bob Thornton made her a target for the paparazzi, as the two announced that they wore vials of one another's blood around their necks. Her relationship with her brother struck many as being just a bit too close, and her offscreen behavior became more and more erratic. She would divorce Thornton, and take up with heartthrob Brad Pitt during the filming of their blockbuster *Mr. and Mrs. Smith* (2004) in which they portrayed male and female killers, husband and wife, their careers unknown to the other. Their on-screen and offscreen chemistry was blazing, as they began a torrid romance in 2005. The two of them then became famous for adopting children, and when she became pregnant with twins they would become the darlings of the gossip magazines. Sadly, Jolie became better known for her offscreen activities than what she was doing on-screen. In fact, there are many people in the business who believe that her offscreen antics cost her an Academy Award nomination for best actress for her performance in *A Mighty Heart* (2007) in which she portrayed the widow of murdered journalist Daniel Pearl.

When she first read the *Changeling* script, she did not want at all to be a part of the film.

"Reading the script made me want to stay away from it as far as possible because I didn't want to think of anything happening to my children," she told MTV in 2008. "I didn't want those scenes. But I couldn't forget it. I found myself telling people the story of the script. And obviously the chance to work with Eastwood was something I always wanted. I guessed, and guessed right, that he would help me through this."

When Eastwood became aware that Jolie was interested in the film, he ordered a stop to the casting procedure, sensing that she was perfect for the part because he saw in her some of the glamour that was so famous in the forties pictures he so loved.

"I think she's one of the few actresses that would have been just as big if she'd worked in Hollywood's so-called Golden Age," Eastwood stated with absolute confidence to the *Los Angeles Times*.

Eastwood continued, "She becomes a publicity magnet; everyone wants to know what she's doing. Because you see her in all the tabloid papers, it's easy to overlook her, and she is really underrated."

With Jolie committed to the film, the film was fast tracked into production as Eastwood and Jolie found an opening in their brutal schedules. Eastwood found that the ranch where the infamous murders had taken place still stood and decided to make a visit to the place, knowing that he would make the film in the California area.

"It was creepy," he recalls in the *Los Angeles Times*, "It looks exactly the same though the house has been slightly modified. We went around back and there were those chicken coops. I don't know if they were the same ones, but they were old, very rustic chicken coops."

The film begins with the disappearance of the boy, and we watch as Christine intensely follows the police search, eventually being told by the police that Walter has been found. A large press event is organized, and she sees her son at the train station and tells the police that who they have found is not her son. Somehow they convince her to take the child home and give it a try, which she does to save them from embarrassment. When she lashes out at the police department by taking the boy back to them, they have her committed. At that time a local reverend (John Malkovich) who knows the corruption that exists within the Los Angeles police force comes to her aid. The film then takes an abrupt turn into the search for a serial killer who may have killed Christine's beloved son. The police have found a killer in Wineville that murders young boys in a chicken coop after raping and torturing them. Was Walter among the boys murdered?

Eastwood does a brilliant job of plunging the audience back into the period, capturing the beauty of the city but also the sense of something terribly sinister lurking under the surface. In many ways the film recalls the dark power of *Chinatown* (1974) and *LA Confidential* (1997), which are films that dealt with the despicable criminal activity in Los Angeles.

The performances in the film are superb, beginning with Jolie who anchors the picture with a quietly powerful performance that is astonishing in its simplicity and ferocious love for her son. The actress tosses aside her vanity for the part, and we the audience benefit from it as we see one of the planet's most beautiful women tone down her good looks to become a woman whose confidence is shattered by events in her life. She comes to doubt everything about the world around her, appearing vulnerable one moment and hard as stone the next. Jolie is clearly on a new level of acting here, going further than she has ever gone before as an actress. Of course, she credits Eastwood.

"It is ridiculously great. It is! I'd come home and be the most annoying person who said, 'It was just so great!' He knows what he wants. He's a great leader, so it works," Jolie would tell MTV, echoing the feelings of just about every actor who has worked with Eastwood in recent years.

"It's not just in the strength or just a sense of cool, he's such a gentleman, when you work on a film with him, he treats every single person on the crew with an enormous amount of gratitude and respect, no matter what they are doing. That kind of leadership and grace is very, very rare," she said about Eastwood.

She admitted that she had to adjust to Eastwood's fast style of shooting, which often included shooting the rehearsals without the actors knowing. Other actors have struggled with this. Meryl Streep found that it was a lovely way to work, but Jolie found it took some getting used to.

"It made me terribly nervous," she told the *New York Times*, "The first day moved so quickly. There are big emotional, heavy things in that movie where it was maximum, two takes. So I woke up in the morning not feeling relaxed. I would make sure I understood where my character was coming from, I was prepared emotionally, my lines were crisp. I was more ready than I'd ever been on a film because that's what he demands. This is how I should always work: I should always be this professional and prepared."

Eastwood smiles with the memory of the shoot, telling the *New York Times* before the film's release, "I can sometimes roll without even saying a word. I'll just motion to the cameraman and he turns it on and there we go. But she (Jolie) understands what things are like, and she was ready."

Changeling marked the first time in many years that Eastwood had made a film for Universal, which decided to take the film to the Cannes Film Festival. The day after the film's premiere, the raves started rolling in, and the film was an immediate contender for major Academy Awards.

"Clint Eastwood's late life renaissance continues at full steam with a typically understated and emotionally wrenching drama based on true events from Los Angeles in 1928. Beautifully produced and guided by Eastwood's elegant, unostentatious hand, it boasts a career best performance by Angelina Jolie who has never been this compelling. Like *Mystic River* in 2003, it should go all the way from the Palais to the Academy Awards next March," raved Mike Goodridge for *Screen International.*

Todd McCarthy, writing for *The Hollywood Bible Variety*, stated, "Emotionally powerful and stylistically sure handed. A thematic piece to *Mystic River* but more complex and more far reaching. As she did in *A Mighty Heart*, Jolie plays a woman abruptly and agonizingly deprived of the one person closest to her. But as impressive as she may have been as the wife of Danny Pearl, her performance hits home more directly due to the lack of affectation—no accent, no frizzed hair or darkened complexion and no attempt to consciously rein in emotions."

"Lurid but never exploitive, pulpy yet consistently classy, Clint Eastwood's doppelganger epic *Changeling* lives up to its name as a case study of dualities," wrote Stephen Garrett for *Esquire.*

"In the twilight of his directorial career, Clint Eastwood continues to make some of his finest films. *Changeling* is a magisterial piece of work. Eastwood never loses sight of the emotions that are driving the story . . . in its unfussy craftsmanship and emotional punch, it shows him at the peak of his powers," wrote Geoffrey McNab of the *London Independent.*

Kirk Honeycutt, a *Hollywood Reporter* critic, greatly admired the film and wrote, "As incredible as it is compelling, *Changeling* brushes away the romantic notion of a more innocent time to reveal a Los Angeles circa 1928 awash in corruption and steeped in a culture that treats women as hysterical and unreliable beings when they challenge a male wisdom. Jolie puts on a powerful emotional display as a tenacious woman who gathers strength from the forces that oppose her. She reminds us that there is nothing so fierce as a mother protecting her cub. So in *Changeling*, Eastwood continues to probe uncomfortable subjects to depict the individual and even existential struggle to do what is right."

Not all the reviews were strong, however, as many critics took exception with Eastwood's new film, and in many cases, seemed angered by the admiration being bestowed upon the director late in his life.

"*Changeling* announces itself as an autopsy of an expansive body of lies that never actually performs, and as such the surprisingly graceless and phony aesthetic is what lingers most," griped Ed Gonzalez for *Slate Magazine*.

The *New York Times* film critic, Manhola Dargis, wrote, "Despite Ms. Jolie's hard work and Eastwood's scrupulous attention, the difficult, fairly one dimensional character fails to take hold."

At the end of the summer there had been hope that *Changeling* would have its North American premiere at the Toronto International Film Festival, the largest and most important of the major fall film events and a place where in recent years most of the Oscar nominees have been launched. Just the year before, four of the five best picture nominees had premiered in Toronto. For bizarre reasons, Toronto decided not to program the film after learning that Angelina Jolie would not travel so soon after giving birth to her twins. It seems that Eastwood himself was not a big enough name for the festival, and their 2008 festival became the weakest it has been in 15 years.

The New York Film Festival programmed the film, and after the screening, the Oscar talk has dropped off considerably, perhaps because all eyes are on Eastwood's second release of 2008, *Gran Torino,* or simply because the film is not generating North American Oscar buzz. However, in the canon of Eastwood films, this film is still among the finest.

Quentin Tarantino has stated that film directing is a young man's job. Obviously he has forgotten to let Eastwood know that because as he hovers near eighty, he is doing some of the finest work of his long career.

29

Gran Torino*

In March of 2008 it was announced that Eastwood would begin shooting a film that would be ready for December 2008 release entitled *Gran Torino*. Speculation started at once that the film was another chance for Eastwood to return to the Harry Callahan character, but those rumors were quickly silenced. What was surprising was the announcement that Eastwood would be acting in the film, his first acting stint since *Million Dollar Baby* (2004), which many in the business assumed would be his last.

Though little is known about the details of the plot, this much I can tell you: The film is being touted as a coming-of-age buddy film about the relationship between an old man and a young boy. Eastwood portrays Walt Kowalski, an ex-Marine who fought in the Korean War, a widower who lives quietly by himself, is cranky toward his neighbors, and likes to be left in peace with his prized possession, a 1972 Gran Torino.

When one of the local neighborhood kids, Tao, attempts to steal the car as part of an initiation into a gang, Walt catches him. After learning Tao was humiliated by the gang members for being caught, he befriends him, allowing him to do odd jobs around his home to make amends for the theft attempt. The old man bonds with the young man, who is trying to find his way, and is more content reading than being part of a gang. When Tao's sister, Sue, is brutally raped by the gang, he feels he must take revenge, but Walt convinces him to allow him, the older man, to take that burden upon himself. Enraged that Sue, who is Walt's friend, has been raped, he takes matters into his own hands, lashing out at the gangs that are growing in power in his neighborhood.

Eastwood shot the film in Michigan in the summer of 2008, with a largely unknown cast. The film gave him the chance to work with more young actors than ever before, and by all accounts he found the experience rejuvenating.

Kowalski offers Eastwood the sort of role he does very well, the miserable older man, isolated and haunted by his past, who will come to terms with it

* Scheduled for release December 2008.

through changing the present. Considering the growth Eastwood has gone through as an actor, there is cause for excitement about this film, and every reason to expect him to deliver yet another excellent performance and a strong film. Rumored to be a drama with elements of comedy, there is much buzz about the film on the Internet, despite the tiny amount of information available.

At this writing little is known about *Gran Torino*, as very few script reviews have been made available, but the sense in Hollywood seems to be, as with *Changeling* (2008), that Eastwood is a double threat for the Academy Awards this year: *Gran Torino* potentially positions him for best actor, while *Changeling* will likely nab him director and producer nominations. Just two years after *Flags of Our Fathers* and *Letters from Iwo Jima* (both 2006), he again finds himself with two major films in release at year's end. Is anyone else of his age in the industry this busy?

Other Eastwood Directing Projects Announced

In 2010 Clint Eastwood will turn 80 years old. Yet in 2008 the man will see two films he has directed, one of which he also stars in, released before Christmas for Academy Award consideration. He shows no signs of slowing down and, in fact, is in the midst of the most creative period of his long career.

At this writing Eastwood has two biographical projects in various stages of pre-production, the first being *The Human Factor*, with Morgan Freeman as Nelson Mandela. Though no date has been announced for either the film's start of production or release, Freeman has committed to the project, and Eastwood has formally announced *The Human Factor* as his next project.

Eastwood has also, with Warner Brothers, purchased the rights to *First Man*, the biography of astronaut Neil Armstrong. In 1969, Armstrong became the first man to set foot on the moon, after which his life spiraled out of control. Again, no production date has been announced, but the film is on Eastwood's slate of projects and should be in theaters within the next two years. No one has yet been cast for the role of Neil Armstrong, and the advances in visual effects that have been made over the last decade or two should please Eastwood.

Filmography

- Films directed in bold

THE FILMS

Revenge of the Creature (1955)

Francis in the Navy (1955)

Lady Godiva (1955)

Tarantula (1955)

Never Say Goodbye (1956)

The First Traveling Saleslady (1956)

Star in the Dust (1956)

Escapade from Japan (1957)

Lafayette Escadrille (1958)

Ambush at Cimarron Pass (1958)

A Fistful of Dollars (1964)

For a Few Dollars More (1965)

The Good, the Bad and the Ugly (1966)

The Witches (1967)

Hang 'Em High (1968)

Coogan's Bluff (1968)

Where Eagles Dare (1968)

Paint Your Wagon (1969)

Kelly's Heroes (1970)

Two Mules for Sister Sara (1970)

The Beguiled (1971)

Play Misty for Me **(1971)**

Dirty Harry (1971)

Joe Kidd (1972)

High Plains Drifter (1972)

Breezy (1973)

Magnum Force (1974)

Thunderbolt and Lightfoot (1974)

The Eiger Sanction (1975)

The Outlaw Josey Wales (1976)

The Enforcer (1976)

The Gauntlet (1977)

Every Which Way But Loose (1978)

Escape from Alcaltraz (1979)

Bronco Billy (1980)

Any Which Way You Can (1980)

Firefox (1982)

Honky Tonk Man (1982)

Sudden Impact (1983)

Tightrope (1984)*

City Heat (1984)

Pale Rider (1985)

Heartbreak Ridge (1986)

The Dead Pool (1988)

Bird (1988)

Pink Cadillac (1989)

White Hunter Black Heart (1990)

The Rookie (1990)

Unforgiven (1992)

A Perfect World (1993)

In the Line of Fire (1993)

The Bridges of Madison County (1995)

Absolute Power (1997)

Midnight in the Garden of Good and Evil (1997)

True Crime (1999)

Space Cowboys (1999)

Blood Work (2002)

Mystic River (2003)

Million Dollar Baby (2004)

Flags of Our Fathers (2006)

Letters from Iwo Jima (2006)

Changeling (2008)

Gran Torino (2008)

*There is a story circulating in Hollywood that Eastwood in fact directed *Tightrope* (1984) but took no credit so as not to humiliate the writer. Because the Directors Guild of America did not credit him for directing the film, I have not included it among the films he has directed.

Awards and Nominations

ACADEMY AWARDS

2006: *Letters from Iwo Jima*
Nominated Best Director
Nominated Best Picture

2004: *Million Dollar Baby*
Won Best Director
Won Best Picture
Nominated Best Actor

2003: *Mystic River*
Nominated Best Director
Nominated Best Picture

1996: The Irving G. Thalberg Award

1992: *Unforgiven*
Won Best Director
Won Best Picture
Nominated Best Actor

THE DIRECTORS GUILD OF AMERICA AWARDS

2004: *Million Dollar Baby*—Won

2003: *Mystic River*—Nominated

1993: *Unforgiven*—Won

THE HOLLYWOOD FOREIGN PRESS ASSOCIATION: GOLDEN GLOBES

2007: *Grace Is Gone*
Best Original Score—Nominated
Best Song—Nominated

2006: *Flags of Our Fathers*
Best Director—Nominated

2006: *Letters from Iwo Jima*
Best Director—Nominated
Best Foreign Film—Won

2004: *Million Dollar Baby*
Best Director—Won

2003: *Mystic River*
Best Director—Nominated

1996: Cecil B. DeMille Award for Lifetime Achievement

1992: *Unforgiven*
Best Director—Won

1988: *Bird*
Best Director—Won

THE NATIONAL SOCIETY OF FILM CRITICS

2003: *Mystic River*
Best Director

1992: *Unforgiven*
Best Director

THE LOS ANGELES FILM CRITICS ASSOCIATION

2006: *Letters from Iwo Jima*
Best Film

1992: *Unforgiven*
Best Director
Best Actor
Best Film

THE NEW YORK FILM CRITICS CIRCLE

2004: *Million Dollar Baby*
Best Director

Bibliography

BOOKS

Beard, William. *Persistence of Double Vision: Essays on Clint Eastwood.* Calgary: The University of Alberta Press, 2004.

Buscombe, Edward. *Unforgiven* (British Film Institute Modern Classic Series). British Film Institue, 2004.

Cook David A. *Lost Illusions: American Cinema in the Shadow of Watergate and Vietnam, 1970–1979.* Los Angeles, CA: University of California Press, 2002.

Ebert, Roger. *The Great Movies II.* New York: Broadway Books, 2006.

Engel, Leonard, ed. *Clint Eastwood: Actor and Director, New Perspectives.* Ann Arbor, MI: Sheridan Books, 2007

Kapsis, Robert E., and Kathie Coblentz, eds. *Clint Eastwood Interviews.* Jackson, MS: University of Mississippi Press Filmmaker Series, 2003

Kitses, Jim. *Horizons West.* London: British Film Institute, 2005.

Kitses, Jim, and Gregg Rickman. *The Western Reader.* New York: Limelight Press, 1999.

McBride, Joseph. *Searching for John Ford.* New York: St Martin's Press, 2003.

Prince, Stephen. *A New Pot of Gold: Hollywood under the Electronic Rainbow, 1980–1989.* Los Angeles, CA: University of California Press, 2002.

Schickel, Richard. *Clint Eastwood.* New York: Vintage Press, 1997.

Thompson, Douglas. *Clint Eastwood: Billion Dollar Man.* New York: John Blake, 2005.

Travers, Peter. *The Rolling Stone Film Reader: The Best Film Writing from Rolling Stone Magazine.* New York: Pocket Books, 1996.

Zmijewsky, Boris, and Lee Pfeiffer. *The Films of Clint Eastwood.* Secaucus, NJ: The Citadel Press, 1996.

PERIODICALS

Ansen, David. "Flags of Our Fathers." *Newsweek,* October 2006.
———. "Letters from Iwo Jima." *Newsweek,* December 2006.
Christ, Judith. "Breezy." *New York Magazine,* October 1973.
———. "Honky Tonk Man." *Newsday,* December 1982.

Corliss, Richard. "Bronco Billy." *Time Magazine*, June 1980.
———. "The Bridges of Madison County." *Time*, June 1995.
———. "The Outlaw Josey Wales." *Time*, June 1976.
Denby, David. "Flags of Our Fathers." *The New Yorker*, October 2006.
"The Eiger Sanction." *Variety*. May 1975.
Frayerling, Christopher. "Unforgiven." *Sight and Sound*, September 1992.
Gleiberman, Owen. "A Perfect World." *Entertainment Weekly*, Nov. 24, 1993.
———. "Flags of Our Fathers." *Entertainment Weekly*, Oct. 20, 2006.
———. "The Bridges of Madison County." *Entertainment Weekly*, June 2, 1995.
Gonzalez, Ed. *Slate*, October 2, 2008.
Goodridge, Mike. *Screen International*, May 21, 2008.
"Honky Tonk Man." *Variety*. December 1982.
Honeycutt, Kirk. "Flags of Our Fathers." *Hollywood Reporter*, October 2006.
———. *Hollywood Reporter*, May 21, 2008.
Kael, Pauline. "Bird." *The New Yorker*, October 1988.
Kauffman, Stanley. "The Bridges of Madison County." *The New Republic*, June 1995.
Kroll, Jack. "Bird." *Newsweek*, September 1988.
Lutey, David. "Space Cowboys." *Screen International*, August 2000.
McCarthy, Todd. "Absolute Power." *Variety*, February 1997.
———. "A Perfect World." *Variety*, November 1993.
———. "Changeling." *Variety*, May 21, 2008.
———. "Flags of Our Fathers." *Variety*, October 2006.
———. "Letters from Iwo Jima." *Variety*, December 2006.
———. "Midnight in the Garden of Good and Evil." *Variety*, November 1997.
———. "Million Dollar Baby." *Variety*, December 2004.
———. "Mystic River." *Variety*, May 2003.
———. "The Bridges of Madison County." *Variety*, June 1995.
———. "Unforgiven." *Variety*, August 1992.
Puig, Claudia. "Flags of Our Fathers." *USA Today Magazine*, Oct. 20, 2006.
Reed, Rex. "White Hunter Black Heart." *Coming Attractions*, 1990.
Saito, Stephen. "Letters from Iwo Jima." *Premiere*, December 2006.
Schickel, Richard. "Honky Tonk Man." *Time*, December 1982.
Schwarzbaum, Lisa. "Letters from Iwo Jima." *Entertainment Weekly*, December 2006.
Travers, Peter. "Letters from Iwo Jima." *Rolling Stone*, December 2006.
———. "Million Dollar Baby." *Rolling Stone*, December 2004.
———. "Unforgiven." *Rolling Stone*, August 1992.
———. "White Hunter Black Heart." *Rolling Stone*, September 1990.

NEWSPAPERS

Abramowitz, Rachel. *The Los Angeles Times*, October 18, 2008.
Attanasio, Paul. "Heartbreak Ridge." *Washington Post*, December 5, 1986.
Bernard, Jami. "Bird." *The New York Post*, September 30, 1988.
Burr, Ty. "Letters from Iwo Jima." *The Boston Globe*, December 15, 2006.
Canby, Vincent. "Heartbreak Ridge." *The New York Times*, December 5, 1986.
———. "High Plains Drifter." *The New York Times*, August 22, 1973.
———. "Unforgiven." *The New York Times*, August 7, 1992.

Carroll, Kathleen. "Unforgiven." *The New York Daily News*, August 7, 1992.

Dargis, Manohla. "Changeling." *The New York Times*, May 21, 2008.

———. "Flags of Our Fathers." *The New York Times*, October 20, 2006.

Ebert, Roger. "Breezy." *The Chicago Sun-Times*, November 18, 1973.

———. "Absolute Power." *The Chicago Sun-Times*, February 28, 1997.

———. "A Perfect World." *The Chicago Sun-Times*, November 24, 1993.

———. "Bird." *The Chicago Sun-Times*, September 30, 1988.

———. "Bronco Billy." *The Chicago Sun-Times*, June 11, 1980.

———. "Flags of Our Fathers." *The Chicago Sun-Times*, October 20, 2006.

———. "Heartbreak Ridge." *The Chicago Sun-Times*, December 5, 1986.

———. "Honky Tonk Man." *The Chicago Sun-Times*, December 15, 1982.

———. "Midnight in the Garden of Good and Evil." *The Chicago Sun-Times*, November 21, 1997.

———. "Million Dollar Baby." *The Chicago Sun-Times*, December 15, 2004.

———. "Mystic River." *The Chicago Sun-Times*, October 15, 2003.

———. "Play Misty for Me." *The Chicago Sun-Times*, November 12, 1971.

———. "Space Cowboys." *The Chicago Sun-Times*, August 4, 2000.

———. "The Eiger Sanction." *The Chicago Sun-Times*, May 21, 1975.

———. "The Outlaw Josey Wales." *The Chicago Sun-Times*, June 30, 1976.

———. "Unforgiven." *The Chicago Sun-Times*, August 7, 1992.

———. "White Hunter Black Heart." *The Chicago Sun-Times*, September 14, 1990.

Guarino, Ann. "Play Misty for Me." *The New York Daily News*, November 12, 1971.

Haskell, Molly. "Breezy." *The Village Voice*, November 18, 1973.

"High Plains Drifter." *London Observer*, October 24, 1973.

Howe, Desson. "Absolute Power." *The Washington Post*, February 28, 1997.

Kempley, Rita. "White Hunter Black Heart." *The Washington Post*, September 14, 1990.

Maslin, Janet. "Absolute Power." *The New York Times*, February 28, 1997.

———. "A Perfect World." *The New York Times*, November 24, 1993.

———. "Bronco Billy." *The New York Times*, June 11, 1980.

———. "Midnight in the Garden of Good and Evil." *The New York Times*, November 21, 1997.

———. "The Bridges of Madison County." *The New York Times*, June 2, 1995.

———. "White Hunter Black Heart." *The New York Times*, September 14, 1990.

Oster, Jerry. "High Plains Drifter." *The New York Daily News*, August 22, 1973.

Reed, Rex. "High Plains Drifter." *The New York Daily News*, August 22, 1973.

———. "Play Misty for Me." *The New York Daily News*, November 12, 1971.

———. "Unforgiven." *The New York Observer*, August 7, 1992

Rosenbaum, Jonathan. "Bird." *The Chicago Reader*, September 30, 1988.

Scott, A. O. "Letters from Iwo Jima." *The New York Times*, December 15, 2006.

———. "Mystic River." *The New York Times*, October 15, 2003.

———. "Space Cowboys." *The New York Times*, August 4, 2000.

Scott, Jay. "Bird." *The Toronto Globe and Mail*, September 30, 1988.

Thomas, Kevin. "The Outlaw Josey Wales." *The Los Angeles Times*, June 30, 1976.

Thompson, Howard. "Breezy." *The New York Times*, November 18, 1973.

Turan, Kenneth. "Absolute Power." *The Los Angeles Times*, February 28, 1997.

———. "Changeling." *The Los Angeles Times*, May 21, 2008.

———. "Letters from Iwo Jima." *The Los Angeles Times*, December 15, 2006.

————. "Mystic River." *The Los Angeles Times*, October 15, 2003.

Weinstein, Archer. "Breezy." *The New York Post*, November 18, 1973.

————. "Honky Tonk Man." *The New York Daily Post*, December 5, 1982.

————. "Play Misty for Me." *The New York Post*, November 12, 1971.

ELECTRONIC SOURCES

Clint Eastwood: Out of the Shadows. DVD. Directed by Bruce Ricker. Los Angeles, CA: Warner Brothers Home Entertainment, 2000.

Charity, Tom. "Letters from Iwo Jima." *CNN*, 2006.

"Interviews with Clint Eastwood and Jeff Daniels." *Blood Work*. DVD. Directed by Clint Eastwood. Burbank, CA: Warner Brothers Home Entertainment, 2002.

"Interviews with Clint Eastwood." *Dirty Harry*, special ed. DVD. Directed by Don Siegel. Burbank, CA: Warner Brothers Home Entertainment, 2008.

"Interviews with Clint Eastwood, Steven Spielberg, Ryan Philippe, and Adam Beach." *Flags of Our Fathers*. DVD. Directed by Clint Eastwood. Burbank, CA: Dreamworks Home Entertainment, 2007.

"Interviews with Clint Eastwood and Ken Watanabe." *Letters from Iwo Jima*. DVD. Burbank, CA: Warner Brothers Home Entertainment, 2007.

"Interviews with Clint Eastwood, Hilary Swank, and Morgan Freeman" and "Oscar Morning After Telecast with James Lipton." *Million Dollar Baby*. DVD. Directed by Clint Eastwood. Burbank, CA: Warner Brothers Home Entertainment, 2005.

"Interviews with Clint Eastwood, Sean Penn, Tim Robbins, Dennis Lehane, and Marcia Gay Harden." *Mystic River*. DVD. Directed by Clint Eastwood. Burbank, CA: Warner Brothers Home Entertainment, 2004.

"Interviews with Clint Eastwood and Jessica Walter." *Play It Again: A Look Back at* Play Misty for Me. DVD. Directed by Laurent Bouzreau. Los Angeles, CA: Universal Home Entertainment, 2001.

"Interviews with Clint Eastwood." *Space Cowboys*. DVD. Directed by Clint Eastwood. Burbank, CA: Warner Brothers Home Entertainment, 2001.

"Interviews with Clint Eastwood and Meryl Streep." *An Old Fashioned Love Story: The Bridges of Madison County*. DVD. Directed by Gary Leva. Burbank, CA: Warner Brothers Home Entertainment, 2008.

"Interviews with Clint Eastwood." *The Outlaw Josey Wales*. DVD. Directed by Clint Eastwood. Burbank, CA: Warner Brothers Home Entertainment, 2001.

"Interviews with Clint Eastwood, Isaiah Washington, James Woods, and Dennis Leary." *True Crime*. DVD. Directed by Clint Eastwood. Burbank, CA: Warner Brothers Home Entertainment, 2000.

"Interviews with Clint Eastwood, Gene Hackman, Richard Harris, and Morgan Freeman." *All on Account of Pullin' a Trigger: Making* Unforgiven. DVD. Directed by Jerry Hogrewe. Burbank, CA: Warner Brothers Home Entertainment, 2002.

Index

About the Author

JOHN H. FOOTE is Director of the Toronto Film School, where he also teaches film history and genre study. He is a nationally known film critic and historian, who writes regularly for *Life and Fashion Magazine* and the *Metroland* syndicate. He is also a frequent guest on CBC Newsworld and Durham Today.